49

Making Good

Making Good

HOW EX-CONVICTS REFORM AND
REBUILD THEIR LIVES

Shadd Maruna

WITH A FOREWORD BY HANS TOCH

AMERICAN PSYCHOLOGICAL ASSOCIATION

WASHINGTON, D.C.

First Printing, September 2000
Second Printing, June 2001
Third Printing, January 2003

Published by
American Psychological Association
750 First Street, NE
Washington, DC 20002

Copies may be ordered from
APA Order Department
P.O. Box 92984
Washington, DC 20090–2984

In the U.K., Europe, Africa, and the Middle East, copies may be ordered from
American Psychological Association
3 Henrietta Street
Covent Garden, London
WC2E 8LU England

Typeset in Goudy by EPS Group Inc., Easton, MD

Printer: Edwards Brothers, Ann Arbor, MI
Cover Designer: Berg Design, Albany, NY
Technical/Production Editor: Jennifer Powers

The opinions and statements published are the responsibility of the authors, and such opinions and statements do not necessarily represent the policies of the APA.

Library of Congress Cataloging-in-Publication Data
Maruna, Shadd.
    Making good : how ex-convicts reform and rebuild their lives / Shadd Maruna.
      p. cm.
    Includes bibliographical references and index.
    ISBN 1-55798-731-9 (alk. paper)
      1. Ex-convicts—Interviews.   2. Ex-convicts—Rehabilitation.
   3. Recidivists—Interviews.   I. Title: How ex-convicts reform and rebuild their lives.
  II. Title.

HV9276 .M37 2000
364.8'0973—dc21

                                 00-058620

British Library Cataloguing-in-Publication Data
A CIP record is available from the British Library.

Printed in the United States of America

To Ashlene, Zara, and all my family,
for never giving up on a persistent offender

If only it were all so simple! If only there were evil people somewhere insidiously committing evil deeds, and it were necessary only to separate them from the rest of us and destroy them. But the line dividing good and evil cuts through the heart of every human being. And who is willing to destroy a part of his own heart?

Alexander Solzhenitsyn (1974)

CONTENTS

ACKNOWLEDGMENTS

A friend of mine likes to use the quote, "Art is 'I.' Science is 'We.'" While I would like to think of this book as equal parts art and science, this project is most definitely "We." There are many voices in this book —the voices of friends, critics, practitioners, other scholars, and most importantly, the individuals who generously contributed their life stories and so much of their time to this research effort. Like the artist, I imposed a sort of order on this cacophony of voices, adding a bit here, taking out a bit there, to make it presentable. Yet, this project never would have been possible if not for all the others who have contributed along the way.

I will start with the money. Over the past 5 years, this study has received generous support from the U.S. Fulbright Commission and the Harry Frank Guggenheim Foundation. More recently, the Joseph Rowntree Foundation (U.K.) has funded a spin-off study that will seek to corroborate the findings of this research with a broader sample of ex-offenders (see Canter, Lundrigan, Maruna, Porter, & O'Keeffe, 1999, for a preliminary report). A fellowship from the University of Chicago / Northwestern University Joint Center for Poverty Research allowed me the time to finish writing up the initial findings. The Foley Center for the Study of Lives and the Institute for Policy Research at Northwestern University contributed in-kind support that went beyond office space and computer time. Finally, much of the fieldwork for this project was conducted as part of four different process evaluations funded by grants from the Merseyside Drugs Council, Merseyside Safer Cities, and the Safer Merseyside Partnership.

Many thanks must go to my Northwestern mentors Dan Lewis and Dan McAdams. The idea for this research project was a product of far too many caffeine-driven conversations with them, and both Dans have left their own distinct imprints on the final product. I also gained a great deal from exchanges with experts like Pam Adelmann, Jack Bush, Shawn Bushway, Stephen Farrall, Barry Goldson, Janet Jamieson, Jim Hilborn, Russ Immarigeon, John Laub, Gil McIvor, Devon Polaschek, Nicole Rafter, Adolph Reed, Mercer Sullivan, Jefferson Singer, and Neal Shover. Most of the kind souls on that list were tolerant enough to read parts or complete drafts of the manuscript years before I was close to making any sense. Ros Burnett, whose Oxford University recidivism study is probably the best of its kind, taught me a great deal about organizing a project of this size and was an extraordinary editor.

I have received tremendous support for this research effort from my new colleagues at University at Albany, State University of New York, and I want to especially thank Hart Blanton, Francois Cooren, Lorraine Hogan, Tom LeBel, Nick Mitchell, Michelle Naples, and Isla Roona for their helpful suggestions for improving the manuscript. I have also learned a great deal about rehabilitation in recent years from Albany's Father Peter Young and his associates, whose New York State ex-offender reintegration program is among the best in the business, and Betty and Rudy Cypser of CURE-NY. Above all, professional thanks must go to Distinguished Professor Hans Toch, my greatest critic and friend.

My hosts and colleagues while in the United Kingdom were extremely generous and need to be thanked for putting up with me for 2 years. Professor David Canter, Laurence Alison, and the team at the Centre for Investigative Psychology at the University of Liverpool provided essential support, guidance, and friendship. The staff and management at the Liverpool branch of NACRO (National Association for the Care and Resettlement of Offenders), especially Tony Riley, Val Metcalf, Dominica Wakelam, Marian Dalton, Patrick McCarten, and Bernadette Loughney, were extraordinarily helpful in introducing me to ex-offenders and Liverpool drinking establishments. I spent the rest of my time learning from Keith Midgley and the staff and students at cutting-edge reintegration programs including the Alternatives to Drugs Programme, the Apex Trust, the Independence Initiative, Next Step, and Transit. Martin Evans, Julian Buchanan, Gillian Hirst, Lynn Irving, Pete Lochran, and all of the other Merseyside Probation staff with whom I worked were very helpful. Finally, Chief Superintendent of Merseyside Police Department Dave Thompson, now "retired" (i.e., completing a PhD and lecturing throughout the country), has been a good friend and an excellent resource on all things Liverpool and all things criminal.

Members of this project's actual research "team" (many of whom have never met each other because they are equally divided on both sides of the Atlantic) have been invaluable. Like all qualitative work, this study produced a veritable mountain of data, and out of some sense of scientific professionalism, I decided that all the data needed to be content coded by at least two "independent" pairs of eyes. This turned out to be an enormous undertaking. I cannot thank all of the people who volunteered to help in this coding nearly enough (since I definitely did not pay them enough). In particular, Louise Porter in Liverpool and Irene Carvalho in Chicago were subjected to an inordinate amount of content coding, which they handled with remarkable ease and good cheer. Laurence Alison, Dave Brookes, Aisling Donnelly, Jen Goldberg, Samantha Lundrigan, Ciaran O'Keeffe, Jeff Reynolds, and Donna Youngs were also enormously helpful in the design of the coding schemes, the fieldwork, and the content analysis. Anna Slater, an author herself, typed over half of the transcripts and was very insightful in her comments and advice.

Of course, my editors at the American Psychological Association, Adrian Forman and Susan Reynolds, deserve much credit for the readability of this book and for encouraging me to finally finish. The benefit of publishing with the APA is that the editors there are not only literary experts but also psychologists. So, they knew just the right combination of client-centered therapy and electric shock behaviorism to keep me going.

Still, Ashelene Aylward gets the most credit for rehabilitating and reforming me as an author. Ash has followed this project from Chicago to the streets of Liverpool, and now to the University at Albany, State University of New York over the last 5 years. I could not and certainly would not have let this research project consume so much of my life over that time had she not believed so deeply in this final product. I cannot thank her enough for her partnership and optimism throughout.

Finally, my greatest debt is to the men and women who agreed to share their life stories and so much of their time with me for the sake of this project. It should be clear to any reader that what these individuals have to add to the literature of criminology is far more interesting and insightful than anything I can contribute. For this reason, I have tried to afford them many chances to speak; I have left their language largely unedited; and I use long, uninterrupted narrative passages more frequently than most publishers would tolerate. In rereading their transcripts many times over, I was struck by the wisdom these individuals shared with me in spite of the often naïve questions I was asking them. Far more than "research participants" or "subjects," these individuals deserve a great deal of credit for developing the ideas in this book. I thank them all for letting me into their lives, and I wish them all the best.

FOREWORD

Probably one of the least memorable moments in the life of the author of this book is when I asked during a job interview whether he had read the *Confessions* of St. Augustine. Whatever he may have thought of this exercise (and I have not dared to ask), it was a left-handed testimonial to the broad range of implications that one tends to see in Shadd Maruna's work.

The study that occasioned my query is reported in this book. Narrowly defined, the subject matter of this study is desistance from crime. Desistance is described in interviews by the desisters themselves. Interview excerpts provide vivid narratives by career offenders who seem to have changed their careers and have discontinued offending. The ex-offenders describe their transmutations, including fresh perspectives and new goals for their lives. A comparison group of unregenerate felons describes contrasting perspectives and goals. This enables Maruna to present a trenchant analysis of the process whereby some chronic offenders manage to become nonoffenders, whereas others do not. The former show us how they have taken charge of their lives, whereas the latter continue to see themselves as passive products of inhospitable circumstance. Unfortunately, the latter type of view is more familiar to us. It is a conception that we often endorse and unwittingly reinforce.

On the average, we social scientists tend not to hold out much hope for offenders—at least for those who by virtue of characterological defects or warped personalities are presumed different from the rest of us. Emphasizing this difference is a time-honored psychometric task, and a frequent concern of forensic psychologists. The mission such psychologists can be assigned dovetails with that of the correctional system, with potentially horrendous effects. Risk assessments undergird risk management, which at the end of the line means incapacitation. What it boils down to is that the process can culminate with a person sequestered for life, or long after his capacity for offending has dissipated.

The enterprise, of course, is not as arbitrary as it may sound. The real world is not a world of double-blind social experiments. As psychologists, when we assess risk, we do so mostly for those who have richly earned our attention. Such entitlement invariably derives from a record of actions that are arguably unambivalently reprehensible. And where offenders raise concerns, the public demands that we assuage these concerns and has faith in our ability to do this. Given this context, it is too much to ask that we operate as if *in vacuo*.

In our upbringing, most of us have also been inculcated with assumptions of immutability based on scientific theory. Personality—the core concept with which psychologists operate—calls attention to continuity of dispositions and reliability of conduct. An even stronger point is made for us by sadder-but-wiser experience. Such experience tells psychologists who work with difficult clients that many of those we had hoped would change have sadly reverted to type. Statistics in our field tend to buttress such experiences: Offender recidivism rates are indecently high, and relapse rates for alcohol or drug abusers, sex offenders, and other people with addictive and obsessive dispositions verge on the astronomical.

But to say that recidivism rates are very high is a far cry from showing that future offending is inevitable or that the future inexorably replicates (or extrapolates) the past. In fact, the opposite may hold: The higher a baseline, the more room we may have for efforts at reform. The word *relapse* has thus come to acquire strangely paradoxical implications. Far from inspiring pessimism or despair, the term provides benchmarks for our interventions: to *prevent relapse* now means to reduce the intervals between relapses and to decrease the probabilities of relapse over time. The knowledge that lapses are par for the course increases our confidence and insulates us against unwarranted discouragement. We are ever cognizant of the fact that change is a long-term process in which the stability of recovery increases reliably over time.

But change is more than discontinuance of undesirable conduct. Maruna points out that those who are reformed have had to relinquish an old self and invent a new one. The individual is only truly reformed when he or she has acquired new purposes, a fresh set of meanings, and a satisfying new role. When we support any of these developments, we buttress change. As one of Maruna's ex-offenders put it, "I really, at the end of the day, want nothing more than someone to say they like my work." Ratifying the new self is a rehabilitative task for positive interventionists.

The most fascinating of new roles that are adopted by people who are reformed is that of change agent. Having undergone a transformation, these people feel competent and motivated to assist others with problems. Maruna calls this orientation a *generative goal*. He points out that it is a useful dynamic in sustaining personal change. He writes that "it is a well-known irony that help-givers are often helped more than help-receivers in a helping relationship." In self-help groups, the process is an established reciprocal one. The reformed person and the person in process of reformation both benefit from their helping transaction. Where professionals act as the reformers, they can recruit recovering clients as associates. The resulting transactions (professional–paraprofessional, paraprofessional–client, and professional–client) can benefit all parties to some measure, and it is not clear who tends to benefit the most.

Where products of a problem become part of the solution of a problem, the process gains credibility. It also becomes less discontinuous, less authoritarian, and more participatory in nature. To recognize these advantages need not mean that we have to undersell the importance of professional expertise or personal skill. An effective paraprofessional has to function as a role model who can capitalize on his or her experience and can deploy native wisdom and formally acquired knowledge. The most impressive of our clients can be selected and trained to perform these functions.

The industry of recovery is expanding and can cumulatively employ a growing number and variety of staff. In substance abuse programs, for example, ranges of paraprofessional skills are being exercised in and out of institutions. There are countless opportunities for all sorts of volunteers in charitable and public service sectors. Religiously motivated groups are playing an increasing role in public policy, which multiplies opportunities for lay participants.

Personal reform comes in many guises, and one of these is that of the sinner-turned-saint. Phenotypically, it is the most extreme form of change, but genotypically, less so. The person's life becomes a morality play and gains value in the telling. As Maruna points out about one of his offenders, "Ironically, although the speaker says that his life has been wasted, by living to tell the tale, he has in fact found a social purpose or meaning for his life: It has produced a 'book' that he can pass on to the next generation."

A transformed life carries all sorts of messages. One of these is cautionary. It says, "I almost didn't make it, and if you embark on a career such as mine, you may end up as I almost did." The opposite message can be a message of hope: "If I made it—as terrible as I was—just about anyone can do it." Other covert messages relate to the process itself. One is a commercial for the change mechanism or intervention that accomplished the change. "Look at me," this message reads, "I am a testimonial to the effectiveness of the intervention." A variant is the introspection, "To get from there to here seems inconceivable. So let me recap how it was done."

The real functions of narratives, however, are those served for the narrator, who has to reconcile the person he or she was with the one he or she claims to have become. The task is daunting because the person the narrator has been is "bad" and the one he or she has become is "good,"

the presumption being one of radical discontinuity. The most inviting solution is to claim that to be really good one has to have been bad: "You
must have been the sort of person I was to have become what I have
become" is the simplest reconciliation formula, which implies the virtue
of an ordeal by fire. The next best solution is to disown one's past, and
many of Maruna's informants opted for this solution. They depict themselves as having been products of destructive forces that they have more
or less recently managed to escape. "Now," they testify, "I am truly free,
and a master (or mistress) of my fate." An acceptable variant is a portrait
of one's real self held captive by one's pretend self, awaiting an opportunity
to escape: "I was dedicated to the life I told you I led," the informant says,
"but deep down inside I have always been the person you now see."

Other messages may have to do with feelings, such as shame, remorse,
or the desire for vindication. To select a missionary career, or a role as
professional helper, becomes a way of atoning for transgressions. It is also
a vehicle for maximizing continuity in one's life because it capitalizes on
past experience as a transgressor (or sinner) to assist or change other persons in the future.

If Maruna had interviewed St. Augustine, he would have heard a
somewhat familiar narrative. He would have been told of an early life of
delinquency, born of association with delinquent peers, whose approval
Augustine valued. Augustine (1968) wrote,

> Amongst my equals, I was ashamed of a less shamelessness, when I
> hear them boast of their flagitiousness, yea, and the more boasting, the
> more they were degraded: and I took pleasure, not only in the pleasure
> of the deed, but in the praise. What is worthy of dispraise but Vice?
> But I made myself worse than I was, that I might not be dispraised:
> and when in any thing I had not sinned as the abandoned ones, I
> would say that I had done what I had not done, that I might not seem
> contemptible in proportion as I was innocent, or of less account, the
> more chaste. (p. 25)

At age 16, Augustine saw himself susceptible to negative peer pressure: "Behold with what companions I walked the streets of Babylon, and
wallowed in the mires thereof . . . for that I was easy to be seduced" (p.
25). He admitted to enjoying his delinquent gang activities, such as larceny,
burglary, and vandalism: "Yet I lusted to thieve, and did it, compelled by
no hunger, nor poverty, but through a cloyedness of welldoing, and a pam-
peredness of iniquity: but joyed in the theft and sin itself" (p. 26). His
argument, however, is that social pressure was ultimately responsible for
his transgressions: "Alone I had never committed that theft, wherein what
I stole pleased me not, but that I stole . . . but when it's said, 'Let's go, let's
do it,' we are ashamed not to be shameless" (p. 30).

St. Augustine wrote, 11 books later—having relinquished his unregenerate self (including a mistress, a tenure-track professorship, and as-

sorted heresies)—about a newfound role as theological change agent. He described this role as follows:

> Now then let Thy ministers work upon *the earth*, not upon the waters of infidelity, by preaching and speaking, by miracles, and Sacraments, and mystic words. . . . But—let Thy ministers work now as on the *dry land*, separated from the whirlpools of the great deep: and let them be a pattern unto the Faithful, by living before them and stirring them up to imitation. (pp. 274–275)

Augustine as reformed reformer can "stir them up to imitation" because he has "lived before them." The ex-offender has experienced the dysfunctional life, and escaped it, and thus makes a plausible and convincing role model.

Hans Toch
Distinguished Professor of Criminal Justice
University at Albany
State University of New York

Making Good

INTRODUCTION:
THE COMMON CRIMINAL AND US

When Anthony Burgess's *A Clockwork Orange* was published in the United States, the book's portrayal of the seductions of crime and the nightmare of state-sanctioned brainwashing fit well with the social and political mood of the country in the 1960s. In 1971, Stanley Kubrick's film version of the book was popularly and critically acclaimed as a philosophical masterpiece. Yet, both the film and the version of Burgess's novel that was published in the United States left out one rather important part of the life story of Alex, the book's gang-leader protagonist—the ending.

The 21st chapter in Burgess's original novel, which like the 21st year in a person's life was meant to symbolize "human maturity," was cut from the American edition of the book and the better-known Kubrick film (Burgess, 1988, p. vi). This omission was hardly a minor one. Burgess explained,

> What happens in that twenty-first chapter? . . . Briefly, my young thuggish protagonist grows up. He grows bored with violence and recognizes that human energy is better expended on creation than destruction. Senseless violence is a prerogative of youth, which has much energy but little talent for the constructive. Its dynamism has to find an outlet in smashing telephone kiosks, derailing trains, stealing cars and smashing them. . . . There comes a time, however, when violence is seen as juvenile and boring. It is the repartee of the stupid and ignorant. My

young hoodlum comes to the revelation of the need to get something done in life—to marry, to beget children, to keep the orange of the world turning in the rookers of bog, or hands of God, and perhaps even create something—music, say. . . . It is with a kind of shame that this growing youth looks back on his devastating past. He wants a different kind of future. (p. viii)

This is certainly not the message that American audiences remember from the book or Kubrick's film. Our version ended as Alex, after being poked, prodded, and drugged in an effort to "rehabilitate" him, is surgically restored to his original self. Alex sarcastically lets us know that he is "cured all right," as he fantasizes about slicing up the whole world with his "cut-throat britva (blade)." Why the different ending? According to Burgess (1988),

My New York publisher believed that my twenty-first chapter was a sellout. It was veddy, veddy British, don't you know. It was bland and it showed a Pelagian unwillingness to accept that a human being could be a model of unregenerable evil. The Americans, he said in effect, were tougher than the British and could face up to reality. Soon they would be facing up to it in Vietnam. My book was Kennedyan and accepted the notion of moral progress. What was really wanted was a Nixonian book with no shred of optimism in it. (p. ix)

The following work also is "Kennedyan" in its exploration of how even the most persistent deviants can change their lives and become productive members of the community. In the 1970s, Americans had learned from Martinson (1974) and others that "nothing works" in efforts to rehabilitate criminals. These pessimistic research findings were frequently and unfairly cited to confirm what we had suspected all along—that criminals are fundamentally different than the rest of us. Despite the best of intentions from do-gooders, no help or therapy in the world could help turn the bad into the good. Once a criminal, always a criminal, after all.

While the proliferation of self-help organizations and literature suggests that many of us believe that we can change our *own* lives, personalities, or behaviors, we do not necessarily extend this belief in the potential to change to others. We tend to view social deviants, in particular, as people with immutable and essentially flawed natures (Gendreau & Ross, 1979). Irwin (1985) called this the myth of the "bogeyman" or the belief in people who are fundamentally and permanently different than "normal" people. Bogeymen go by many labels: *sociopaths, incorrigibles, unamenables, career criminals, superpredators, scum.* They are the ubiquitous bad guys in every action film, who can be casually butchered to the delight or indifference of the audience (because, after all, they are the bad guys). Although the precise criteria for being a bogeyman remain elusive, we tend to "know them when we see them." The mark of Cain in its many forms is apparently difficult to hide.

The occasional reactions generated by my own research illustrate the prevalence of this belief in the permanence of criminality. Like Leibrich (1993, p. 30), I faced a "Greek chorus of doubt" when I told colleagues and criminal justice practitioners that I was interviewing ex-offenders who have "gone legit." I was repeatedly asked, "How can you prove they are really clean?" or "How do you know they're not just lying to you?"

In all likelihood, this suspicion probably did not concern the use of self-report methodology but instead had more to do with the subject matter. The idea that bad people can become essentially good seems to contradict a fundamental belief of contemporary society. Indeed, on those occasions in which I would introduce one of my ex-offender informants to such skeptics, the new reaction was almost always along the lines of, "Yeah, but he's not a *real* criminal, though. He's a great guy who just got into trouble." Under a paradigm of criminal essentialism, once someone has reformed, this is a priori proof that he or she was never *really* a criminal from the start (Lofland, 1969, p. 289). Therefore, it is almost impossible to contradict the idea that "real criminals" cannot change.

The creation of bogeymen may serve a distinct social purpose. If there is no common enemy, no Them, perhaps there can be no Us. Yet creating a Them also essentially relieves Us from having to examine ourselves for signs of deviance. If crime is something that wicked people do, we need not worry that our own behavior is wrong. Despite occasional transgressions, we do not expect to be treated like "some kind of common criminal." In the black-and-white world of good guys and bad guys, one is either a good person who makes some forgivable mistakes or a common criminal who deserves no sympathy.

An equally dark side of this equation, of course, is that once a person finds him- or herself on the wrong side of that line, the bogeyman stigma is likely to persist even when deviant behaviors do not. Ambiguous labels such as "criminal" or "thief" connote both what a person is likely to do in the future and "what one has done at any one time, even though this is not a pattern and the doing has been abandoned" (Sagarin, 1990, p. 802). The belief in people who are permanently and fundamentally bad almost necessitates their segregation from mainstream society (Newman, 1975). Only with the ready acceptance of the existence of bogeymen or incorrigible offenders could selective incapacitation and policies like "three strikes and you're out" be easily justified (Gottfredson & Hirschi, 1986).

Irwin (1985) argued that the myth of the bogeyman has its most profound influence in societies passing through uncertain times. If this thesis is correct, late 20th-century American society must be experiencing highly uncertain times. In what they aptly referred to as the "waste management" model of corrections, Feeley and Simon (1992) argued that the role of the correctional system is no longer to "correct" or even punish but rather incapacitate and control those presumed to be chronically bad. The number of inmates in state and federal prisons has skyrocketed from less than 200,000 in 1970 to almost 1.5 million by the close of the century (Ziedenberg & Schiraldi, 1999). Including inmates of local jails, the United States incarcerates around 2 million of its citizens, who account for around one fourth of the total number of prison inmates in the world, all at a cost of around $40 billion to taxpayers (Ziedenberg & Schiraldi, 1999).

Unfortunately, although research findings consistently contradict the bogeyman myth that drives this incarceration mania, academic criminology has at times acted as an active coproducer of the discourse of criminal essentialism. Most obviously, despite the evidence that criminal behavior is widespread throughout the population and that most criminal careers are short-lived and sporadic, criminological research continues to focus on the static differences between offenders and nonoffenders as if these were "types" of people. A special fascination has been reserved for the infamous 5% or 6% of the male population that seems to account for over half of all recorded crimes (see Gottfredson & Hirschi, 1986, for a critique). The criminologist who is willing to give this group a sensationalist label like "superpredators" can be assured media exposure and a mass audience. Bogeymen may not really exist, but they certainly sell a lot of books.

Burgess (1988) attributed the continuing appeal of his book *A Clockwork Orange* to this public hunger to believe there really are an alien species of criminal monsters among us. "Unfortunately, my little squib of a book was found attractive to many because it was as odorous as a crateful of bad eggs with the miasma of original sin" (p. x). Burgess wrote,

> Let us have evil prancing on the page, and up to the very last line, sneering in the face of all the inherited beliefs, Jewish, Christian, Muslim and Holy Roller, about people being able to make themselves better. Such a book would be sensational, and so it is. But I do not think it is a fair picture of human life. (p. ix)

Indeed, it is not. The pessimistic notion of the irredeemable criminal simply does not fit one of the best established empirical findings in criminology: Almost everyone who is labeled as a superpredator eventually "goes straight"—or desists—from crime. How they manage to do so is the subject of this book.

THE ROAD AHEAD

I am interested in "false positives"—people who "should" commit crime, according to common wisdom and our best predictive calculations, but do not. In the eight chapters that follow, I outline the beginnings of a new understanding of *desistance* from crime—the process by which stigmatized, former offenders are able to "make good" and create new lives for themselves. This analysis is largely based on the findings of the Liverpool Desistance Study (LDS), a qualitative investigation of desistance that involved long-term field observations and hundreds of casual and in-depth interviews with British ex-convicts between 1996 and 1998.

Although "new," the theoretical understanding developed in this book originates in an ongoing dialogue with a wide variety of previous research findings on the process of offender rehabilitation, recovery from addiction, and adult personality development. I have done my best to synthesize much of what is known about the experience of personal reform, illustrate this phenomenon with data from the LDS, and offer suggestions for how the LDS findings might help improve the provision of support services for individuals undergoing this self-transformation. Ultimately, it is these individuals whom I hope to benefit with this book and with my research.

The premise of this book is that to successfully maintain this abstinence from crime, ex-offenders need to *make sense* of their lives. This sense-making commonly takes the form of a life story or self-narrative (McAdams, 1985, 1993; Sampson & Laub, 1995). "Individuals confront ambiguity, change, and contradictions throughout their lives, (and) constructing a coherent personal narrative on sometimes disorderly lives is one of the dominant struggles that life-course research has uncovered" (Sampson & Laub, 1995, p. 156). According to McAdams's theory of the life story identity, modern adults create this internalized life story—or personal myth— to provide their lives with unity, purpose, and meaning. The construction and reconstruction of this narrative, integrating one's perceived past, present, and anticipated future, is itself the process of identity development in adulthood. Individuals who are unable to construct this sort of consistent narrative out of their lives may suffer depression, anxiety, or other problems. In his research on the self-narratives of chronically addicted men, Singer (1997) found,

> What is missing from the identities of men suffering from chronic addiction is a belief that their lives are embedded in the same world and reality to which the rest of us belong . . . Most [of us] have stories that, despite unhappiness or tragedy, make sense. [T]he chronically addicted . . . continue to feel [an] otherness about the apparent illogic of their stories. (pp. 278–279)

Therefore, I argue that to desist from crime, ex-offenders need to develop a coherent, prosocial identity for themselves. As such, they need to account for and understand their criminal pasts (why they did what they did), and they also need to understand why they are now "not like that anymore." Ex-offenders need a coherent and credible self-story to explain (to themselves and others) how their checkered pasts could have led to their new, reformed identities. Lofland (1969) called this the "question of congruence":

> How can an apparently discontinuous life trajectory be made a related, meaningful train of events? . . . What kinds of perspectives most facilitatively or most easily integrate and make meaningful a life that is experienced as discontinuous, radically changing and full of shame and guilt and that is felt or feared to be worthless? (p. 282)

The entirety of this book can be read as an elaborate, empirical response to Lofland's rhetorical question. There are, of course, many paths to reform and recovery. Some individuals "find God," some "burn out," some just drift away from the lifestyle. Yet, there appear to be significant commonalities in the subjective orientations or life perspectives of people who are desisting from crime. The purpose of my research on ex-offender narratives has been to identify the common, psychosocial structure underlying these self-stories, and therefore to outline a phenomenology of desistance.

As such, this research is intended as a supplement to research on the structural correlates and predictors of desistance (e.g., Sampson & Laub, 1993). Subjective aspects of human life (emotions, thoughts, motivations, and goals) have largely been neglected in the study of crime, because the data are presumed to be either unscientific or too unwieldy for empirical analysis (Groves & Lynch, 1990; Toch, 1987). Although we know that individuals respond to situations differently on the basis of their interpretations and outlooks (Caspi & Moffitt, 1995), these individual differences have not received the same attention as the more easily measured structural factors influencing criminal behavior. Narrative research methodology makes it possible to empirically examine the cognitive mediators between these environmental influences and individual behavior.

At the same time, although the data for this study are psychologically analyzed, these narratives cannot be understood outside of their social, historical, and structural context (Bertaux, 1981; Hagan, 1998). Self-narratives are developed through social interaction. Appraisals from those around us, modeling, and structural obstacles and opportunities all influence the process of identity change (Becker, 1964; Felson, 1985). Moreover, each person adopts a self-story based on the limited range of interpretations or narrative archetypes "proposed, suggested and imposed on him by his culture, his society and his social group" (Foucault, 1988b, p. 11).

The identity stories fashioned by the participants in this research can be seen as rational adaptations within existing paradigms of public discourse (Henry & Milovanovic, 1996). According to Foote and Frank (1999), "The social availability of preferred stories, and the assimilation of experience to these narratives, is *how power works* [italics added]. The power of the dominant discourse is to include some stories as tellable and to exclude others as marginal and abnormal" (p. 177). The narratives collected as part of the LDS, therefore, say as much about subcultural and societal pressures facing ex-deviants (and how these can be *resisted*) as they do about individual competencies and inclinations.

Additionally, the LDS findings have intriguing implications for the applied world of correctional policy and practice. After all, the vast majority of work that is carried out in the name of offender rehabilitation and treatment—from cognitive therapy to Alcoholics Anonymous—focuses on changing offender self-perspectives. Self-help and professional counseling inevitably involve exploring one's life history, listening to the personal testimonies of others, and revising one's social outlook. In particular, an exciting, new wave of correctional programming is based on understanding and correcting the "cognitive distortions" that can lead to criminal behavior (Bush, 1995; Ross & Ross, 1995). These activities can surely benefit from a research-based model of the self-narratives that seem most supportive of successful desistance from crime.

WHAT DID WE FIND?

The findings from this research may surprise many of those working in corrections and offender treatment. As Irwin (1970) argued, "Criminal ex-convicts do 'straighten up their hands,' but they do not approach the model of the reformed man held by behavioral scientists or prison administrators" (p. 176). Not that the sample members failed to display any cognitive distortions. Far from it. In fact, interviewees displayed an exaggerated sense of control over the future and an inflated, almost missionary, sense of purpose in life. They recast their criminal pasts not as the shameful failings that they are but instead as the necessary prelude to some newfound calling. In general, the highly positive accounts bore almost no resemblance to the ugly realities of the ex-offenders' lives (as one understands them in criminological research).

The catch is, these distortions were made by the ex-convicts who were going straight—the "reformed" ex-cons—not those who were still committing crime. The active offenders I interviewed, on the other hand, seemed fairly accurate in their assessments of their situation (dire), their chances of achieving success in the "straight" world (minimal), and their place in mainstream society ("need not apply"). That is, if accuracy is measured in terms of a correspondence with popular views, then it is the desisting ex-offenders whose narratives seem the most out of step with reality (see Seligman, 1991, for parallels in the study of depression).

I describe this process of willful, cognitive distortion as "making good." To make good is to find reason and purpose in the bleakest of life histories (Frankl, 1984; Taylor, 1983). In many ways, this resembles an organic version of Rotenberg's (1987) proposal for therapeutic "rebiographing" or "rehabilitative storytelling," in which former deviants are encouraged to actively "correct" their pasts "for the sake of psychological continuity and cognitive congruity" (p. 49). By "selectively and creatively reinterpreting past events to suit future aspirations," the ex-offender is able to justify one's past while also rationalizing the decision to go straight (p. 50). Rotenberg called this a "legitimate historical rehabilitation method" through which the "failing parts in a person's history are contracted while the reinterpreted reconstructed parts are expanded to create a more congruent life story dialogue between the future-oriented present new 'I' and the past 'thou'" (p. 65).

By "making good," not only is the desisting ex-offender "changed," but he or she is also reconstituted. As with first becoming deviant, "the former identity stands as accidental; the new identity is the basic reality. What he is now is what, after all, he was all along" (Garfinkel, 1956, pp. 421–422). Creating this sense of order out of disorderly lives may be of particular importance to those who are trying to maintain an important life change such as desisting from crime.

LAYOUT OF THIS BOOK

I begin chapter 1 by reviewing what is known about desistance. The irony here is that, although the relationship between aging and the abandonment of criminal behavior is one of the oldest and best-known findings in criminological research (dating back at least to Quetelet, 1833/1984), it is also one of the least understood phenomena in the field (Moffitt, 1993). Recently, criminologists have sought to explain the aging-out phenomenon by pointing to normative, biological changes and predictable social transitions during the life course. Although turning points such as turning 30 or getting married can indeed inspire a person to decide to change, making this decision is only half the battle. These explanations can be therefore strengthened by research on the subjective or cognitive process by which an ex-offender is able to maintain the resolve to change over time and in the face of life's predictable setbacks.

Chapter 2 describes the Liverpool Desistance Study, a recent examination of this subjective process. The LDS involved two carefully matched samples of ex-offenders: one group that is still active in criminal behavior and the other that is actively going straight. Using narrative methodology, the life stories of these ex-offenders were content analyzed and compared quantitatively and qualitatively for the systematic differences between the two groups that might hold the clues to understanding desistance as a psychosocial process. Further discussion of the sampling procedure, research methodology, and analysis can be found in the appendix.

Part II of this book is titled "Two Views of a Brick Wall." The two views refer to the overall worldview of the active offender sample and the worldview of the desisting sample. The "brick wall" is of course the situation all of the sample members face as long-term, persistent offenders and ex-convicts.

Chapter 3 paints as "objective" a picture of this social situation as possible. As I say in the title of this chapter, "Sample Prognosis: Dire," things do not look too good. The risk factors and structural obstacles facing all of the participants include the following: impoverished backgrounds replete with physical and emotional abuse; long criminal histories and the stigma that accompanies them; long-term use of addictive substances like alcohol and heroin; personality traits that favor adventure and excitement over routine and responsibility; and residence in an area notorious for its limited economic opportunities. All of the sample participants face roughly these same obstacles, yet over half of the sample is making good and avoiding the lure of criminal pursuits.

Chapter 4 describes the "reactive person–environment interactions" (Caspi & Moffitt, 1995) that characterize the way habitual offenders view and respond to their circumstances. This perspective is described as a "condemnation script." The persistent offenders who agreed to participate in this research shared a sense of being doomed or fated to their situation in life. They sought temporary comfort in criminal pursuits, because they felt they had little chance of achieving success in the "straight world." Indeed, from what we know about the causes of criminal behavior, they might just be right. Yet, in this case, this rational realism probably does the individual a disservice (see also Alloy & Abramson, 1979).

The good news is that a person's past need not be a life sentence (Sampson & Laub, 1993; Seligman, 1993). Chapter 5 outlines the overall self-story—sometimes called the *macronarrative* or *Gestalt* (Harvey, Weber, & Orbuch, 1990)—that seems to best characterize the prototypical self-story told by desisting ex-offenders. The "redemption script" outlined in this chapter is the heart of this book and the primary contribution to the research literature from the LDS. In this narrative, rather than "knifing off" or hiding away their past lives in crime, interviewees sought to turn their past lives into something positive using a form of "tragic optimism" (Frankl, 1984). Even the most shameful of pasts can be "put to use" as a sort of moral tale to help guide others in the right direction. In this way, the former deviant becomes a "wounded healer"[1] (Nouwen, 1972) and a role model for others.

---

[1] I first heard this term from Father Peter Young of Albany, New York, who may have been among the first to use the label in the field of ex-offender reform and recovery—a subject he knows a little something about after over 30 years in the business.

This model contradicts many of our images of how reformed ex-offenders think—and how we think they *should* think (Irwin, 1970). For instance, the narratives displayed little evidence of the aging ex-offender who burns out through sheer exhaustion, the defiant rebel who gets his spirit broken by the System, or the repentant sinner who is shamed into reform. In Part III, I analyze these alternative models of the reformed self, implicit in much correctional practice and policy, in light of the findings from this research.

At least since Glueck and Glueck (1937/1966), researchers who study desistance from crime have suggested that the study of how people reform "on their own" could aid in the improvement of professional activities conducted in the name of offender reform (e.g., Rex, 1999; Uggen & Piliavin, 1998). In other words, "Can educators, psychologists, correctional workers, and others devise means of 'forcing the plant,' as it were, so that benign maturation will occur earlier than it seems to at present?" (Glueck & Glueck, 1937/1966, p. 205). The LDS is not an applied study, nor was the intent to evaluate any specific correctional programs. However, as a considerable part of correctional practice involves trying to change the self-narrative of inmates, the content of desisting self-narratives can be a useful benchmark for analyzing these efforts.

Chapter 6 explores the rehabilitative capacity of "work," probably the oldest idea in the reform of criminal offenders (Simon, 1993). The theme of "productivity" and the agentic themes of achievement and accomplishment are common in the narratives of desisting ex-offenders. In fact, these are among the themes that best distinguished desisting narratives from those in the active group. Importantly, however, the content of the work valued in the desisting narratives is specific. Desisting ex-offenders emphasize the desire to make some important contribution to their communities, and in particular to individuals like themselves who find themselves in trouble with the law.

Chapter 7 addresses the sticky issue of "Shame, Blame, and the Core Self." A considerable amount of correctional work with offenders involves "shaming" and other efforts to convince offenders to "take responsibility" for what he or she has done wrong. Although desisting interviewees do admit that many of the things they had done in the past were "stupid mistakes," they frequently blame this behavior on circumstances, their social situation, and other factors such as addiction and delinquent friends. Overall, they present themselves as good people "deep down" who were thrust into bad behaviors. This seems quite different from the repentant sinner model, yet some level of self-protection may be necessary to account for long years of offending behavior. Equally, a "love the sinner, hate the sin" approach to shaming might improve the effectiveness of such interventions (e.g., Braitwaite & Mugford, 1994).

Finally, although desisting narrators often make excuses for past criminal behavior, they portray themselves very much in control of their current and future life direction. This change in personal agency is frequently attributed to empowerment from some outside source. In the last chapter, "The Rituals of Redemption," these social and interactional processes of empowerment and reintegration are explored in the desisting narratives. Reformed ex-offenders emphasize that their reform has been "certified" by a variety of authorities. In fact, rituals involving exoneration from judges, family members, and others are salient scenes throughout the narratives. Such rituals, if they were to be institutionalized as part of reintegration practice, might improve efforts to reintegrate ex-offenders into society.

FINAL CAVEATS

All of the research participants who have offered their life stories for this project were nonrandomly identified because they fit the profile for what has been called the "career criminal" or "persistent offender." That is, each has at some point in their life been engaged in a sustained period of very high-frequency offending. These persistent thieves—perhaps wrongly (see Gottfredson & Hirschi, 1986; Weitekamp, Frieze, Kukla, Reed, & Rest, 1987)—have been the obsession of criminologists and the criminal justice system since at least the Philadelphia cohort study (Wolfgang, Figlio, & Sellin, 1972). They represent the infamous 5% or 6% of offenders who are responsible for over half of all recorded crimes. It should be noted, however, that these offenses tend to be relatively "ordinary" crimes such as burglary, theft, and drug sales, and very rarely more serious offenses like rape or murder. This too is consistent with what is known about persistent offenders in general (e.g., Weitekamp et al., 1987). Obviously, it is far easier to sustain a career in stealing car radios over the span of a decade than it is to engage in a sustained pattern of homicidal behavior. The infamous 5 or 6% are not serial killers but petty thieves, vandals, and punks.

As such, the sample participants tend to be young, working-class "street" offenders—or what Shover (1996) referred to as the "deskilled criminal Lumpenproletariat"—and not offenders from the much more lucrative worlds of corporate, white-collar, and political crime. The purpose of this targeted sampling is not to lend credibility to the myth that only the poor can be career criminals. Instead, these individuals were chosen precisely *because* they are the people who are most susceptible to the public imputation of permanent or essential deviance. Street offenders, and not their corporate counterparts, are typically the bogeymen whom society labels "sociopaths" or "incorrigibles." Their transition away from criminal behavior, therefore, was deemed the most interesting conversion to explore in this study of self-change.

Moreover, we already know a good deal about how people who have middle-class social networks and "noncriminal identity interests" (Waldorf, Reinarman, & Murphy, 1991) can abandon criminal behavior. The white-collar or corporate deviant can fall back on family savings, a college education, or the support of well-connected friends to aid their transition out of crime. Witness the mainstream success of ex-offenders like Michael Milken or Oliver North (a recent news report gushed "Forget junk bonds. These days, financier Michael Milken is making his money from the boom in internet stocks"). There is little mystery in how such people manage to avoid re-arrest. The socially excluded street offenders in this sample face far more obstacles to reintegration, because in most cases they were never integrated in the mainstream in the first place. The self-transformation they describe is a more extreme and, I think, theoretically interesting case of self-change than moving from junk bonds to internet stocks.

Still, it is hoped that the ramifications of this research are not limited exclusively to ex-convicts. At the most abstract level, this research is an exploration of how *all* people can sustain radical changes in entrenched patterns of behavior. Although one should be careful about overgeneralization, past research on other examples of self-change (e.g., losing weight, quitting smoking, and overcoming alcoholism) has uncovered "robust commonalties in how people modify their behavior" (Prochaska, DiClemente, & Norcross, 1992, p. 1110). Also, the motivational themes and perspectives herein described by reformed ex-offenders will be familiar and meaningful to even the least deviant among us on some level.

This may be especially true because, whenever possible, the argument of this book is presented in the words of this study's participants themselves. As Conway (1998) argued,

> If we think of Rousseau offering statistical calculations of the likelihood that his experience correlates closely with that of other men of his generation in France, we see his claims to be a "new man" differently. But his autobiography tells us, sometimes in too much detail, just how it felt to him. And that magical opportunity of entering another life is what really sets us thinking about our own. (p. 18)

This "magical opportunity" for empathetic understanding is the explicit goal of this project, and some might suggest a fair ambition for the social sciences in general (see esp. Bertaux, 1981; Matza, 1969). Although not as comforting or sensational as the myth of the bogeyman, it is hoped that the realization that the Them are a lot like Us is closer to what Burgess (1988) meant by a "fair picture of human life."

I

DISSECTING DESISTANCE

Desistance from crime is an unusual dependent variable for criminologists because it is not an event that happens, rather it is the sustained *absence* of a certain type of event (in this case, crime). There is an old joke along the lines of "stopping smoking is easy—I do it every week." The same can be said for persistent offenders, who often make several pronouncements that they plan to "go legitimate" or "go straight" only to find themselves returning to criminal behavior. Quitting crime or terminating a criminal career, then, also seems to be quite easy. The difficult part is to "go straight" and *stay* that way. Equally difficult is the process of measuring and accounting for the sustained maintenance of inactivity.

It is argued here that sustained desistance most likely requires a fundamental and intentional shift in a person's sense of self. The study of desistance may therefore similarly require something of a shift in the way that criminal behavior is studied and analyzed. This section is an attempt to summarize what is currently known about desistance and what gaps the Liverpool Desistance Study (LDS) is intended to fill.

Understanding how the process of desistance works has always been important but may be even more so in the present era of unprecedented incarceration. In the United States, it is estimated that over 500,000 inmates, many of them struggling with problems of substance abuse and addiction, will be released from correctional facilities every year for at least the next decade (Travis, 2000). Among these, approximately two-thirds are likely to be re-arrested in the 3 years following their release (Reno, 2000). Accordingly, the question of how to improve the process of ex-offender reentry or reintegration will be among the most important issues facing the country in the next few decades. There seem few better ways to start this discussion than by first understanding successful cases of desistance from lives of crime and addiction.

1

DEFINING DESISTANCE

One of the "staples" of criminological research, dating back to before the turn of the 20th century, is the concept of the chronic, incorrigible, or "hardened" criminal fated to a lifetime of criminality (Gottfredson & Hirschi, 1986, p. 214). The early positivists in criminology suggested that these natural-born criminals were apelike, biological throwbacks who had not fully evolved as human beings (Rafter, 1997). Behavior reform was essentially deemed impossible for this population. Lombroso (1911), for instance, wrote that "Atavism shows us the inefficacy of punishment for born criminals and why it is that they inevitably have periodic relapses into crime" (p. 369).

Although the age of criminal anthropology with its "radical naivetés" has largely given way to social and psychological understandings of crime, the notion of intractable criminality is still very much alive in criminology and popular thought (Foucault, 1988a, p. 145). Glaser (1964) wrote,

> Despite this shift from hereditary to environmental interpretations of crime, there still is a tendency to think of the person whose experiences make him [or her] a criminal as distinctly different from the noncriminal. Theories for the explanation of criminality, from "multiple causation" to "differential association" to "containment," all seem to imply that when the totality of influences making for criminality exceed the totality of influences making for noncriminality, the person becomes a criminal. . . . The implication is that once criminality results

from this process, it usually is a fairly steady state, not readily or quickly reversed. (p. 466)

In fact, Gove (1985) has argued that *all* of criminology's major theoretical perspectives either explicitly or implicitly suggest that criminal behavior is "an amplifying process that leads to further and more serious deviance" (p. 118; see also Hirschi & Gottfredson, 1983, p. 553). Even labeling theory suggests that once a person internalizes a deviant label, the stigma is "almost irreversible" (K. Erikson, 1962, p. 311). "No systematic effort has been made to specify the social mechanisms which might operate to 'return' the stigmatized secondary deviant to a 'normal' and acceptable role in the community" (Trice & Roman, 1970, p. 539).

As such, criminology has faced a significant challenge in recent years. After all, although it is true that most adult offenders showed signs of being delinquent children, the majority of juvenile delinquents do not become adult offenders (McCord, 1980). By the time they reach age 28, around 85% of people called "offenders" seem to stop offending by most estimates (Blumstein & Cohen, 1987). For most individuals, participation in "street crimes" like burglary, robbery, and drug sales (the types of offenses of most concern to criminologists) generally begins in the early teenage years, peaks in late adolescence or young adulthood, and disappears before the person reaches age 30 (see Figure 1.1).

Some even argue that this well-known "age-crime curve" has remained virtually unchanged for at least 150 years (Gottfredson & Hirschi, 1990; but see Greenberg, 1994; Steffensmeier, Allan, Harer, & Streifel, 1989). Of course, the age-crime relationship apparent in official records like Figure 1.1 does not itself prove that offenders mature out of criminal behavior. For instance, as offenders age, they may simply become more adept at not getting caught by the police, or else they just spend more time incarcerated (and therefore are not getting arrested). Alternatively, older offenders may simply slow down their offending to a level at which they are rarely apprehended or move into a less risky type of criminal activity, such as white-collar offending.

Still, although these hypotheses may explain some portion of the official age–crime relationship, the same pattern emerges in longitudinal research using self-report data (e.g., Farrington, 1992), long-term ethnography (e.g., Sullivan, 1989), and life history studies (e.g., Shover, 1985). There is little doubt among the research community today that the vast majority of delinquents and adult offenders reliably desist from offending behavior in later life (Rutherford, 1992).

Matza (1964) was among the first to illustrate how this widespread phenomenon of desistance from crime contradicts the majority of sociological and psychological theories of criminal behavior. In what he called an "embarrassment of riches," Matza posited that criminological theories

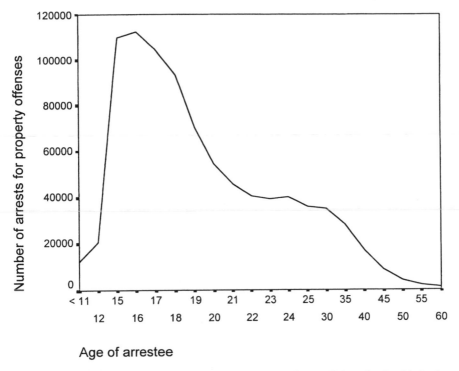

Figure 1.1. Arrests for property offenses by age. From *Crime in the United States*, 1995, by the U.S. Department of Justice, Federal Bureau of Investigation, 1996, pp. 218–219.

vastly overpredict criminal behavior partially because they fail to acknowledge the temporary and contingent nature of criminality. Matza concluded that instead of viewing criminality as a permanent property of individuals, one should conceive of deviance as something that individuals sporadically "drift" in and out of during certain periods of the life course.

In the same year that Matza's (1964) *Delinquency and Drift* appeared, Glaser (1964) described a typical offending history as a "zigzag path" between crime and noncrime. In his exhaustive study of former prisoners, Glaser found that there was little support for the idea that criminality was a stable trait.

> These are the cases that justify the maxim that no human being should ever be regarded as hopelessly criminal. Today all are law-abiding and orderly, yet a decade or less earlier most were condemned as psychopaths. They include men who were considered the most criminal and intractable prisoners in the entire federal system. (p. 56)

Consequently, Glaser concluded his book with a challenge to the field of criminology:

> This view of criminality as generally an oscillating behavior pattern suggests that it may be more fruitful, for rehabilitation objectives, to

shift the focus of criminological theories from [a] search for the processes that make for persistence in crime to [the] development and test
[of] a theory on the conditions that promote change from crime to
noncrime and back again. (pp. 466–467)

While the Matza/Glaser challenge might be seen as the catalyst for
the new "criminal career" or "developmental criminology" paradigm (e.g.,
LeBlanc & Loeber, 1998; Thornberry, 1997), the research community has
probably not approached the sort of theoretical understanding they advo-
cated.[2] In one of the most thorough analyses of the topic, Moffitt (1993)
argued that the aging-out phenomenon remains "at once the most robust
and least understood empirical observation in the field of criminology"
(p. 675). Similarly, Hirschi and Gottfredson (1983) said that the age–crime
relationship "easily qualifies as the most difficult fact in the field" (p. 553).

WHAT IS DESISTANCE?

One obstacle to understanding desistance from crime is the lack of a
clear definition of just what this thing is that we hope to understand. It
might be that the model of desistance used in the research literature to
date has hindered our understanding of the phenomenon (Bushway et al.,
2000; Laub & Sampson, 2000; Maruna, 1998).

Desistance as a Termination Event

As is reflected in the language of "burnout" and "spontaneous remis-
sion," the criminal career literature traditionally imagines desistance as an
event—an abrupt cessation of criminal behavior. This assumption is made
explicit in both the statistical models favored in criminal career research
(e.g., Barnett, Blumstein, & Farrington, 1987) and on the rare occasion
that researchers define desistance in the literature. For example, in the most
enlightening, contemporary discussion of the subject in the criminological
literature, Shover (1996) defined *desistance* as "the voluntary termination
of serious criminal participation" (p. 121). Another recent, comprehensive
review of the subject describes desistance as the "moment that a criminal
career ends" (Farrall & Bowling, 1999). In this version of desistance, one

---

[2]Gottfredson and Hirschi (1986) and Shover (1996, p. 124) have both argued that criminal
career research continues to focus primarily on identifying born criminals (although now called
"career criminals" or "life-course persistent offenders")—a practice that was criticized by Glaser
(1964) and Matza (1964). Rife with false positives, false negatives, and false promises, this
prediction literature has been "plagued with high hopes yet weak results" in attempts to
predict who will become career criminals, according to Sampson and Laub (1995, p. 150).
Gottfredson and Hirschi (1986) wrote, "The 20–20 hindsight of career criminal research turns
out to have been misleading. When asked to identify career criminals in advance of their
criminal careers, the research community requests additional funding" (p. 217).

quits crime in much the same way as one resigns from a legitimate occupation. Accordingly, there has been a sustained focus on turning points, conversion experiences, and the life events that can cause this decision to "take this job and shove it."

Unfortunately, the career metaphor misses a fundamental fact about criminal behavior pointed out by Matza and Glazer: It is sporadic (Luckenbill & Best, 1981). Therefore, "termination" takes place all of the time. For example, a person can steal a purse on a Tuesday morning, then terminate criminal participation for the rest of the day. Is that desistance? Is it desistance if the person does not steal another purse for a week? A month? A year? Farrington (1986) warned that "even a five-year or ten-year crime-free period is no guarantee that offending has terminated" (p. 201). Most researchers who use terms like *cessation* or *termination* seem to imply that this is a permanent change. Yet, such permanence can only be determined retrospectively (Frazier, 1976)—presumably after the ex-offender is deceased.

More critically, even if we do decide to study only dead desisters, we *still* have no real understanding of how to measure the termination "moment." For instance, suppose we know conclusively that the purse-snatcher in the previous example (now deceased) never committed another crime for the rest of his long life. When did his desistance start? Is not the voluntary termination point or concluding moment the very instant when the person completes (or terminates) the act of theft? If so, in the same moment that a person becomes an offender, he also becomes a desister. That cannot be right.

Alternatively, one could model the termination point as the moment when the person decides to quit the life of crime. So, in the case of the dead purse-snatcher, perhaps he gets apprehended by the police and this failure leads him to decide that crime is a bad idea. Research on this decision-making process (e.g., Cusson & Pinsonneault, 1986) is often referred to as the *choice* or *rational choice* model of desistance. Indeed, when analyzed in retrospective accounts, this reasoning does indeed appear to be very rational. When researchers ask former deviants *why* they quit offending, they typically receive answers like "Because I was sick of the lifestyle," "I burnt out/hit rock bottom," "It was time to do other things," "I had no alternative but to quit," and a variety of quite rational-sounding, self-interested reasons (Waldorf, 1983; W. G. West, 1978).

Yet, deciding to desist and actually desisting are two very different things. As one of the interviewees in my research stated,

> Well, whenever you're in prison you see the light so to speak. "Oh, I'm never going back." So I was all that, "Oh, I'm never going back," and I done well for a while. I managed to get a job and stuff, but things started going back to the old routine. (male, age 24)

This point was empirically confirmed in an Oxford University study of recidivism (Burnett, 1992). When the researchers asked a sample of prison inmates whether they wanted to go straight, over 80% responded, yes, they were sick of the life of crime and would love to desist. Twenty months after being released from prison, almost 60% of the sample reported reoffending. Sitting in a prison cell or riding in the back of a police van, apparently, many an ex-offender decides that crime does not pay. Understanding the rationality of such decisions, however, should not be confused with understanding the *process* of going straight and *staying* that way.

Smokers can relate. Ex-smokers who give up smoking usually quit because it is bad for their health. Very rational. Yet, most smokers who give up smoking also resume smoking again in a few days (or hours) after they decided to quit for this quite rational reason (Prochaska & Di-Clemente, 1992). So, understanding *why* people give up smoking (because it is unhealthy) is not the same as understanding *how* people who make this decision actually maintain their resolve against short-term temptations. It is my contention that the latter question is the more important one in the study of desistance.

Although the metaphor of the "moment of clarity" conversion experience is embedded in Western discourse, research on how people change entrenched patterns of behavior contradicts the image of self-change as a moment or event (e.g., Baskin & Sommers, 1998; Maruna, 1997; Pickles & Rutter, 1991; Prochaska & DiClemente, 1992). DiClemente (1994) argued that achieving a lasting personality change can take between 7 and 10 years. Hence, the gestation period for being "born again" may actually take longer than the 9 months it took the first time around.[3] Even in the literature of Alcoholics Anonymous (AA), which popularized the "hitting bottom" idea of recovery, it is clear that a person's "first experience of 'bottom' is unlikely to make him [or her] amenable to the AA identity" (Lofland, 1969, p. 252). The "dramatic white-light conversion" described by AA co-founder Bill Wilson has been criticized as an unlikely and unhelpful parable even by members of AA themselves (O'Reilly, 1997, p. 103).

> Most commonly, [conversion in AA] is represented not by a moment of abrupt change at a single point in the past, some cataclysmic disruption of the cognitive universe, but rather by an account of gradual accommodation to AA folkways and a set of adjustments . . . to everyday life without a drink. (O'Reilly, 1997, p. 120)

---

[3]A similar paradigm shift is taking place in sociological research on religious conversions (e.g., Neitz, 1990; Richardson, 1985). The model of the instantaneous conversion based on Paul's experience on the road to Damascus is being replaced by a framework that sees individuals more as the agents of their own conversion.

While "turning points" and rational decisions ("moments of clarity") may serve an important symbolic and psychological function, their value to the understanding of desistance has probably been overstated. Trice and Roman (1970) argued that many "hitting bottom" stories may be exaggerated to set the stage for impressive "comeback accomplishments" (p. 543). Furthermore, as Knupfer (1972) pointed out, individuals often give "strangely trivial reasons" for giving up deviant behaviors (see also Biernacki, 1986). Most importantly, nothing inherent in a situation makes it a turning point. One person's reason for changing their life (e.g., "hitting bottom" or else finally making the "big score" in the crime game) might be another person's reason to escalate offending ("Now I have nothing to lose" or "See how easy this is?"). As such, randomly assigning identical turning-point experiences to addicts and offenders, in the hope that this would trigger self-transformation, might be a formula for disaster.[4]

Like the person who makes a New Year's resolutions to give up chocolates, the ex-offender who decides he or she wants to desist from a life of drugs and crime often loses his or her resolve when faced with temptation and frustration. Consider the testimony of two of the recovering heroin users I (SM) interviewed as part of my research:

> SM: After one of these prison sentences, did you say to yourself, "I ought to get off this (heroin)?"
>
> Interviewee: Oh yeah, yeah I wanted to get off it definitely. I've come out of prison and I haven't touched it, you know what I mean, I have done that like. I've stayed off it, I think I stayed off it for 6 months, and that's the longest I've stayed off it. Completely off it, smack and methadone both. Then, I had all troubles with me ex-girlfriend, you know, who I had the baby to, and then like, she stopped me seeing the baby you know, and shit like this. And everything just built up and that was it. I had one (hit) and got back into the swing dead easily. (male, age 26)

As another interviewee explained:

> Lots of heroin users, people on drugs, even coke, will wake up one morning and think, "I'm sick of doing this every day. I've got to stop," and then they'll want to stay away from everyone. So if you get a few of them urges where they want to come off it and then you get this big turning point and you think "That is it. I am not going to use no

---

[4]Lofland's (1969) notion of "disorienting episodes" probably better captures the role of these significant episodes in ex-offenders' lives than the notion of the "turning point." In a disorienting episode, individuals are forced to reconsider their typical patterns of behavior and become "amenable" to going straight or making some other change (Lofland, 1969, p. 252). Indeed, turning points have been similarly recast as "triggering events" in a recent reformulation of the sociogenic argument (Laub et al., 1998). Like a disorienting episode, a triggering event can cause a person to question one's direction; it is not, however, seen as a cause of desistance.

more." And, you've just got to try and do it, 'cause if you don't, you do go (back to drugs) like that [snaps his finger], and I've done a few of them (relapses). I've done a couple of days and couple weeks and a couple of months (of abstinence), and then I'll get some slap in the face, and I've done years on it (heroin) again. This is the longest I've ever been off now, going on a year and a half. (male, age 33)

Desistance as a Maintenance Process

Desistance might more productively be defined as the long-term abstinence from crime among individuals who had previously engaged in persistent patterns of criminal offending. The focus here is not on the transition or change, but rather on the maintenance of crime-free behavior in the face of life's obstacles and frustrations—that is, when "everything builds up" or one receives "some slap in the face." This alternative definition can be inferred from the only context in which the word *desist* is ever heard outside of criminology: the "cease and desist order." The call to *cease and desist* is a request to stop what you are doing (cease) and refrain from doing it again (desist).

The emphasis on refraining is also apparent in the colloquial terminology used for the desistance process. Although ex-offenders do not describe themselves as "desisting," they do talk about "going straight," "making good," or "going legit" (Irwin, 1970). These phrases imply an ongoing work in progress. One *goes* legit. One does not talk about having *turned* legit or having *become* legit. The "going" is the thing.

This language is meaningful. During a focus group with a dozen ex-offenders, for instance, I was admonished for using the term *rehabilitation* (Maruna, Naples, & LeBel, 1999). "We don't like the word 'rehabilitation'; we prefer 'recovery,'" I was told. Although synonymous at first sight, the two terms differ significantly in their linguistic implications. A person can be rehabilitated by a program or by a treatment professional, yet recovery is an individual, agentic, and purposeful process. Like "going legit," recovery is also distinctly subjective and frequently considered an ongoing process (as in the Twelve-Step notion that former alcoholics are always "recovering"). A person works at recovery, like he or she "goes" legit.

Borrowing from Foote and Frank's (1999) eloquent definition of *resistance*, then, desistance is "no end state where one can be; rather, it is a perpetual process of arrival" (p. 179). This definitional distinction will have acute implications for the study of desistance. The study of termination or cessation triggers the question of *why*. If a watch stops ticking or a heart stops beating, we look for the variable or variables that caused this change. Specifically, we look for new things that happen at about the same time as the termination event that could be responsible for the change. The study of maintenance, on the other hand, requires a different explanation, this time sparking the question of *how*. How do some watches keep ticking (despite taking whatever licking)? How do some hearts keep beating when faced with stress and trauma? Ironically, then, the study of desistance might best be construed as the study of *continuity* rather than change—continuity of nondeviant behaviors. Continuity research focuses on the personality variables, interactions, and environmental consistencies that allow for long-term persistence in various behaviors (see especially Caspi & Moffitt's [1995] review), and not for "causes."

Importantly, the ability to *maintain* abstinence might be wholly unrelated to the initial cause (or one's initial reason) for *ceasing* the behavior in the first place. Felton Earls and his colleagues wrote, "Initiating change is but the first step. The second step involves maintaining the change . . . (and) the skills required for initiating behavior change are usually different from those required for maintaining it" (Earls, Cairns, & Mercy, 1993, p. 291). Similarly, in their research on alcoholism, Amodeo, Kurtz, and Cutter (1992) speculated that "negative" or "avoidant" motives, such as fear of arrest, physical deterioration, family breakup, or job loss, might be the most common incentives for "putting down the bottle." Yet, more positive or "approach" motives such as a sense of purpose in life or a commitment to occupational success might be more influential in *maintaining* sobriety (p. 709). Avoidant motives can be powerful catalysts for action, they suggested, but they may not be enough to sustain long-term resolve against powerful temptations.

In terms of criminal offending, there is no great mystery as to *why* a person would choose to avoid crime. The material and personal benefits resulting from most criminal behavior are miniscule, the risks are high, and prisons and jails are generally miserable places to spend one's life (Gottfredson & Hirschi, 1990; Shover, 1996). The bigger question is *how* exoffenders are able to make good in the face of widespread social stigma, limited career opportunities, and social exclusion. Abstaining from crime under these highly criminogenic circumstances requires some explanation.

EXPLANATIONS OF DESISTANCE

The two most often cited explanations of how desistance is maintained fall into the dichotomy of ontogenetic and sociogenic paradigms (Matsueda & Heimer, 1997; Sullivan, 1996). According to ontogenetic explanations, the young offender eventually "ages out" of crime, with the "sheer passage of time" turning the offender into a responsible adult (Glueck & Glueck, 1940). According to the sociogenic accounts, what every delinquent needs to turn him or her around is "a steady job and the love of a good woman"—or man, presumably.

There are at least two other plausible stories for how people desist, yet both have fallen so far out of favor in the past three decades that they are hardly ever mentioned in discussions of desistance from crime. The first, the *medical model story*, suggests that offenders desist when they are "fixed" or corrected by psychotherapy or offender rehabilitation. The second, the *specific deterrence story*, says that offenders get sent to jail, learn their lesson, and resign themselves never to go back.

A growing body of evidence suggests that correctional interventions, especially addiction treatment programs, can in fact be very effective in reducing overall rates of recidivism (Andrews & Bonta, 1998; McGuire, 1995). Yet, even the most extreme partisans on either side of the punishment–rehabilitation debate do not suggest that either state rehabilitation or punishment can account for most ex-offenders desisting in any consistent way. The rehabilitation workers I spoke to during the fieldwork for this project maintained the philosophy that "If I can just help one kid out of 20 turn his life around, I will be successful." On the other hand, the prison officers, on the front lines of the specific deterrence business, told me, "When we release some kid, I like to say, 'See you in a few weeks,' because they always come back."

In fact, in the United Kingdom, 53% of all inmates discharged from prisons in 1993 were reconvicted within 2 years (Kershaw & Renshaw, 1997). Among people who received community penalties in 1993, the 2-year reconviction rate was almost identical, at 57% (Kershaw, 1997). This well-known fact that "they" frequently do "come back" after being "corrected" or "deterred" is precisely the reason both stories have been assigned a minor role in the scientific understanding of desistance. Although no one believes that the state plays no role in the desistance process of ex-offenders, criminologists tend to look elsewhere, to forces like the labor market, to the family, and to the offender himself or herself, to account for this highly-predictable change in behavior.

"Growing Out of Crime"

One of the first social scientists to address the question of age and crime was Adolphe Quetelet (1833/1984), who argued that the penchant for crime diminishes with age because of the "enfeeblement of physical vitality." In 1919, Goring similarly described the process of aging out of crime as a "law of nature," comparing desistance to a biological process such as puberty. Sheldon and Eleanor Glueck (1940) included elements of this biology-based notion of desistance in their theory of "maturational reform," in which they argued that an intrinsic criminal impulse naturally declines after age 25. In this model, "Father Time" has an "inevitable effect upon biologic and psychologic processes" (Glueck & Glueck, 1937/1966, p. 15). Hence, "Aging is the only factor which emerges as significant in the reformative process" (Glueck & Glueck, 1940, p. 105).

Criminology's explanatory efforts "have not progressed appreciably" since the Gluecks' pioneering work, according to Shover (1985, p. 77). In fact, contemporary researchers have explicitly sought to resurrect the idea that desistance is due primarily to the "inexorable aging of the organism" (Gottfredson & Hirschi, 1990). Gottfredson and Hirschi (1990) suggested, "Crime declines with age. Spontaneous desistance is just that, change in behavior that cannot be explained and change that occurs regardless of what else happens" (p. 136; cf. Wilson & Herrnstein, 1985, p. 145). According to proponents of this view, the effect of age on criminal behavior is "direct," natural, and invariant across social, temporal, and economic conditions (Hirschi & Gottfredson, 1995, p. 135).

Usually implicit in such views is that physiological qualities of the aging individual account for the change (see Cline, 1980; Gove, 1985). For instance, one version of the biological argument is that the decline in criminality over time is linked to the decline in the production of testosterone over the life span. However, the link between testosterone levels and criminal behavior is anything but clear. Recent evidence suggests that in early adolescence, when differences in testosterone levels among boys are substantial, higher levels of testosterone are linked to social dominance and popularity but are actually *conversely* related to physical aggression (Schaal, Tremblay, & Soussignan, 1996). Second, even in animal studies in which it seems clear that higher levels of testosterone correlate with higher levels of aggressive behavior, it is still not clear that the testosterone causes the aggressive behavior. Just the opposite seems to be true, according to Sapolsky (1997):

> Study after study has shown that if you examine testosterone levels when males are first placed together in the social group, testosterone levels predict nothing about who is going to be aggressive. The subsequent behavioral differences drive the hormonal changes, rather than the other way around.[5] . . . Similarly, fluctuations in testosterone levels within one individual over time don't predict subsequent changes in the levels of aggression in that one individual. (p. 45)

This last point may be the most critical for the understanding of desistance: Although testosterone levels do decrease gradually with age,

---

[5]Sapolsky (1997) explained this frequent confusion between correlation and causation as a case of "physics envy" among scientists and scholars. **Sapolsky:** Because of a strong bias among certain scientists, it has taken forever to convince them of this point. Suppose you're studying what behavior and hormones have to do with each other. How do you study the behavioral part? You get yourself a notebook, a stopwatch, a pair of binoculars. How do you measure the hormones and analyze the genes that regulate them? You need some gazillion-dollar machines; you muck around with radiation and chemicals, wear a lab coat, maybe even goggles—the whole nine yards. Which toys would you rather get for Christmas? Which facet of science are you going to believe in more? The higher the technology, goes the formula, the more scientific the discipline. Hormones seem to many to be more substantive than behavior, so when a correlation occurs, it must be because hormones regulate behavior, not the other way around. (p. 46)

the age–testosterone curve is far from parallel to the sharply peaking age–crime curve (Farrington, 1986). As such, even if hormones play a role in criminal behavior, they do not by themselves seem to help explain why such behaviors decline so rapidly in young adulthood. The same can be said for other known, physiological changes in the human species. For instance, physical strength does not tend to peak until age 30, not 17, and the decline in physical abilities in adulthood is nowhere near as steep as the decline in criminal behavior seems to be (Adams, 1997).

Dannefer (1984) argued that explanations like the Glueck's maturational reform theory commit an "ontogenetic fallacy" by assuming that changes in behavior reflect the natural and universal "properties of the aging organism" rather than social or institutional processes (see also Greenberg, 1981; Sampson & Laub, 1993). Although aging certainly plays some role in the process of desistance, critics suggest that maturational reform explanations fail to "unpack" the "meaning" of age (Sampson & Laub, 1992). Age indexes a range of different variables, including biological changes, social transitions, and life experiences. For age to be a meaningful explanation of social behavior, according to this argument, one must ask which features indexed by age "constitute the mediating mechanisms" at work in this process (Rutter, 1996, p. 608; see also Matza, 1964; Wootton, 1959).

"A Steady Job and the Love of a Good Woman"

Beyond maturational reform, the next most influential understanding of the desistance process is the theory of social bonds or "informal social control." Social bond theory suggests that varying informal ties to family, employment, or educational programs in early adulthood can partially explain changes in criminality during the life course. Trasler (1980, cited in Gottfredson & Hirschi, 1990) wrote, "As they grow older, most young men gain access to other sources of achievement and social satisfaction—a job, a girlfriend, a wife, a home and eventually children—and in doing so become gradually less dependent upon peer-group support" (p. 135).

Sampson and Laub (1993) argued that these bonds provide individuals with a stake in conformity and a reason to go legit. Conversely, the theory predicts that those individuals who lack these bonds are the most likely to stay involved in criminal and delinquent behavior because they have the least to lose from social sanctions and ostracism.[6] Warr (1998)

---

[6]Substantial research confirms that desistance from crime is at least weakly correlated with stable employment (Glaser, 1964; Horney, Osgood, & Marshall, 1995; Laub, Nagin, & Sampson, 1998; Mischkowitz, 1994; Sampson & Laub, 1993; Shover, 1985), getting married (Farrington & West, 1995; Gibbens, 1984; Laub et al., 1998; Meisenhelder, 1977; Mischkowitz, 1994; Rand, 1987; Rutter, Quinton, & Hill, 1990; Sampson & Laub, 1993; Warr, 1998; Zoccolillo, Pickles, Quinton, & Rutter, 1992; but see Wright & Wright, 1992), completing education (Farrington, Gallagher, Morley, St. Ledger, & West, 1986; Rand, 1987), and becoming a parent (Hughes, 1998; Leibrich, 1993; but see Rand, 1987).

emphasized the second half of Trasler's formula, arguing that it is the pulling away from juvenile peer groups at the end of adolescence that is most facilitative of reform.

The standard criticism of sociogenic theory is that these arguments tend to downplay individual-level selection effects.[7] Critics like Gottfredson and Hirschi (1990), for instance, scoff at the notion that "jobs somehow attach themselves" to individuals, and they emphasize that "subjects are not randomly assigned to marital statuses" (p. 188). Because individuals self-select into "treatments" like "attachment to the labor force" and "cohesive marriages," they argued, the direction of causality or influence is difficult to determine. Gottfredson and Hirschi rejected the notion of peer group influence on similar grounds that "birds of a feather flock together." In other words, association with delinquents may be a product of one's delinquent tendencies rather than a cause.

A more serious challenge to sociogenic explanations is that, although occasionally modeled as "events" that can be sequentially ordered, the primary dependent and independent variables of the social bond model (good marriages, labor force participation, and desistance from crime) are all purposeful, ongoing social interactions with no fixed natures. In Irwin's (1970) colorful terms:

> The wife or old lady, who originally seemed so charming and beautiful often loses her charm and beauty. Debts mount, petty differences between husband and wife emerge, and the pleasant experiences between the two become rarer. . . . Often, after the passage of time, the family scene degenerates into an ugly, bickering, nagging routine, a far cry from that visualized from prison. (p. 144)

Just as desistance involves ongoing maintenance ("going legit"), stable marriages and labor force attachments also require constant care and feeding. Marriages, friendships, and careers are probably better understood as social constructions or processes than as stable conditions or events.

For this reason, sophisticated versions of sociogenic theory increasingly hold that the relationship between social ties and desistance has "strings attached" (Uggen, 1996). Sampson and Laub (1995), for instance, argued that employment "by itself" does not affect desistance. Rather, "employment coupled with job stability, commitment to work, and mutual ties binding workers and employers" reduces criminality (p. 146). Similarly, Rutter (1996) wrote, "Marriage as such has no very predictable effect. It all depends on the sort of person whom you marry, when you marry,

---

[7]Indeed, the exogenous nature of the institutional effects on individual behavior is an explicit assumption of sociogenic theory. According to Laub et al. (1998), "'Good' things sometimes happen to 'bad' actors" (p. 237) and "We emphasize that turning points are "triggering events" that are, in part, exogenous—that is, they are chance events. If these events were entirely the result of conscious calculations or enduring patterns of behavior, we could not argue for the independent role of social bonds in shaping behavior." (p. 225)

and the sort of relationship that is achieved" (p. 610). Finally, Loeber, Stouthamer-Loeber, Van Kammen, and Farrington (1991) argued that educational opportunities do not correlate with desistance, but "attitudes towards education" do (p. 71). Hence, desistance depends not only on the existence of social attachments but also on the perceived strength, quality, and interdependence of these interactions (Laub & Sampson, 1993; West, 1982).

SUPPLEMENTING THE POSITIVIST APPROACH: A PHENOMENOLOGY OF REFORM

In a qualitative study of ex-offenders in New Zealand, Leibrich (1993) could not find "any obvious external differences in the social environment of those who were going straight and those who were not" (p. 137). Instead, she attributed desistance to "major cognitive changes" experienced by her sample (p. 86). "Although there do seem to be some differences between people who are going straight and those who are not, the differences do not lie in simple facts of life, but rather in the way that people *interpret* their lives" (p. 199). In other words, as in the well-known aphorism among offenders that "You rehabilitate yourself" (Meisenhelder, 1977), families, jobs, age, or time cannot change a person who does not make a personal effort to change on the inside. Adams (1997) similarly noted,

> Thinking of criminal reform as self-initiated socialization highlights a side of the equation often ignored by researchers. Substantial and lasting changes in criminal behavior rarely come about only as a result of passive experience, and such changes are best conceptualized as the outcome of a process that involves significant participation by the offender, who, in many respects, acts as his or her own change agent. (pp. 334–335)

Both ontogenetic and sociogenic forces play crucial roles in the desistance process. No one can deny the importance of aging and societal attachments in the process of desisting from crime. Yet, Leibrich and Adams are not alone in arguing that what seems to be missing from both approaches to desistance is an understanding of the phenomenology of desistance (see also Clarke & Cornish, 1985; Cusson & Pinsonneault, 1986; Farrall & Bowling, 1999; Shover, 1996).

According to Caspi and Moffitt (1995), the fundamental tenet of phenomenological research is that different individuals exposed to the same environment experience it, interpret it, and react to it differently. "Each individual extracts a subjective psychological environment from the objective surroundings, and that subjective environment shapes both personality and subsequent interaction" (p. 485). Psychology's dramatic paradigm shift from behavioristic determinism to a more cognitively sophisticated understanding of human action (e.g., Chomsky, 1959) passed "largely unnoticed by criminologists" until very recently (Clarke & Cornish, 1985, p. 160). However, with the ascendance of rational choice understandings of crime, phenomenological and sociocognitive research into "criminal thinking" is resurgent (new books by Baumeister, 1997, and A. Beck, 2000, may trigger or signal a coming wave). Additionally, cognitive theories of criminal decision making have recently had a profound impact on the applied fields of offender therapy (e.g., Andrews & Bonta, 1998; Bush, 1995; Hollin, 1989; McGuire, 1995; Ross & Ross, 1995) and substance abuse counseling (e.g., Ellis & McInerney, 1992).

Phenomenological criminology is an attempt to understand criminal decision making through an examination of the offender's self-project—the self-image they are hoping to uphold (Toch, 1969), the ends they aim to achieve (Shover, 1996), and their strategies for creating meaning in their lives (Irwin, 1970; Shoham & Seis, 1993). In his phenomenology of crime, Katz (1988) described this as the "foreground of crime." Whereas most criminology focuses on the "background" of crime (the social, biological, and psychological characteristics that predispose one to criminal behavior), foreground research focuses on the "underlying cognitive mechanisms by which information about the world is selected, attended to, and processed" (Clarke & Cornish, 1985, p. 147).

Importantly, this sort of phenomenological approach should not be seen as competing with sociogenic and ontogenetic explanations but rather as a "supplement to the positivist approach" (Toch, 1987). Burnett (1992) wrote,

> Investigations into the correlates of offending and recidivism have been helpful in producing tools for prediction but are unable to answer more specific questions about how these correlates interact across time or how they impact on offenders' motivations, rationalizations and responses to opportunities to re-offend. . . . Knowledge of offenders' construction of their situation is essential to a fuller understanding of why there are different incidences of re-offending in apparently similar circumstances. (p. 181)

Analyzing the subjective experience of going straight can only strengthen criminology's understanding of the roles of social bonds and aging in the desistance process (Farrall & Bowling, 1999; Laub & Sampson, 1993).

The Gluecks, for instance, were not comfortable with the idea that biology alone could explain desistance, so they added an element of emotional or psychological maturation to their concept of maturational reform. "It was not achievement of any particular age, but rather the achievement of adequate maturation regardless of the chronological age at which it occurred that was the significant influence in the behavior change of our criminals" (Glueck & Glueck, 1945, p. 81). Unfortunately, the Gluecks left this notion of "maturity" dangerously vague, and their explanation was deemed tautological (Wootton, 1959, p. 164). Aware of this shortcoming, the Gluecks explicitly urged future researchers to "dissect maturation into its components" (Glueck & Glueck, 1940, p. 270) and "go more deeply into what might be denominated the content of age" (Glueck & Glueck, 1945, p. 79).

The best-developed theoretical argument in this tradition can be found in the work of Neal Shover (1983, 1985, 1996), who attributed desistance from crime, in part, to changes in "identity, self-concept and the framework employed to judge oneself and others" (Shover, 1983, p. 208). According to Shover (1996), the primary elements of this process include:

1. The "acquisition of an altered perspective on their youthful self and activities" (p. 131).
2. A growing awareness of time (p. 132).
3. A "revision of aspirations" to include goals such as "contentment, peace, and harmonious interpersonal relationships." (p. 134)

Similarly, Gove (1985, p. 128) linked desistance from crime to the following internal changes:

1. A shift from self-absorption to concern for others.
2. Increasing acceptance of societal values and behaving in socially appropriate ways.
3. Increasing comfort with social relations.
4. Increasing concern for others in their community.
5. Increasing concern with the issue of the meaning of life.

The subjective changes hypothesized by Shover and Gove provide the foundations for a phenomenological understanding of how ex-offenders go legit (and stay that way) that is consistent with existing qualitative research on the lived experience of criminal desistance (e.g., Adler, 1993; Baskin & Sommers, 1998; Burnett, 1994; Graham & Bowling, 1995; Hughes, 1998; Irwin, 1970; Jolin, 1985; Leibrich, 1993; Lofland, 1969; Maruna, 1997; Meisenhelder, 1982; Shover, 1985). Research on people who have overcome addictions also indicates that similar cognitive and subjective changes play a key role in the maintenance of change (Biernacki, 1986; Denzin, 1987; DiClemente, 1994; Kellogg, 1993; O'Reilly, 1997; Ronel, 1998; Singer, 1997; Stephens, 1991; Thune, 1977; Vaillant, 1983; Waldorf, 1983). Describing a wide range of samples, from probationers in New Zealand to heroin addicts in San Francisco, these studies suggest that there might be remarkable similarity in the explanations and self-understandings of ex-deviants.

When such persons are asked to "dissect maturation," the responses almost always stray away from behavioral manifestations (e.g., an absence of crime) and define maturity as a new way of "looking at the world" or constructing reality:

> My ideas, habits, the way I see life has changed. I used to have no purpose to the day and I didn't try to do anything. Now, I have a purpose and I'm realistic. I know the pros and cons. I used to be angry . . . never used to enjoy things like nature. . . . I'm more accepting now. (New York interviewee in Maruna et al., 1999)

So-called "maturation"[8] seems to refer to a transformation in what Gottfredson and Hirschi (1990) called "criminality" or the propensity/inclination toward criminal activities (Bushway et al., 2000). The psychological profile of the "mature" (the desisting mindset?), therefore, seems at least as important to understand as the nature of criminality. Both frames of mind seem to characterize people we call criminals at varying times in their lives.

---

[8]The word *maturity*, in this sense, is meant differently than the passive process of maturation implied in the ontological model. Maturing into an adult role requires motivation, effort, and a desire to change (Peele & Brodsky, 1991). As such, maturation need not refer to biological age. Colloquially, in fact, the term *maturity* is most often applied to those whose behavior is *not* in accordance with age expectations ("The student is a very mature teenager" or "The professor can be very immature for his age"). This usage implies that maturity might be a malleable personality attribute or "frame of mind" rather than a quality inherent to any particular age. However, because "maturational reform" has become associated with ontogenetic or age-related understandings of desistance, words like *maturity* probably should be used cautiously and sparingly. Additionally, some commentators have expressed concern that use of the term connotes an infantilization of deviants. In regard to maturational theories of overcoming drug addiction, for instance, Waldorf et al. (1991) wrote, "The 'maturing out' hypothesis smuggles into scholarship . . . an insupportable assumption about abstinence . . . rooted in temperance-era moralism: that fully developed human beings do not desire to alter their consciousness with drugs" (p. 236).

2

THE LIVERPOOL
DESISTANCE STUDY

Although a variety of subjective factors have been uncovered in "exploratory" studies of reformed deviants, the link between desistance and this change in self-concept has rarely been established empirically (Burnett, 1992, and Shover & Thompson, 1992, are two rare tests of subjective theory). In particular, since Glaser's (1964) pioneering work, strikingly little research has compared the clandestine thought patterns and personal beliefs of desisting ex-offenders with those of persisting offenders to isolate the subjective perceptions that correlate with desistance.[9]

The challenge facing phenomenological researchers, of course, is that

---

[9] The typical phenomenological desistance study (e.g., Cusson & Pinsonneault, 1986; Maruna, 1997) locates a group of desisting ex-offenders and identifies the self-perceptions and social perspectives common across the sample. Yet, without contrasting these findings to a comparable sample of active offenders, one cannot isolate what aspects of self-concept are directly related to desistance. For instance, one of the findings common to this type of desistance research is that individuals who make good have learned from repeated failures that criminal behavior is too risky. Desisting ex-offenders are said to become more cautious and more sensitive to the likelihood of their apprehension. In the United Kingdom, one says, "I lost my bottle" (nerve). While it seems logical that this subjective change encourages desistance from crime, this might also be a normative change common to all individuals as they pass out of their teenage years, including those people who do not desist from crime (see Irwin, 1970). In fact, in a rare comparison between desisting and persisting ex-offenders, Shover and Thompson (1992) were unable to find any significant correlation between perceptions of risk and the continuation of criminal behavior. Without such comparative research, one cannot know for certain what subjective changes matter the most in going straight.

subjectivity is by its nature rather messy. Abstract concepts such as identity and the self are difficult for researchers to reliably study, and when they do, their findings are equally difficult for readers to interpret and evaluate. Becker (1998) wrote,

> As a rule, our research does not have anything very new to say about self-conceptions or identity.... At worst, the researcher announces triumphantly that what was studied was indeed a case of the development of identity or the adaptive character of social organization. That kind of result isn't useful to anyone.... The advice they offer is too general. (p. 125)

The Liverpool Desistance Study (LDS) was explicitly intended to overcome some of the inherent vagueness of self-identity research. The LDS is an empirical analysis of the phenomenological or sociocognitive aspects of desistance. The study involves a systematic comparison between the self-narratives of desisting ex-offenders and those of a carefully matched sample of active offenders. By isolating the ways in which members in these two groups differ in their worldviews and self-perspectives, this research is an attempt to specify the cognitive adaptations and self-schemas that may help ex-offenders make good and stay that way.

To do so, the LDS takes advantage of the recent theoretical and methodological insights in narratology (Greimas, 1990) or the "narrative study of lives" (Josselson & Lieblich, 1993; McAdams, 1985). The primary data in such research are the stories that individuals tell to account for their behavior. The narratologists' interest in these narratives is not so much the facts they contain (what happened in their lives) but rather in the meanings the individuals attach to such facts—how they choose to frame the events of their lives.[10]

Therefore, although the narratives collected in this research are largely retrospective accounts of past events, this is *not* a retrospective study. In other words, this is not a research study that looks at people who have "already desisted" and asks them how they did it or what "made them change." This is a study of people who were actively making good or going straight right before my eyes as I interviewed them. This maintenance (the "going"), in the face of structural obstacles and temptations, is what interested me.

---

[10]As such, this research is not intended (nor suited) to "test" more structural theories of desistance (e.g., social bonding, special deterrence, and treatment effectiveness). Although phenomenological research can supplement our understanding of how changes in the environment affect individual cognition, these findings can do little to prove or disprove the overall importance of jobs, marriage, or rehabilitative treatments for the wider population. More traditional methodologies, using correlations and large-scale random samples, are far better suited than narratology for this purpose.

DESISTANCE AND SELF-NARRATIVES: A RATIONALE

The narratives that desisting people tell are thought to be of scientific interest for several reasons. First, an emerging body of research suggests that internal self-narratives are used to guide and organize human behavior patterns. According to M. B. Scott and Lyman (1968), "Since it is with respect to deviant behavior that we call for accounts, the study of deviance and the study of accounts are intrinsically related, and a clarification of accounts will constitute a clarification of deviant phenomena" (p. 62). Second, self-narratives are dynamic. Many factors might drive human behavior (genetics, personal background, age, and all the other usual suspects), but most of these cannot be "corrected" or "treated" by social workers or the criminal justice system. In theory, self-narratives could be. Finally, self-narratives are explicitly contextual. Stories are cultural artifacts. One of the best ways to understand a particular subculture or group at a particular point in time is to analyze the stories that members of that group are telling. Similarly, understanding the stories that ex-offenders use to interpret their lives should help us understand how Western society constructs criminality at this moment in history.

Although the method has been largely abandoned today, life history narratives have played a critical role in the development and analysis of theories of criminal behavior (Becker, 1966; Bennett, 1981). Discussing life histories like *The Jack-Roller* (Shaw, 1930), for instance, Clifford Shaw (1929) argued, "So far as we have been able to determine as yet, the best way to investigate the inner world of the person is through a study of himself through a life-history" (p. 6). Indeed, the window to a person's "inner world" that self-stories provide has inspired a new paradigm in psychology referred to as the narrative study of lives. Sarbin (1986) even suggested that the narrative should be the "root metaphor" or organizing principle for the field of psychology as a whole.

Traditionally, however, criminologists have used life story narratives for their sociological rather than psychosocial content. Shaw, for instance, "made no attempt to pursue the implications of the Jack-Roller's idiosyncratic point of view for an understanding of his involvement in delinquent conduct" (Finestone, 1976, p. 101). In fact, when hermeneutic or psycholinguistic analysis was included in the Chicago School's life story research, according to Bennett (1981), it was merely "inserted to placate the psychologists who headed the institute for Juvenile Research" (p. 190).

Building largely on McAdams's (1985, 1993) notion of the "personal myth," theorists in sociology (e.g., Giddens, 1991), criminology (e.g., Canter, 1994), addiction research (e.g., Singer, 1997), and psychology (e.g., Bruner, 1987) have recently started to view the life story as more than a retrospective record of life events. The self-narrative is increasingly understood as a critical part of an individual's personality and inner self. Giddens

(1991) wrote, "A person's identity is not to be found in behavior, nor—important though this is—in the reactions of others, but in the capacity to keep a particular narrative going" (p. 54). Identity is the human being's answer to the existential question, "Who am I?" and, as such, provides life with a sense of meaning (Singer, 1997).

The narrative identity can be understood as an active information-processing structure, a cognitive schema, or a construct system that is both shaped by and later mediates social interaction. Essentially, people construct stories to account for what they do and why they did it. These narratives impose an order on people's actions and explain people's behavior with a sequence of events that connect up to explanatory goals, motivations, and feelings. These self-narratives then act to shape and guide future behavior, as people act in ways that agree with the stories or myths they have created about themselves (McAdams, 1985).

This position is largely consistent with the understanding of self and identity developed in social interactionism (Felson & Tedeschi, 1993), rational choice (Clarke & Cornish, 1985), attribution theory (e.g., Felson & Ribner, 1981; Weiner, 1991), social learning (Akers, 1985; Bandura, 1989), and other sociocognitive approaches to understanding deviance and sense-making. In fact, almost 40 years ago, Cressey (1963) argued that "Criminals and delinquents become dishonest because of the words available to them" (p. 151):

> A great deal of evidence supporting the importance of verbalizations in criminal and non-criminal conduct is found in the literature, but it never has been systematically collected and published. . . . Lindesmith reported that if a person habituated to drugs talked to himself in certain ways he will become an addict. . . . Becker showed that perception of the effect of marijuana was determined by the kinds of words given to the smoker by users. (p. 151)

Probably the best-developed narrative theory in criminology is Sykes and Matza's (1957) theory of neutralization techniques. According to Sykes and Matza (1957), "Much delinquency is based on what is essentially an unrecognized extension of defenses to crimes, in the forms of justifications[11] for deviance that are seen as valid by the delinquent but not by the legal system or society at large" (p. 666). As one of the most frequently cited theories in criminology (Wolfgang, Figlio, & Thornberry, 1978), this theory has inspired a substantial body of research on the use of excuses and justifications to account for socially objectionable behaviors. This research has confirmed, probably beyond question, that people who commit crimes of all types—from deer poaching (Eliason & Dodder, 1999) to hate crimes

---

[11]In Sykes and Matza's (1957) original formulation, they outlined five major "techniques of neutralization": denial of responsibility, denial of injury, denial of the victim, condemnation of the condemners, and appeal to higher loyalty.

against the Amish (Crider, Byers, & Biggers, 1997)—rely on a variety of a posteriori rationalizations to justify their behavior to others and themselves.

Still, criminologists continue to disagree on whether these "techniques of neutralization" suggest cognitive orientations that "precede deviant behavior and make deviant behavior possible" (Sykes & Matza, 1957, p. 667) or whether they are just after-the-fact rationalizations unrelated to the original offending (Hindelang, 1970). Hirschi (1969) suggested that both positions might be true. When individuals are caught breaking some norm, they may create a retrospective justification to rationalize the act. The use and acceptance of such justifications, in turn, may allow the individuals to continue or even accelerate offending behavior. Hirschi (1969) described the development of neutralizations, therefore, as a "hardening process" that facilitates continued criminal behavior (p. 208). Akers (1985), who disagreed with Hirschi on most issues, reaches much of the same conclusion in his discussion of the "definitions" favorable to crime:

> Initial acts may and do occur in the absence of definitions favorable to them; rather the definitions get applied retroactively to excuse or redefine the initial deviant acts. To the extent that they successfully mitigate others' or self-punishment, they become discriminative for repetition of the deviant acts and, hence, precede the future commission of the acts. (p. 60)

Consistent with the Thomas Theorem, "If (persons) define situations as real, they are real in their consequences" (Thomas & Thomas, 1928, p. 572), self-stories represent personal outlooks and "theories of reality," not necessarily some objective reality (Epstein & Erskine, 1983). For instance, a person might commit certain acts of violence that would be deemed senseless by outside observers. Yet, these acts might be perfectly rational in terms of that person's self-narrative (Canter, 1994; Shover, 1996).

Consider the real consequences described by the following individual interviewed as part of the fieldwork for this project:

> I said, "Give me the fucking chain back," and he pulled a knife out at me and his friend had got this baseball bat.... I went home, and just couldn't sleep, you know. I kept waking up at, like, 2 a.m., saying, "I can't deal with this." My girl was telling me to calm down, let it go. But I kept thinking to myself, "This is going to have to be something big." This isn't going to be just a fist fight. This is going to be big.... Everybody in the scene knew I was looking for him.... (Eventually) I met him at the pub. I brought this knife and I stabbed him.... Unless you actually grew up in that situation, you wouldn't understand what I was going through. Common sense is just different in that situation. You just don't have the same common sense. Lying in bed, really, I think about it a lot. "If this, if that," but then the "ifs" go away and you just have to say, "This is the real you." I had no

choice really. You do nothing and you get written off the scene altogether. Street-wise, that's suicide—you're back to the bottom of the ladder, you're nobody. Sensible-wise, of course, that's the best thing that could happen to you. That means taking the alternative route with the suit and job and all. But I've got a rough streak in me somewhere. . . . I had to do it. (male, age 27)

According to narrative theory, only by understanding the way this man understands himself and his interpretation of the "common sense" of the streets can one begin to understand why he attempted murder. Furthermore, only by changing this self-story ("This is the real me," he says) can the person change his behavior (see A. Beck, 2000; Bush, 1995).

Unlike personality traits, which tend to be largely stable over time, a person's narrative identity can and does change throughout life. In fact, one's self-story has to be "routinely created and sustained in the reflexive activities of the individual" (Giddens, 1991, p. 52). Eschewing strict developmental stage theories, narrative theorists generally argue that identity is a lifelong project that individuals continuously restructure in light of new experiences and information (McAdams, 1993).

As such, questions may be raised as to which comes first. Do changes in a person's self-narrative occur causally prior to desistance from crime or does desisting from crime simply lead someone to change their identity story? Probably both. Like neutralizations, self-narratives should be understood as factors that help to sustain desistance. The development of a self-story favorable to desisting from crime could be seen as "hardening" the individual's resolve to stay out of trouble. This hardening of change, and not the moment of change, is the process that we are trying to understand when we study desistance.

Changes in objective and subjective deviant careers occur together in an interactional process with neither acting necessarily as a "cause" of the other (Shover, 1983). Laub and Sampson (2000) wrote, "There is presently no way to disentangle the role of subjective versus objective change as the cause of desistance. It is probably the case that both are present in the change process" (p. 67). Desistance is best understood using a model of co-determinacy, whereby cause and outcome are not conceived as discrete entities but are "interrelated and overlapping, such that some part of cause is constituted by some part of the event produced in part by it and vice versa; but all of the event is not all of the cause (and vice versa)" (Henry & Milovanovic, 1996, p. 126).

Finally, although various categories or types of self-stories may be identified, narrative theory does not seek to divide *persons* into static "types," or what Canter (1994) described as a "cafeteria view of life stories."

> This pulls the framework back into the realms of static characteristics. Instead of having distinguishing ear lobes, criminals can be recognized by the particular heroes they endorse. Life is not that simple. Narra-

tives are moving targets that change their shape in response to life circumstances. (p. 312)

This dynamic and contextually contingent quality makes the narrative domain of human personality an ideal level of analysis for the understanding of long-term behavioral patterns like desistance.

SEEKING OUT DESISTANCE STORIES

The original design for this study was relatively clear. I would locate a group of "desisters," then seek out a matched group of "persisters" or active offenders who had more or less the same background as the desisters. Both groups would participate in life story interviews, and the narratives would be content analyzed and compared quantitatively for the differences in their self-perspective, outlook, and personality that might be related to the process of desisting from crime.

"Desisters," "Persisters," and the "Real World": A Caveat

It needs to be said that this initial design was, in retrospect, more than a little naïve. While I had never met anyone who identified themselves as a "desister" or a "persister," I assumed that such people could be easily identified in a random sample of ex-offenders (through parole, corrections, etc.). After all, in articles such as "Delinquency Careers: Innocents, Desisters, and Persisters" (Blumstein, Farrington, & Moitra, 1985), these neat labels are used to dichotomize the entire population of ex-offenders. Unfortunately, like every researcher who enters the field in search of these persisters or desisters, I soon reached the conclusion that such classification is purely a convenience for statistical classification and "hides a tremendous amount of variation" (Glaser, 1964, p. 54). To be blunt, most of the persisters one finds do not seem to really persist, most desisters do not seem to really desist, and, honestly, it is getting harder than ever to find any "innocents."

Individuals in the real world do not tend to fall into the neat dichotomies of desisters–persisters, innocents–offenders, victims–victimizers, or prosocial–antisocial consistently constructed in political and criminological discourse (Henry & Milovanovic, 1996; Young, 1996). From Glueck and Glueck (1940, pp. 269–270) to Leibrich (1993, pp. 34–35), field research has found that there are multiple degrees or flavors of criminality and desistance. Leibrich (1993) decided that instead of the dichotomy between going straight and being crooked, it was possible for one to be "going curved" or "straight enough." Burnett (1992) proposed an ingenious, sixfold typology of ex-offenders (Converts, Nonstarters, Avoiders,

Hedonists, Survivors, and Earners) and also suggested the possibility of such categories as Waverers, Ambivalents, Provisionals, Drifters, and Rebounders.

Irwin (1970) divided the outcomes of his sample into the categories that are most meaningful to the ex-offenders themselves. He suggested that "success" to the ex-offender has more to do with "doing good" or "doing poor" (economically and socially) than it does with the means by which one gets there (by going straight, marginal, or crooked). Thus, one can be "Straight, but doing poor," "Marginal, but doing good," or even "Crooked, but doing good," in Irwin's typology (p. 195).

The point is, when researchers seek desisters and persisters among ex-offenders, we frequently find instead that "Those who have lived in both the criminal and the conventional social worlds may walk a zigzag path between the two" (Glaser, 1964, p. 54). The only thing more difficult than finding "pure desisters" among ex-offenders, in fact, is finding "pure criminals." Burnett (1992) wrote,

> Those (ex-convicts) who were firmly committed to criminal behavior, both in word and deed, were a minority in this study, and unwavering, unerring desistance was equally rare. The more typical property offender takes a hesitant, faltering path, vulnerably poised between the attractions of alternative directions. (p. 107)

This is, of course, Matza's (1964) finding of "drift," whereby most of the persons researchers call criminals or deviants are neither fully deviant nor fully straight, but rather "flirt now with one, now with the other" and commit to neither (p. 59).

A Hidden Population

Randomized samples of probationers, parolees, or other arbitrary convenience samples of ex-offenders will turn up many times more waverers and ambivalents than desisters or persisters (Burnett, 1992; Leibrich, 1993). And, of course, taking a "random" sample of career criminals or desisting people is impossible, as the universe from which it would have to be drawn is unknown and unknowable. Therefore, this project used a targeted, theoretical sampling technique (Watters & Biernacki, 1989) in an effort to specifically identify members of the interest populations: people actively committed to a criminal lifestyle and former offenders committed to a straight life. These interviewees were identified through ethnographic fieldwork (34%); recommended by probation officers, social workers, or reintegration workers (40%); or suggested by other ex-offenders through a "snowball sampling" technique (26%).

As such, the two samples that were finally identified for this project should not be seen as representative of the entire population of ex-offenders in the United Kingdom or anywhere else. The LDS samples are not suitable for making generalizations about the distribution of desistance in some population or subpopulation. Instead, the groups were hand-selected to maximize the likelihood of identifying individuals at the two extremes of a long process of change, or two ends of a spectrum between unequivocal successes and failures. The individuals known in the literature as "converts" (Burnett, 1992) or "pivotal normals," (Lofland, 1969) and the equally rare persisting offenders known as "hedonists" (Burnett, 1992) or "pivotal deviants" (Lofland, 1969), were intentionally oversampled. Compared with the ubiquitous "quasi-desisters" or "wavering" ex-offenders, such pure types are not easily identified in random samples of ex-offenders, in parole offices, or in prisons.

Of course, this is not to say that the more common ex-offenders have never in their lives been fully committed "pivotal deviants." Nor should one assume that the average ex-offender, floating between crime and non-crime, has no chance of making a full conversion to a straight life. To the contrary, he or she almost certainly will. The zigzagging does not last forever (Glaser, 1964, p. 56). Whether this sample is representative or not, therefore, depends on the lens one uses to look at desistance. From a cross-sectional perspective, at any given point in time, converts or reformed ex-offenders will be a minority among populations of ex-offenders. Yet, in the lens of the life course, most long-term offenders at some point were fully committed to offending like the persisting sample, and will *eventually* make good like the members of the desisting sample.

When they do, of course, they will likely be neither obvious nor easily available to researchers. Reformed ex-offenders do not belong to any registered organization, and they sometimes go to extremes to hide their criminal pasts. Finding a sample of desisting persons to study this process, therefore, was among the most difficult tasks I faced.

Operationalizing Desistance

Equally difficult was the task of defining and operationalizing the target concepts of this research: *desisting* and *persisting*. In what Becker (1998) called an "intimate and continuing dialogue . . . between data and image," my working definitions for these processes actually emerged during the collection and analysis of the life histories. According to Becker, the method of analytic induction "always involves . . . a mutual clarification of the conceptual solution to a research problem (e.g., how do people get to be addicts) and the definition of what constitutes the problem and its embodiment in real life (e.g., how to define an addict and addiction)" (p. 200).

One example of this mutual clarification in the LDS involved the notion of the "career offender." Without a career in crime there could be neither persistence nor desistance. Unfortunately, *career criminal* is a term that is frequently used, but rarely defined. The U.S. Department of Justice (1983) suggested the career criminal is "a person having a past record of multiple arrests or convictions for serious crimes, or an unusually large number of arrests or convictions for crimes of varying degrees of seriousness" (cited in Gottfredson & Hirschi, 1986, p. 215). Therefore, career criminals should not be confused with professional criminals, if "professional" implies membership in elaborate underground organizations like the Mafia, involvement in upper-level drug distribution, or participation in the lucrative world of corporate or white-collar crime. The career criminal label is usually used simply to refer to people who commit a lot of crime over a span of several years.

While still vague, this definition at least makes it clear who is not included. The person who in a moment of passion commits a "once-off" crime and lands in prison, for instance, may be an offender but is certainly not a career criminal. During the sampling process for this project, I met and interviewed several of these individuals, whom Irwin (1970) labeled "square johns." One was a travel agent who assaulted a man whom he found in bed with his girlfriend. Another interviewee, in his early 40s, was convicted of assaulting his brother in a family argument. Neither of these individuals had any previous convictions or arrests, and neither interview was included in the quantitative analysis for this research project.

Of course, these low-rate offenders are the most common "successes" in any sample of ex-offenders. Indeed, if one's interest was in predicting who will successfully stay out of trouble among a group of convicted offenders (e.g., Greenwood, 1983), these are definitely the types of persons one should bet on. But is this desistance? To desist from something, one presumably needs to have been a quite regular participant in the activity. For instance, someone who smokes two or three cigarettes a year does not talk about "quitting" smoking.

The question becomes one of where to draw the line. Do ten crimes constitute a career? Fifteen crimes? Twenty crimes? Fortunately, this impossible question never emerged in the sampling procedure. All of the individuals with whom I came in contact had a criminal history consisting of only one or two serious crimes, or else they had massive criminal histories involving repetitive, habitual offending lasting for years (see Moffitt, 1993). Every person included in the present sample offended on at least a weekly basis for some stretch of at least 2 years. This effectively solved the first problem of defining the "career criminal" concept for the purposes of this study.

The next example of Becker's mutual classification involved determining which of these career offenders could be described as persisting and which were desisting. Previous criminal career research has tended to hold a "persistent until proven innocent" policy. Under this framework, an individual needs to maintain Boy Scout-like standards of purity to earn the label *desisting* but needs little more than a few brushes with the law to be labeled a *persistent offender*. For instance, Farrington and Hawkins (1991) required 11 years of crime-free behavior for someone to qualify as desisting from crime. Everyone else, importantly, is considered to be persisting. Therefore, if one of their sample members were to commit a crime at age 22, they would still be considered a "persistent offender" at age 32 (Bushway et al., 2000).

I assumed that to be considered "persisting," at a minimum, the individual needed to admit that he or she would be carrying on with criminal behaviors. Twenty of the career criminals I interviewed readily admitted that they would. On the other hand, a few of the individuals recommended to me as potential desisting or persisting representatives told me at the time of the interview that they had recently offended (usually in the past few weeks) but were trying to stay out of trouble in the future. These cases created a need to better define my criteria. Some previous researchers would consider such recent offenders to be persisters (e.g., Farrington & Hawkins, 1991) and others would consider them desisters (e.g., Liebrich, 1993; Meisenhelder, 1982). I considered them somewhere "in between" desisting and persisting (e.g., Matza, 1964).

I have no grounds for doubting the sincerity of their desire to change, so I could hardly categorize them as active offenders. After all, my goal was to identify a mind-set consistent with the continued pursuit of illegal activities, and these individuals might not be planning to commit any future crimes. At the same time, I was not convinced that what the person was doing could be considered desistance, or maintaining an abstinence from crime, in any meaningful sense. If anything, they were flirting with desistance or trying abstinence on for size. Like the "once-off" offender interviews, these cases were not included in the quantitative comparison between active and desisting offenders.

All of the 30 remaining interviewees said that they would not be committing crimes in the future and reported over a year of crime-free behavior. Members of the desisting sample generally estimated that they had probably been "clean" for 2 to 3 years.[12] Long-term follow-up studies of inmates after release suggest that most official recidivism occurs in the first year out of prison (R. A. Beck & Shipley, 1989; Hoffman & Meierhoefer, 1979; Irwin, 1970). Moreover, this figure is based on *reconviction* data, not self-reports. Every member of the desisting sample reported offending (e.g., selling drugs, burglarizing shops, and stealing cars) on a daily

---

[12]Such precise estimates are always highly suspect. Unlike members of Alcoholics Anonymous, who often can provide the number of days, months, and hours since their last drink, most desisting offenders drift away from criminal behavior gradually (Bushway et al., 2000; Laub et al., 1998). As such, few can provide precise dates and times for the "beginning" of their desistance in any meaningful sense.

or weekly basis in the not-so-distant past. For such individuals, 12 months of drug-free, crime-free, and arrest-free behavior is a significant life change worthy of examination. This abstinence from criminal behavior does not guarantee the change is "permanent," but it accurately captures the process I am interested in studying.[13]

Importantly, though, the primary qualifications for inclusion in the matched samples were subjective. First, individuals had to identify themselves as long-term habitual offenders. If they never thought of themselves as offenders (i.e., if they were "square johns" who committed a few crimes), then desisting from crime is hardly interesting (or possible). Second, they had to identify themselves as either successfully "going straight" or else actively persisting with criminal pursuits. Again, if an individual does not think that he or she is going straight or actively offending, then they probably are not (Irwin, 1970, p. 179). After all, these are usually considered to be intentional behaviors.

Because of the nature of the sampling technique used, the interviewee also had to be known (to parole officers, reintegration workers, friends, or associates) as someone who was going straight (or persisting). In a few cases, this "second opinion" was a helpful reassurance. Still, despite others' concern that I might be "duped" by crafty or self-protective interviewees, research suggests that offender self-reports are generally more reliable than most alternatives. In fact, Nagin, Farrington, and Moffitt (1995) warned that researchers who rely on official data to study desistance may be the ones being duped. "While (sample members') official criminal records ceased many years before, they were still committing criminal acts, such as stealing from their employer, according to the self-reports" (p. 112). Because "almost all published findings about criminal careers rely on official data," the LDS's use of self-report data and the reports of significant others is a useful corrective (Nagin et al., 1995, p. 135).

Matching the Samples

In total, 55 men and 10 women were formally interviewed for this project. Of these, 30 were classified as desisting, and 20 were considered to be persisting. The remaining 15 interviews were not included in the quantitative analysis because, on examination of their offense histories, these individuals did not match the criteria for either group.[14] Like the

---

[13] This implies that there might be a mathematical formula that could differentiate between "real" desistance and less interesting random fluctuations in individual crime rates. In fact, quantitative criminologists are busily working to concoct such a formula based on changes in an individual's rate of offending over time (e.g., Bushway et al., 2000). Of course, ex-offenders themselves make similar, if more subjective, calculations and are probably well able to discern between the "real deal" and a temporary lull between crimes (see Irwin, 1970).

[14] No potential interviewee was turned down because he or she did not meet the criteria I was looking for. To do so would indeed encourage interested participants to distort their criminal histories in order to qualify. I interviewed everyone who was recommended to me.

majority of ex-offenders with whom I came in contact during fieldwork, these individuals fell somewhere in between committed offending and committed desisting. Still, these narratives were not abandoned. All of their interviews were qualitatively analyzed and were a useful benchmark for understanding the desisting and persisting scripts.

Following Glaser (1964), the desisting and the persisting samples were intended to be matched, as closely as possible, on variables such as age, gender, types and number of crimes committed, age of criminal onset, parents' occupation, national origins, and high school completion (see Appendix and chap. 3). Therefore, the samples were purposely matched on several variables that are correlated to one's likelihood of desisting from crime. Research consistently shows that age is the strongest predictor of desistance (Wilson & Herrnstein, 1985). The mean age for LDS participants was 30 years old (M = 30.7 desisting group, M = 30.6 persisting group). The extent of a person's prior criminal record and the likelihood of becoming a recidivist are directly correlated (Glaser, 1964), and the earlier a person begins offending, the longer criminality typically lasts over the life course (McCord, 1980; Moffitt, 1993).

Nonetheless, these background variables provide little understanding about how desistance occurs and tell us even less about how policy can encourage it. Trying to explore the impact of these independent variables in a small study like this would only confuse the effort to understand desistance as a developmental process. Without a random sampling, this study cannot answer questions regarding who desists and when and is not intended as part of this prediction-based literature. Instead, the purpose of the project is to explore the question of how the process of desistance works for those who do desist. Matching the two groups on background variables allows for a comparison of more dynamic, developmental variables across the groups.

DATA COLLECTION

The dynamic "variable" of most interest to me was the self-narrative. Although a variety of methods have been proposed for accessing these internalized identity stories (see Denzin, 1989; Singer & Salovey, 1993), most involve intensive, semistructured interviews in field settings. Importantly, the transcribed life story documents produced in such research are not themselves the self-narratives that guide an individual's behavior. The stories people tell social scientists about themselves, however, are assumed to hold the outlines of their internalized self-narratives in the same way that answers to an attitude survey or a pencil-and-paper personality test serve to represent a person's beliefs or personality (McAdams, 1993). Life story interviews provide rough indicators of the internal self-story that the person actually lives by. These narrative transcripts can therefore be quantitatively coded and systematically compared for cross-case similarities and differences in theme, tone, style, motivation, and characterization.

The multiphase interview protocol for the LDS usually lasted 2 to 3 hours and was designed to provide personological profiles of each participant. The interviews included a standardized personality trait questionnaire, a criminal behavior checklist, and a social background survey. The main focus of the interviews involved allowing the participants to "tell their story."

In an effort to ensure some consistency across the interviews, I facilitated each conversation myself. Using a modified version of McAdams's Life Story Interview (McAdams, 1993), supplemented by open-ended questions regarding crime and corrections-related experiences, I asked each participant to describe his or her life as if he or she was writing an autobiography. Interviews were structured so as to be comparable across the samples, yet participants were allowed to follow whatever tangent they felt appropriate. Whenever possible, the interviews took place at the homes of participants and in privacy. Interviews were tape-recorded and transcribed. Participants were compensated for their time, and after the interview I encouraged them to discuss their own theories of rehabilitation and reform (many of which have had a profound impact on my own thinking).

This interview data have been supplemented by 18 months of ethnographic field observations at a variety of rehabilitation and resettlement programs in the Liverpool area. This fieldwork included informal discussions with ex-offenders, current offenders, police officers, social workers, prison staff, and probation officers concerning the process and possibility of offender reform, and their own strategies or theories in regard to promoting rehabilitation. I was able to observe numerous one-on-one and group counseling sessions and met individuals at every stage of the reintegration process—from those just beginning to contemplate reform to persons who have been "legit" for a decade or more. As a volunteer for the National Association for the Care and Resettlement of Offenders and the Alternatives to Drugs Programme, I was allowed weekly exposure to the unfolding dramas in the lives of individuals trying (sometimes unsuccessfully) to avoid the temptation to reoffend.

Also, following the interviews, I made every effort to remain in touch with sample participants and several became friends. The participants were aware that I was interested in keeping tabs on how they were doing, and this "longitudinal monitoring" did not seem to negatively affect our relationships. The additional facts about desistance and/or criminality that I learned during this time were added to the field notes I was keeping but did not alter the original interview data.

Becoming a part of the social and symbolic worlds of ex-offenders in these ways allowed me to observe more than "snapshots" of the desistance process. I met three participants' mothers (two agreed to be interviewed on tape), most interviewees' partners, and many of the children who received credit for interviewees' transformations. Finally, my "fieldwork" also included living for a month in an inner-city men's hostel where some of the participants were identified. All of this rich exposure to the lives of sample members has supplemented the findings from the narrative interviews and contributed to this understanding of desistance.

DATA ANALYSIS

The data collected in this inquiry were analyzed both inductively and deductively for patterns in the way participants in each group interpreted and defined their lives. The goal was to construct a single, composite portrait of the desisting self—the identity narrative that seems to best support desistance from crime (see chap. 5). To understand this narrative, a similar portrait needed to be constructed for active offenders outlining the identity factors that allow for continued involvement in criminal behavior (see chap. 4).

These prototypical portraits were constructed using the constant comparative method of analytic induction, defined by Ragin (1994) as "any systematic examination of similarities that seeks to develop concepts or ideas" (p. 93). During this case-by-case analysis, emerging portraits of the "universal" desistance and persistence narratives were contrasted with and improved by subsequent cases in the sample. Each "negative case" would trigger adjustments to the model to fit all the previous cases as well as the outlier (Becker, 1998). Eventually, a point of "saturation" was reached in which new cases were not adding to the model's explanatory power (Bertaux, 1981).

The final product therefore highlights the commonalities, not the differences, in how desistance is experienced and understood. As others have suggested, desistance may not be a unitary phenomenon. Women may desist differently from men. People with darker skin may desist differently from people with lighter skin. Timing during the life course, geography, age cohort, crime specialization, height, weight, and wind direction all may affect the way that desistance works. Although interesting questions, these issues are best left to large-scale, randomized research. Qualitative research is best suited for exploring similarity, not for establishing systematic differences (Ragin, 1994).

Still, the LDS qualitative analysis has been supplemented by a deductive and comparative analysis between two groups (desisters and persisters). Select aspects of the narratives were content-coded by two graduate students, blind to all identifying information on the participants, for quantitative validation of the hypothesized differences between persisting and desisting narratives. This content analysis used well-established content dictionaries to code for narrative themes like generativity (Stewart, Franz, & Layton, 1988) and agency (McAdams, 1992); the use of excuses, justifications, and other neutralizations (Schonbach, 1990); and the use of contamination and redemption sequences in the life stories (McAdams, Diamond, de St. Aubin, & Mansfield, 1997). This coding process is described in detail in the appendix. The goal of this comparative analysis was to determine what aspects of the common desistance narrative are unique to ex-offenders who avoid crime and what aspects are shared by active offenders. The former may hold the clues as to how ex-offenders can desist from crime.

II

TWO VIEWS OF A
BRICK WALL

The situation facing recidivist offenders is something like a brick wall. It is surmountable but is enough of an obstacle to make most turn around and "head back." In this scenario, "back" refers to back to crime, back to the lives they are familiar with, but mostly back to prison—where recidivist offenders seem to go again and again.

The reasons for this repeat offending in the face of such failure are reviewed in the following three chapters. Chapter 3 reviews what Katz (1988) referred to as the "background factors" behind this persistent offending for the members of the Liverpool sample. The risk factors reviewed here will come as no surprise to those who work with or research criminal offenders: poverty, child abuse, detachment from the labor force, the stigma of social sanctions, low educational attainment, few legitimate opportunities in the community, serious addictions and dependencies, high-risk personality profiles and, of course, long-term patterns of criminal behavior. Although this last "risk factor" might seem circular, the best predictor of future criminal behavior is always past criminal behavior. And, this sample has plenty of that.

The next two chapters, on the other hand, describe what Katz (1988) referred to as the "phenomenological foreground of crime": the motivations, personal projects, and perspectives of individual ex-offenders. It is here that the LDS sample diverges.

The ex-offenders in this sample need a logical self-story to help them deal with their own feelings of culpability, external stigma, and the potential emptiness and void of their lives. Sample members face the stigma not just of having offended but also the stigma of growing up poor and failing to achieve Horatio Alger–like achievements by their own bootstraps. They face internal questions of shame, blame, guilt, and culpability for their offending and also for the state of their lives. Finally, like everyone else, they struggle to fill their lives with some pursuit that is worth living for.

In chapters 4 and 5, I argue that the different responses to these three phenomenological challenges differentiate desisting offenders from their still active counterparts in crime. Essentially, desisting interviewees have constructed a meaningful story to redeem themselves. Without this story, it is argued, they would likely interpret the brick wall facing them as reason enough to turn back.

3

SAMPLE PROGNOSIS: DIRE

Although each participant in this research project has a unique personal history and faces a singular life situation, the common characteristics, shared by interviewees across both persisting and desisting samples, need to be understood as well. Standard for criminological discourse, this discussion is largely based on a deficit model, illustrating all of the handicaps and obstacles faced by the sample, rather than emphasizing the group's collective strengths and abilities. (Chapter 5 will be more comforting for those looking for a ray of hope.) There is no denying that sample members have several strikes against them if they hope to stay out of trouble. Nonetheless, I should say, the most consistent personal trait among interviewees in this study, by far, was a superlative sense of humor and an interpersonal assertiveness that would make most stage performers jealous. Both traits were probably honed in years of study in pool halls, playgrounds, group homes, and prisons, where each had to survive, sometimes literally, on their wit, charm, and domineering social presence.

STRIKE 1: CRIMINOGENIC TRAITS

A standardized, personality test was administered to the sample of reformed ex-offenders and the matched sample of active offenders in the Liverpool Desistance Study (LDS). This questionnaire, the Big Five Index

(John, Donahue, & Kentle, 1991), was designed to measure the five over-arching traits thought to make up a person's basic disposition: agreeable-ness, conscientiousness, extroversion, neuroticism, and openness to experience. In a comparison of the two samples in this study (Maruna, 1998), the personality traits of desisting ex-offenders did not differ significantly from those of active offenders—even on traits thought to be related to criminality (e.g., Eysenck, 1989).

However, the personality traits of LDS participants (in both the desisting and persisting samples) do differ significantly from adult norms. John et al.'s (1991) sample of adults in the general population scored 3.77 on agreeableness and 3.58 on conscientiousness. The combined LDS samples averaged 3.22 on agreeableness and 2.68 on conscientiousness (T = 5.83 and T = 8.34, respectively, p < .001). These relatively stable personality traits, therefore, do seem to be predictive of the onset of long-term criminal behavior but do not seem to be predictive of desistance (Farrington & Hawkins, 1991; Nagin et al., 1995). In other words, desisting ex-offenders may retain many of the personality traits typical of active offenders even though they are able to avoid crime.

This finding is consistent with what is known about personality traits in general: They are generally stable over time (McCrae & Costa, 1987). Gottfredson and Hirschi (1995) wrote, "Enhancing the level of self-control appears possible in early childhood, but the record suggests that successful efforts to change the level later in life are exceedingly rare, if not nonexistent" (p. 33). To some degree, this has been borne out in previous empirical research on crime in the life course as well. For instance, Laub, Nagin, and Sampson (1998) found that measures of extroversion, egocentricity, and aggressiveness in childhood failed to differentiate persistent offenders from persons who desisted from crime by the age of 32. Osborn and West (1978) found that repeat offenders who desist from crime "retained some traits typical of delinquents, most notably their relative high scores on the scale of 'antisociality'" (p. 447). Finally, Charland (1985, cited in Loeber & LeBlanc, 1990) found that desisters who had previously committed serious crimes continued to display "profound personality deficits" (based on numerous trait measures) even after offending had ceased.

This paradox is also well known among ex-offenders. Irwin (1970) wrote, "The criminal very often changes his life, refrains from the type of criminal life he once followed; but he does not become a 'square'" (p. 175). In conversations and interviews, the trait that participants in both groups (desisting and persisting) most commonly used to define themselves was "antiauthority" or nonconformist. This self-perceived trait is largely subsumed under the *conscientiousness* measure (which includes items such as "Is a reliable worker" and "Perseveres until the task is finished") and the *agreeableness* measure (which includes items such as "Likes to cooperate with others").

The participants in this study described themselves as persons who dislike taking orders and refuse to be "obedient," especially if obedience means happily accepting a menial, low-paying job. "They are the men and women who rebel against the grinding routine of life—the dulling, numbing experience of going to the same mindless job every day" (Rubin, 1976, p. 34). Even participants who had completely given up crime still thought of themselves as adventurous, rebellious, and independent. While this cluster of personality traits might make sample members well suited for careers as artists, athletes, or even venture capitalists, they also raise the chances that an individual will engage in criminal activities when facing certain circumstances.

STRIKE 2: CRIMINOGENIC BACKGROUNDS

The experience of growing up in economically disadvantaged circumstances has affected the lives of almost all of the participants in this sample. Eighty percent of the participants in both desisting and persisting groups said that they grew up in an area "considered dangerous or bad." Over 80% of the desisting group and 75% of the persisting group reported that their parents had been unemployed, sporadically employed, or employed as unskilled laborers. Additionally, over half of the participants (63% desisting, 45% active) grew up in single-parent families.

Shover (1996, p. 30) wrote, "No other aspect of their circumstances is so profoundly important for virtually every aspect of their lives" as the fact that these individuals have grown up in poverty. One participant in this study explains:

> We were poor. Basically one of those stories. We had nothing, and I was the eldest and I had all the responsibility. Um, I think the thing that sticks out in my mind is, you're looking at the early '70s, and it's not, I don't suppose, in the '40s when poor was poor. I think when you were poor in the '70s not everybody around you was, so you stuck out more. Go back 50 years ago and everybody seemed to be, you know, at a certain level everybody was poor. But in the '70s it wasn't like that really, so I'd be a liar to say that I wasn't self-conscious of the fact I knew we were poor. (male, age 32)

Additionally, over a third of the sample members in the two groups (37% desisting, 35% active) reported having been abused or severely neglected as children. Although alarming, these numbers alone do not do justice to the childhoods described by interviewees:

> But um, all through this, all through the beatings and stuff I used to approach teachers, um, and nobody ever believed me that this was happening. Um, and I went to the Vicar once, the local Priest and

nothing happened. They just all said I was a liar and stuff. I remember one day, um, [my stepfather] tried to beat me up, but he was really drunk and I'd curled up in a ball in the corner. The only piece of me that was available was the right side of me leg, and he just kicked it for about half an hour. And, er, I was in school the next day, I could hardly walk. And, I kept having to go the toilet and take me trousers down, 'cause I had, er, what they call a blood bruise, where the blood's seeping through the skin, from me knee to me hip. And, me trousers kept sticking to it, so I had to keep going and wiping it with this piece of toilet paper in the toilets. And, um, one of the teachers found me, and I told them that me step-dad had done this to me. And, I remember I always used to think that "Something would get done now— they'll either take me away or take him away." But nothing, ever. I feel a bit envious now, of you know, the way social workers behave now, the way they're quite intrusive into families, and I sometimes wish like, that somebody would have done that with me. I might not have gone down the road I went down. (male, age 30)

Another participant explained:

I was like the black sheep of the family. I used to get beat up a lot by [my stepmother]. Really beat up badly. Black eyes, kicked all over the house. I got stabbed once. You know, bottles on my head. My brother and sister left after a month to live with me mother. I tried, but [my father] kept coming back for me. (male, age 40)

The participants in this sample frequently said that they consider childhood experiences of abuse to be the "lowest point" in their lives, even though many have experienced the worst punishments the state can allow for their crimes. The following interviewee, for instance, had experienced both child abuse and serious trauma in prison:

> SM: What do you consider to be the lowest point or worst time in your life?
>
> Participant: Having to be in the bed and thinking, "Is me Dad going to come in pissed [drunk]?" We used to sit there and say, "Which one [of us kids] is gonna be next [to be hit]?"
>
> SM: *So, you consider this time worse than your experiences in prison?*
>
> Participant: That was well worse than prison. Well worse. (male, age 29)

About a quarter of the participants in the two groups (27% desisting, 25% active) said that they were placed into foster care homes because of abuse or trouble in their family homes. Many of these individuals subsequently found that their treatment in care was even worse than what they had experienced at home:

There was a lot of sexual abuse—even from the female house parent. We were there for five or six years. It wasn't known then that children were regularly abused and that. You know, we were put out at weekends to various couples and that. I guess now it was what you'd call a pedophile ring. (male, age 39)

It is not difficult to understand how almost all of the narrators developed an intense sense of injustice as young people. As one interviewee, who described being physically abused by a priest at school, explained,

They're abusing their position of authority and all that like, and they're showing no respect for us, you know what I mean, or anything. So why should we show it back like? . . . This teacher started like putting chairs over me head and all that like, so that's when I started thinking like, "Fuck authority" like. You can understand what I mean, like this is what they're going to do to me like, well ten times more back like. . . . I think that's when I started to rebel, you know what I mean. (male, age 26)

A Record "as Long as Your Arm"

A consistent theme throughout the narratives was a feeling of being "cheated" out of a childhood because of early obligations to family and a lack of opportunities. Most of the interviewees took the opportunity, therefore, to live something like a replacement childhood during their late teenage years and early 20s. Two thirds of the sample (63% desisting, 65% active) left school at 16 years old without gaining any qualifications (i.e., without the equivalent of a high school diploma). Most said they were deeply involved with informal delinquent gangs by this time. The average age of first arrest, a measure often considered "age of onset" of criminality, was 15 years old for the desisting group and 14 years old for the persisting or active group. Almost all of the participants (87% desisting, 95% active) said that their teenage friends "broke the law regularly." For the most part, the criminal pursuits reported by members of this sample were nonviolent property offenses. Among the most common criminal pursuits were burglary, 73% (73% desisting, 70% active); car theft, 58% (53%, 60%), and drug sales, 50% (47%, 50%). Smaller numbers of participants in both groups were involved in more violent crimes. Over half had been involved in regular street-fighting (53% desisting, 70% active), and about one third of the sample admitted to assault (30%, 40%) and armed robbery (23%, 45%).

Almost every interviewee said that at its peak his or her involvement in crime was a daily or at least weekly activity. Also, all of the interviewees enjoyed some significant stretches of time without getting caught. In fact, three of the most financially successful offenders in this sample spent the least amount of time in prison in the sample. Nonetheless, on the whole, sample members have experienced more than their share of time in the criminal justice system. Although such estimates are highly inexact, participants guessed that they had been arrested, on average, about two dozen times (26 desisting, 25 active). Both groups in the sample have spent significant time in prison (3.7 years and 3.9 years, respectively), and all of them have had experience with community corrections (probation or parole) at some point. As such, they certainly fit the description of persistent offenders or "great pretenders" (Shover, 1996) who consistently fail to be deterred by criminal justice sanctions.

> I got charged and I got bailed, and so by this time I'm withdrawing really bad and I need drugs, you know, I need some smack [heroin]. So I went behind the [name of shopping mall], you know, attempting to rob something out of a van, and this copper comes along and goes, "I don't believe it," collars me. So I've been nicked [arrested] twice in one day. (male, age 25)

> They [a judge] said I've been arrested 73 times. They call me a "professional shoplifter." They said I was a professional shoplifter, and I was standing there and I'd been in the cells all night, in custody, and they said I was a professional shoplifter. Seventy-three charges. [She shakes her head in disbelief.] Most of them are drug related. (female, age 32)

Most of the interviewees could be best described as street crime opportunists or "generalists," who generally made a living selling drugs or stolen goods but will occasionally consider burglary or robbery "jobs" if the expected take is high enough. At the time of the interviews, most of the active offenders were receiving very low monetary returns for their offending. Yet, almost all of the interviewees described better financial times when they were making and spending around £300 (U.S. $500) per day on party pursuits. These sporadic windfalls might have been exaggerated, yet the cost of maintaining a serious heroin addiction (at £10 to £15 a bag) over the span of a decade, as many sample members did, requires a substantial income, legal or illegal.

Addiction and Crime

Almost every LDS participant (93% desisting, 95% active), in fact, admitted to regular drug use at some point in their lives, and two thirds of the two groups (67% desisting, 65% active) said that they had at some point been addicted or dependent on alcohol or drugs. This overlap is hardly surprising. In fact, Zamble and Quinsey (1997) argued that serious substance abuse is so entangled with repeat offending that the two processes may be "inseparable." This link is empirically demonstrated in the recent Columbia University study on drugs and crime (Belenko, 1998):

> The more prior convictions an individual has, the more likely that individual is a drug abuser: in state prisons, 41 percent of first offenders

have used drugs regularly, compared to 63 percent of inmates with two prior convictions and 81 percent of those with five or more convictions. (p. 7)

Simply put, persistent offending in the face of repeated failure and incarceration is highly irrational behavior and demands a particularly strong motivating force. A perceived need for expensive, illegal substances apparently fills this role. (In Glueck and Glueck, 1937/1966, pp. 178–183, alcoholism serves the same purpose.) Of course, addiction is neither a necessary nor a sufficient cause of persistent offending. There are huge numbers of individuals who consume drugs and alcohol in high quantities and who do not regularly engage in criminal behaviors. These tend to be relatively affluent individuals, who can support their habits through employment or family savings. Considerable research has looked at how these largely middle-class people become addicted and can overcome their addictions (Waldorf et al., 1991). Their stories are not included in this study. Although purchasing illegal drugs or driving under the influence of alcohol are themselves crimes (and things that LDS sample members did regularly), no one was included in this study on that basis alone.

Additionally, there are a small number of persistent offenders who neither drink heavily nor use drugs. I met one such individual, who was involved in armed robbery for years and felt he was "above" the use of addictive substances. Although his case is probably unique, LDS participants almost always said they began offending before trying heroin, cocaine, or other heavy-end drugs. The onset of criminality, therefore, cannot be easily blamed on drug use. Participants usually only became exposed to these substances after firmly establishing themselves in deviant subcultures involved in burglary, fighting, or other delinquent pursuits. In a few cases, in fact, interviewees said that they first came in contact with heroin in juvenile offender institutions, borstals, or jails.

It is interesting that several interviewees described actually scaling down their criminal pursuits after realizing that they were addicted to heroin. Whereas the risk of imprisonment is not taken very seriously by 19-year-old toughs, unspoiled by peaceful living conditions, the threat of withdrawing from heroin in a jail cell without bathroom facilities is an enormous threat to persons addicted to heroin. Although continuing to offend, new heroin users said they frequently scaled their criminal involvement down from crimes like armed robbery to less risky crimes like shoplifting:

> Well, I hadn't really shoplifted up to when I got on to this shite [heroin]. I used to do decent graft [serious offending] and earn a good few bob [a lot of money], you know what I mean? And then as it goes by, you start getting a bit more scared and wary. 'Cause, like, if you go grafting, you think, "Hang on. I could do that," and then you think,

"Well, what I'll do is I'll go and do a bit of shoplifting—just get enough to get a bag to sort meself out." (male, age 38)

Finally, criminal pursuits sometimes are difficult to give up even after a person stops using drugs. One desisting participant explains,

I wouldn't mind, but I'd been off the gear [heroin] for a couple of weeks. I hadn't touched it and I thought, "What am I still shoplifting for?" It was just because I was used to the money. . . . I shoplifted every day and I made 200 pounds [U.S. $300] every other day. . . . I was used to having a lot of money all the time. (female, age 26)

Despite these important caveats, for the vast majority of this sample, drug use and criminal behavior were indeed largely "inseparable" (Zamble & Quinsey, 1997). For individuals who spend years as both drug abusers and criminal offenders, this seems to be the case anyhow. When I asked interviewees if they could continue one without the other, most thought the question to be ridiculous. If one wants to recover from drug addiction, he or she had better stop selling drugs and hanging around with armed robbers. Likewise, if one wants to desist from stealing things, he or she had better lay off the smack (or else, as I was continually told, "win the lottery"). The study of desistance, therefore, is almost necessarily a study of abstaining from both types of behavior.

The division between the study of crime and the study of addiction has always been an arbitrary split dictated by bureaucratic and disciplinary boundaries, rather than substantive concerns. While criminologists on one side of a campus are busily modeling the criminal careers of a group of burglars, on the other side of campus, medical researchers might be studying the same individuals as victims of addiction. Sometimes this is literally the case. The original "professional thief," Chic Conwell, was himself an addict, who went on to act as a research informant not just for Sutherland's landmark criminology research (Conwell & Sutherland, 1933) but also for Lindesmith's (1947/1968) classic study of addiction and opiates. The same is true for a sample of Boston men who have played a role in a classic study of criminal etiology (Sampson & Laub, 1993) and, separately, the natural history of alcoholism (Vaillant, 1995).

The point is that most long-term, recidivist offenders in this sample and elsewhere can be seen as either addicts or criminals (or, most accurately, as both) depending on one's perspective. According to a report by the U.S. General Accounting Office in 1991, somewhere between 70% and 85% of prison inmates are in need of some level of substance abuse treatment. This number is surely growing as increasingly punitive drug laws fuel the expansion in imprisonment. From 1980 to 1995, for instance, the proportion of federal prisoners in the United States who were drug law violators jumped from 25% to 60% (Belenko, 1998). Feeley and Simon (1992) concluded, "With drug use so prevalent that it is found in a majorities of arrestees in some large cities, it can hardly mark a special type of deviance" (p. 462).

Addictive substances like cocaine, heroin, and whiskey are all widely available and aggressively promoted in the neighborhoods from which the individuals who fill the prisons tend to be drawn. Moreover, the "risk factors" that predispose someone to experiment with these substances are generally the same as the factors that promote involvement in crime or violent behavior (Farrington, 1991). As such, there has been a call among leading scholars to acknowledge the "generality of deviance" and to break down the walls between specialist divisions like drug abuse research, violence research, and property crime research. Theorists such as Hirschi and Gottfredson (1994) and Tittle and Paternoster (2000) would have us, instead, study social deviance as a general construct that includes all of these different behavioral manifestations.

According to this argument, so-called "drug offenders" do not specialize in drug crimes, any more than "violent offenders" specialize in violent crimes. Knowing that an individual has committed a deviant act of Type A (e.g., interpersonal, property crime, drug-related) does not help us predict what specific type of crime he or she will commit at a later time. More generally, however, past deviance is certainly predictive of further deviance. The participants in this research sample know this fact only too well, unfortunately.

STRIKE 3: CRIMINOGENIC ENVIRONMENTS

Finally, nearly all of the participants (92%) grew up in Liverpool, England, which may be unique even among inner-city areas for its lack of adequate employment opportunities. This was especially the case during the 1980s, when the members of this sample were coming of age. The European Union has since assigned Liverpool "Objective One" status as one of the poorest areas in all of Europe and made the area the target of a scattering of regeneration projects.

Howard Parker began his 1974 ethnography of Liverpool's "downtown adolescents," *View From the Boys*, by asking, "Liverpool, what does it mean to the outsider—football, strikes, a peculiar accent as if everybody's got a clothes-peg on their nose, the Beatles, a famous port, a working-class conurbation?" Twenty-five years later, although the influence of labor unions and football remains, outsiders have attached several new connotations to the city and its people. To the outsider today, Liverpool[15] is prob-

---

[15]Several of the interviews and much of the ethnography in this study took place outside of Liverpool's city boundary in the boroughs that make up the region known as Merseyside (which surrounds the River Mersey). Yet, outsiders generally refer to the entire area covered in this study as "Liverpool," and I will do the same, interchanging the names Liverpool and

ably best known for unemployment, the riots, drugs, and crime. (Because this is a book about crime and deviance, I focus on these negative perceptions rather than Liverpool's more positive reputation as a world capital of popular music, artistic innovation, and good humor.)

The "boys" in Parker's ethnography are now the fathers of a new cohort of "down-town adolescents" who, according to interviewees, are even more streetwise than the generation Parker describes. Certainly, Liverpudlians (also called "Scousers") in the 1980s and 1990s faced an environment with far fewer job prospects, more drugs, and more guns than that faced by young people in the 1960s and 1970s. As one research participant stressed to me, "What you have to concentrate on in your report is that Liverpool is a poverty place. Liverpool is a hard place, especially when you have a record" (male, age 25).

The advent of containerization in the shipping industry during the 1970s and 1980s led to the tragic demise of the city's traditional male job provider, and the world-famous port city became instead infamous for the tens of thousands of dockworkers who suddenly found themselves out of work. The massive layoffs on the docks combined with mine closings and general capital flight to cripple Liverpool's once booming economy, leaving working-class men in particular largely redundant. According to the census, the male unemployment rate was a staggering 20.8% in 1991. In addition, a fifth of Liverpool's male population, between 16 and 64 years old, simply dropped out of the workforce altogether.[16] The unemployment rate for adult women under 59 was 9.5% in 1991. Over one third of the female population was out of the labor force, and one third of the city's employed women worked only part time or on a government scheme (Office of Population Censuses & Surveys, 1992).

These harsh economic conditions, combined with a perception of

---

Merseyside. I take this liberty because the entire area of Merseyside is larger and much more heterogeneous than the areas covered in this study.

[16]Because of this dire employment situation, this sample contains a much higher number of unemployed people than other samples of desisting ex-offenders (e.g., Sampson & Laub, 1993). Only 5 of the 30 desisting participants and none of the persisting participants were in full-time employment at the time of the interviews, and only one of these could be considered a well-paying job. Therefore, the desisting participants in this study were going straight without the benefit of high replacement salaries. Most of them were surviving on "the dole" (Job Seekers Allowance) and the income from sporadic temporary work.

Offender reintegration programmers in Liverpool are quite frank about the probability that even with additional job training, ex-convicts may never find work in the area. **SM:** If I'm an ex-con, and I work hard at this training program, and gain some skills at computer work or that sort of thing, at the end of the day, am I even going to be able to find a job?

Programmer: No. No, I'm not going to pretend they are. But, going back to what you asked before about what we [a reintegration program] can do for people, is, if they want to make a change, right, people gain an awful lot of confidence just through—for want of a better word —our caring and empathetic sort of thing. I've seen people change because of that. One thing I'd never say is, "You're going to get a job if you come to us," because that would be a load of bollocks. The jobs aren't there. But I mean, you can still—I really believe that you can—avert people away from crime by changing their state of mind. By giving them some value in themselves. Giving them some worth."

brutality among the police, motivated a mass protest in 1981, which became known as the Liverpool or Toxteth Riots.[17] The resulting media coverage earned Liverpool a largely undeserved reputation as one of Britain's "dangerous places" (Young, 1996). The *Independent* newspaper wrote,

> It seems to be Liverpool's destiny always to be setting new benchmarks for urban barbarity. The city that brought you the Toxteth riots, Heysel, the murder of James Bulger and, last spring, the rape of a five-year-old girl by a fourteen-year-old boy, has in the past year staked a plausible claim to being the gun capital[18] of the country. (Popham, 1996, p. 1)

Property crime is a widespread problem in Liverpool, as it is in many British cities. According to the 1996 International Crime Victimization Survey, people living in England and Wales face the highest risks in the industrialized Western world of being burgled or having their car stolen. More than a third of respondents in England and Wales reported having been a victim of such crime in the past year, compared with only one quarter of U.S. respondents and a little over a tenth of Swedish respondents (Travis, 1997). Liverpool faced especially dire rates of property crime throughout the 1980s. In 1987, for instance, the reported level of property crime for the city was nearly double the national average for England and Wales (Parker & Newcombe, 1987). Since then, Liverpool's crime rate has been dropping steadily to levels below those of similarly sized cities like Manchester. Ironically, though, according to Parker and Kirby (1996), one frequently cited (but discredited) explanation for this decrease has been dubbed the "Scousers Abroad" theory. This hypothesis suggests that instead of slowing down their activities, Liverpool's notorious thieves were simply traveling longer distances to offend.[19]

---

[17]Although the media framed the event as a sort of "race riot," police officers who were involved in the confrontations characterized the protests as class-based, political, and highly organized. "They wanted to start the revolution right here in Liverpool, and maybe they should have, but we weren't going to let them," one senior officer told me. Several nonpolice participants in the riots said they capitalized on the chaos to redistribute wealth in their own interest. As one White interviewee, who was involved in looting, said, "Everyone made money in the riot—everyone." Even "mothers of my friends—little old ladies," he said, could be seen "pushing shopping carts" full of stolen goods to their homes.

[18]Although Liverpool may be one of the United Kingdom's "gun capitals," private gun ownership is illegal, and guns play a far less significant role in the city's crime scene than they do in equivalent areas in the United States. For instance, only 15 of the 50 sample members said that they had ever owned a real gun. (My British friends laugh when I tell them this was a surprisingly low percentage to me.)

[19]Based far more on reputation than reality, a Liverpool accent is considered in some quarters to be tangible evidence of criminality. Almost every Liverpudlian can tell a story about being discriminated against because of his or her accent when traveling outside of the city. A rehabilitation worker, for instance, described bringing his family to a southern resort town and having his preadolescent children removed from a store because the store manager assumed they were there to steal. Although one should be very careful with comparing prejudices, some of the parallels to racism in the United States are unavoidable. For instance, on several occasions, I was told recycled versions of racist jokes in which the word "Scouser" was substituted for the word "Black" in the American versions of the joke. Twice, for instance, I was asked, "What do you call a Scouser wearing a suit?" ("The defendant," of course.)

Perhaps most importantly, Liverpool experienced an unprecedented "epidemic" of heroin use beginning around 1981 or 1982 (Pearson, 1987). As one Liverpudlian described the situation, "You go on these [public housing] estates and see the young people and everyone looks like they're from the 'Dawn of the Dead,' walking around like zombies all day long" (male, 40s, *field notes*). Although heroin was almost unheard of in Liverpool in the 1970's, by the mid-1980s, according to almost every interviewee in this sample, "It was suddenly everywhere."

Parker and Kirby (1996) estimated that Merseyside now has the largest collective heroin-using population in the United Kingdom. Although the total number of regular heroin users is unknown, health authorities estimate the number to be somewhere between 16,000 and 18,000. Not only is this level of heroin use higher than most other urban areas around the world, this epidemic is also specific to the generation of Liverpudlians growing up in the 1980s. According to Parker and Kirby (1996), "Today's equivalent young adults [to those who experimented with heroin in the 1980s] hold largely anti-opiate and anti-injecting views but regard all other drugs, with some ambivalence about crack cocaine, as acceptable for 'dabbling' with" (p. 3).

Participants in this sample are keenly aware of their unique misfortune of growing up in the wrong place at the wrong time:[20]

> I was 17 [when I started using heroin]. I can't explain it to people now, but we were the guinea pigs. No one knew. No one knew what it did. Because of the way I'd been brought up, I was doing things I shouldn't be doing anyway, and I was fascinated by it. I just started taking it. But I didn't know what it was when I first started. It was only months later when I thought "What's happening here? What's come over me?" And the urge is there then and you need to do it, you just need it. (male, age 33)

Another participant explained:

> Yeah, and what happened with me was, it was like a certain age— about two years younger or two years older—and I wouldn't be where I am. [Heroin] didn't affect my older brother and it hasn't affected me younger brother. I was at the age—I left school in 1983. In '83, '84,

---

[20]Using almost identical language, almost every interviewee described a time in the early 1980s when there was a "drought" on marijuana across Liverpool. Yet, during the same period every drug dealer in the city suddenly seemed to have this new substance, generally referred to only as "smack," that was supposed to be "a lot like pot." Only after becoming addicted to the new drug (which was largely smoked or "chased" rather than injected) did they even realize they had been using heroin, some said. Several interviewees offered possible theories for this sudden appearance of heroin in the early 1980s, the most interesting of which linked the deluge to the unemployment-inspired riots that took place just a year before. "Opium for the masses," the interviewee suggested, "to quiet us down." Today, interviewees say, the "smackhead" or heroin addict is considered the "lowest of the low" among the criminal hierarchy in Liverpool. Unlike nonaddicted thieves, persons addicted to heroin will allegedly "take the eyes out of your head, you know, rob their own mothers, little grannies like" (male, age 38).

and '85, if you look back, that was when the big heroin thing took over, and I was ripe for it. See what I mean? Me older brother only two years in front of me, he didn't get affected by it. He left school and had his head together a bit by then. I was right at that stupid age when no one can tell me what to do. I'm 16 and I know best. And the younger brother had me as a role model and thought, "Well, I won't end up like him." (male, age 29)

The other overrepresented "type" in this sample is something known as the "Scallie" and apparently found only in Liverpool. Although not easily defined, the Scallie[21] is the reason outsiders often give for avoiding the Liverpool area. According to an interviewee, a Scallie is a "wannabe":

Being a Scallie is all about attitude, isn't it? It's wearing the clothes. The shirt untucked. It's about trying to look like you're the man. You're the coke dealer. You're the big thing. [But] half of them aren't doing anything [illegal], like. They're standing on the street corner, or they're going to the pubs. But it's about trying to be that image, isn't it? (male, 40s, *field notes*)

Despite all of these singularities, the most striking feature of the setting for this research, as numerous interviewees pointed out, is that "things are the same wherever you go." The similarities between the Scallies in this sample and the "gangbangers" in Chicago or the "cholos" in Southern California probably far outweigh the differences between these stereotyped groups (Katz, 1988). They are all primarily working class, primarily male outcasts with limited economic options and a penchant for risk and excitement. Although one should not overgeneralize, the participants in this Liverpool sample probably have similar counterparts in many parts of the world.

THE STRUCTURE OF RECIDIVISM

All of these risk factors tend to point an individual in one direction: prison. Of course, this official sanctioning does not make these risk factors go away, and probably makes the person's situation much worse. When individuals with the above described "strikes" against them leave prison,

---

[21]Taking a nod perhaps from stories of so-called juvenile superpredators, the British tabloid press and Liverpool's detractors have recently discovered something called "Super Scallies," who allegedly have outdone even the most notorious of Liverpool's bad boys. Like other terms of derision aimed at youths, "Scallie" is often just a word used to describe any working-class Liverpool youth, delinquent or not. Of course, Liverpool is internationally known as the birthplace of four young Scallies who changed the world with their music. Although one should not read too much into the Beatles phenomenon, the psychological impact of this historical foursome on the city of Liverpool does go beyond tourist shops and museums. After all, growing up in a city where the local heroes were four rebellious young lads surely had some effect on the way the participants in this sample define success.

they return to a situation just as bad as the one that prompted their initial offending. Even worse, they return to society stigmatized as a law-breaker and therefore further excluded from legitimate opportunities for success.

McArthur (1974) wrote, "The released offender confronts a situation at release that virtually ensures his failure" (p. 1). Although the enormous difficulties faced by ex-convicts after their release have been consistently and extensively documented for the past 100 years, the mechanisms for ex-offender reintegration have not improved greatly in that time (cf. Booth, 1903; Hegell, Newburn, & Rowlingson, 1995). As a parole officer explained during the fieldwork,

> [When someone is released from prison] they get a discharge grant— the standard is £47 and the maximum is something like 100 quid— but most of them get out here and find themselves with nothing, like. Nothing to do, nowhere to go, no money. So they reoffend, and we grab them up and say, "How dare you?" and put them right back in prison. . . . It does feel a bit sick to be part of a system that does that to human beings, you know. (Male, 40s, *field notes*)

This gloomy assessment quite accurately captures the experiences described by most of the participants in this sample:

> When I came out [of prison] with my £35 . . . I was skint [broke]. I had a rail warrant [train ticket]. The first thing I thought was, "Could I sell the rail warrant?" I thought, "This is great, I've never been more likely to need to commit a crime [than the day I get out of prison]." I thought, "Fucking hell, I've got £35. What am I going to do? I have a room in [inner-city Liverpool] and the landlord is a guy who used to buy dope off me years ago." This—the indignity is mortifying. (male, age 49)

The ex-offender reintegration schemes that do exist can only go so far in opening up opportunities for ex-offenders when the economy is weak and prejudice is high. As one reintegration worker explained, "We get them to the starting gate, and then you find out that gate is locked" (male, 40s, *fieldnotes*).

With considerable emotion, interviewees described being targeted by the police as "usual suspects" and said they were frequently "stitched up" for crimes they did not commit. One interviewee was strip-searched by the police after meeting with me in a downtown pub. Suspected heroin users are pulled into police vans, told to strip and bend over, as every inch of their bodies are searched for the drug. Interviewees said that this frequently happened during periods in which they had been trying to desist, which only provided additional incentive to return to drug usage. After all, "If you are going to get harassed either way, you might as well at least get the buzz" (male, 30s, *fieldnotes*).

Sampson and Laub (1995) explained that prior deviance "incrementally mortgages the future by generating negative consequences for life chances" (p. 147). Interviewees referred to this as the "vicious circle," whereby decisions made in youth continue to haunt them in their young adulthood.

> I really tried to stay out of trouble, but it's very difficult, you know. Like once you're into a routine and the people you're hanging about with and everything, and plus you're always getting hassled by the Police. And, the thing I always explained to people was, you know, it was about this time that I left home, I was about 16, about then, that I left home. Me mum and dad had had enough of me basically so I was kicked out because—well they kicked me out anyway—and I was on the streets for a very long time, about 10, 12 months. The thing I always explain to people is, our "brilliant" government brought this new rule in that between the ages of 16 and 18 you're not entitled to any [welfare] benefit, you've got to work. So because I was homeless, I couldn't get a YTS job (Youth Training Scheme, a government-sponsored program), and like I couldn't get benefit, but I still had like over £1,000 in fines that I had to pay at £8 a week. So I'm stuck in this rut. I've got to pay these fines or I've got to go to jail, and I've got to live as well. So, I was committing more crimes, going back to court and getting more fines, and it was just a vicious circle. So the next thing I ended up back in prison again. (male, age 25)

Deviant behavior in this sense can be seen as generating its own continuity by spawning a "chimera" of action–reaction sequences (Patterson, 1993). As Janet Reno (2000) asked in her discussion of the obstacles ex-offenders face during reentry, "Is it anyone's surprise that nationwide two-thirds are rearrested within 3 years of release?"

4

READING FROM A
CONDEMNATION SCRIPT

The obstacles that interviewees say prevent them from making good are not delusions or figments of their imagination. Making an honest living is not easy for a poorly educated, poorly connected, working-class ex-convict with a massive criminal record, weak family ties, and no savings. This is especially true when one lives in a city where almost half of the male population is either unemployed or has stopped looking for work altogether. The potential appeal of crime in such situations is obvious, when interviewees say they can "go like that" [snaps fingers] and have "all the money you want" by entering the illegal drug trade (male, age 26):

> The reality is I'll never be able to get a straight, decent job unless I was working for myself or something. So, it looks like I'm back to crime, doesn't it? I mean, I'd love to go to work for £200 a week plastering walls, but I just can't see it. I'm now a single man. I've met people from all over the world, who have offered me [illegal] jobs all over the world . . . so, it looks like that's what I'm going to do. Isn't it? (male, age 28)

As logical as this reasoning might sound, though, persistent criminal behavior still requires some explanation. As easy as the money can be in the world of drugs and crime, this pursuit almost inevitably leads to imprisonment and renewed cycles of poverty and stigma. Although a first-time delinquent may overestimate his or her chances of escaping this fate, surely every inmate sitting in prison has started to guess that crime does not pay.

To understand how repeat offending makes sense in the face of such deterrence, one must understand the mind-set or self-perspective of the recidivist actor. A vast literature explores this terrain "inside the mind" of deviants, spanning both sociology (e.g., Katz, 1988; Lofland, 1969; Shover, 1996; Sykes & Matza, 1957) and psychology (e.g., Andrews & Bonta, 1998; Blackburn, 1998; Dodge, 1993; Hollin, 1989; Ross & Ross, 1995; Singer, 1997; Toch, 1969, 1993). The behavioral manifestations of interest to these researchers differ. For instance, Dodge discussed conduct disorder in children, Singer studied alcoholism, and Toch focused on adult violence. Nonetheless, remarkable similarities can be found in the phenomenology of all these deviant behavior patterns. Bush (1995), in fact, suggested that almost all deviants share an "antisocial logic" or a "small set of cognitive habits that define their orientation toward life" (p. 144).

The basic structure of this logical self-narrative can be outlined by examining the life stories provided by participants in the Liverpool Desistance Study (LDS). Although this is a study of how ex-offenders can stay away from crime, the LDS includes the narratives of 20 active offenders to serve as a reference point or a contrasting sample for the "desisting" group. The assumption guiding this research is that the two groups (desisting and persisting offenders) represent similar individuals in different stages of the process of change (e.g., Prochaska & DiClemente, 1992) and not two starkly different "types" of people (e.g., adolescent-limited vs. life-course persistent offenders). In other words, from everything we know about crime and the life course, all of the active sample members will almost surely desist in the near future (Gottfredson & Hirschi, 1986).

DOOMED TO DEVIANCE

The long-term, persistent offenders in this sample generally said that they are sick of offending, sick of prison, and sick of their position in life. Several talked at length about wanting to go legit or at least doing something different with their lives (see also Burnett, 1992). Yet, they said that they feel powerless to change their behavior because of drug dependency, poverty, a lack of education or skills, or societal prejudice. They do not want to offend, they said, but feel that they have no choice.

In trying to find a sample for this research project, I was prepared for difficulty in finding ex-offenders committed to a straight life. I imagined that finding ex-offenders committed to a criminal lifestyle, on the other hand, would be much easier. This did not turn out to be the case. Like Matza's delinquents, most of the adult offenders I contacted lacked any sort of enthusiastic commitment to crime. Even among those included in the persisting sample, hand-picked for their willingness to admit to active criminal involvement, most only begrudgingly accept the labels society has applied to them: "I'm a thief, but if there was some other way, I'd do that. [pause] I guess I'm just a thief—no more, no less" (male, age 28).

I characterize the narrative of persistent offenders as a *condemnation script*. The condemned person in the story is the narrator (although he or she reserves plenty of condemnation and blame for society as well). Active offenders in this sample largely saw their life scripts as having been written for them a long time ago. In a description of "ontologies of the self," Hankiss (1981) called this a "self-absolutory" narrative strategy, in which a negative present follows linearly from a negative past.

When asked to describe "some of the important turning points in your life," for instance, persisting interviewees often described only events that took place in childhood. One 25-year-old answered that the time he was sexually attacked as a small boy was his life's turning point. As we had discussed this event earlier in the interview, I did not ask for further details, but rather asked, "Any other turning points, important episodes since then?" He responded, "Just that really, everything else was normal." Another 36-year-old respondent said that her father was her turning point. I asked what she meant by this, and she explained, "Just being treated the way I was by him and that."

The turning points described by active offenders tended to take on the quality of life sentences for these narrators:

Participant: I was always on the border of being a good guy and drifting into the other side. I mean, I can fit in with anybody—with either group—I can adapt. I could have gone either way. But the judge, he decided for me. . . . One day I was on the way to work, and I had a fight. The judge sent me to remand for it. Since then, I've applied for other jobs and just—nothing. I eventually found a job working in a warehouse and stuff, but like life had mostly just straightened itself out after that, you know? Just prison, prison, prison, prison from then on.

SM: What happened on that first conviction? What was it for?

Participant: I'd been taking some drugs—coke, snorting, you know —and I couldn't get to sleep, right. I'm sitting there, watching "Santa Barbara" and shit at 9 a.m. and still can't sleep. And, I got to get to work. On the way, I just clashed with a geezer [claps his hands] and a fight sort of started. That was the deciding factor in my life. Now

I wish I'd just taken that day off work, called in sick or whatever. (male, age 27)

Participants in the persisting or active offender group largely see no real hope for change in their lives and have generally accepted the fate that has been handed to them.

[My ex-wife] said, like, "If you got off heroin now, I'd come back," you know, but I'm happy the way I am. I'm just happy to plod along, and I know I've got a habit. I'm at the stage now where I'm resigned to the fact that I'm an addict and I'm going to be an addict to the day I die, and nothing's going to change that. (male, age 33)

It was just—we were completely like opposites. Me old fella [father], like, he—like I'm complacent like—but me old fella like, he used to be an alcoholic, and he tried to stop drinking and he stopped. He used to smoke, and he decided to stop and he stopped. You know what I mean, if he decided he was going stop then he stopped. If he said he was going to do something, he'd do it and then that would be the end of it. Whereas me like, I'll say something, and I'll half mean it and you know, I mightn't do it. . . . The fact that I look like me old fella, you know, I just couldn't be me old fella, you know what I mean. We are just completely different people. (male, age 32)

To refer to the active offenders in this sample as "persistent" misses this ubiquitous feeling of helplessness among active offenders. Attached to the word *persistence* in a thesaurus, one finds synonyms like *tenacity, perseverance, resolve, determination, pluck, grit* and, most ironically, *purpose*. Decidedly none of the above, the persistent offender's orientation toward life is far more like what de Charms (1968) described as the "Pawn" self. Whereas "Origins"—or people with high self-efficacy—feel that they are masters of their own fates, Pawns feel that life outcomes are largely dependent on circumstance and chance events. As such, Pawns are unlikely to search for meaning in their lives and lack a "language of agency" or self-initiative (Larson, 2000). In the Pawn's version of causality, "shit happens."

SM: What do you see in your life, say 5 or 10 years down the road?

Participant: I'm scared to think that far ahead actually. Right now, I'm just living one day at a time actually. You can't afford to look any further I suppose, 'cause you just don't know what's around the next corner. You know what I mean? (male, age 38)

Some cognitive-based theories suggest that this weak sense of personal control may be linked to depression, substance abuse, and possibly criminal behavior (e.g., Bush, 1995). We were able to empirically examine this hypothesis using the two samples of narratives in the LDS. Turning-point episodes offered by interviewees in both groups were extracted and were content analyzed by two independent raters using McAdams's (1992) coding scheme for measuring agentic themes (self-mastery, status–victory, achievement–responsibility, and empowerment) in life narratives. In a test of proportions, the narratives of active offenders were found to be five times more likely (χ^2 = 10.3, df = 1, p < .001) than the desisting offender stories to be completely lacking a "language of agency" (Larson, 2000) in their descriptions of life turning points. This coding scheme and the details of the content analysis can be found in the appendix under "Agency Content Analysis."

ESCAPING THE BURDEN OF CHOICE

This lack of self-efficacy may encourage offending in several ways. First, a person who subscribes to a Pawn story of self might seek out situations that can reinforce and even enhance one's sense of self-victimization (Caspi & Moffitt, 1995; Rotenberg, 1978, p. 95). As one desisting interviewee said in retrospect, "I offended to be caught; I didn't stop" (male, age 28). According to Shover (1996), imprisonment in particular can "crystallize and strengthen a conception of oneself as a person who has been treated unfairly by authorities" (p. 181). This may be precisely what the persistent offender consciously or unconsciously wants.

SM: So what did you do when you got out [of prison]?

Participant: I went home, and when I got home, as soon as I got home, me brother picked me up and took me home, and me brother was sat in the living room on his own, and I walked in to him and I said, "Take me back." Believe it or not like, I did. He said, "What?" and I said "Go ahead, take me back." I said, "It's not for me, this life," and that's the truth like. I said, "Take me back," and he said, "No." I said, "Take me back like, I'm not ready for this life." (male, age 26)

The cycle of "just prison, prison, prison" helps to maintain a coherent sense of oneself as a victim of society, which for the active offenders in this sample may be the only life script they know (see Epstein & Erskine, 1983).

At the same time, as indicated in their scores on the personality trait questionnaires, the individuals in this sample tend to be repelled by authority, regulation, and outside control. Therefore, they may feel the indignity of being controlled by circumstance more deeply and painfully than others, and therefore be motivated to try to regain some control by offending. Indeed, this idea is central to Matza's (1964) theory of delinquency among adolescent males. Matza argued that being "pushed around" puts a young man in a "fatalistic mood," whereby he starts to "see himself as an effect" rather than a cause (p. 88; cf. Bush, 1995). This sense of irresponsibility frees him from moral constraints. In such situations, delinquent behavior can be viewed as a way of "restoring the mood of humanism" or allowing the individual to feel in control of a situation (see also Hollin, 1989).

Singer (1997) described a similar process in his discussion of individuals experiencing chronic alcoholism:

> Convinced that failure, relapse and death are his inevitable fate, the chronically addicted man chooses to say, "I might as well do the damage to myself before life does it to me." At such moments the individual turns his capacity for self-mastery against himself. His only sense of control is the harm he can do to his body and to those people who still love him. . . . There are two avenues to a sense of agency that any individual can travel—one is the independence gained by success, the other the freedom of total loss. (p. 39)

The "freedom of total loss" can be understood as a way of avoiding the burden of responsibility that accompanies free choice. Rather than self-destruction, this can be considered a form of self-protection for those with a vulnerable or shame-prone sense of self (Baumeister, 2000; Khantzian, Halliday, & McAuliffe, 1990). Intentionally failing may be less stressful on a person's ego than trying to succeed and failing anyway. Sabotaging one's life chances with alcohol and other drugs, therefore, may be "the best available excuse for not living up to expectations" (Baumeister, 1991, p. 154).

The following story, told by a 25-year-old male (who incidentally had stolen a television set in the hour prior to our interview) illustrates this possibility in sharp detail:

> Participant: I got nicked [arrested], goes in, does me turkey [heroin withdrawal] in jail, and it was fucking, very rough. I got sent to [prison], down near London from Liverpool—no visits, no letters, no nothing. . . . Gets out. And, as soon as I got out the first thing on me mind was smack [heroin]. I had, like, I took some money off a couple of the lads, getting out, I had like £300 [approximately U.S. $500] in me pocket, I had another £200 waiting for me on the way home. . . . I bought a bottle of whiskey, 4 tins of lager, and just got bevvied [liquored] up on the train going home. As soon as I got home, it was just smack, rocks [crack cocaine], smack, rocks.

> SM: Had you done rocks before?

> Participant: Yeah, been doing them on and off, not as often, but this day when I went home I had £500 to spend, and I'm

spending it, I'm going to have a good day of it, but I thought I'll have one day of it and then pack it in. So anyway, I gets through the money, I'm just injecting it, and I was injecting this bag into me arm, and [my friend] said "Your face has just turned blue," and I've gone, boomph [claps hands] on the deck and died. Three times I died on the way to hospital. Got brought 'round and you don't remember nothing about it. I just, one minute I was there at [my friend]'s, pumping gear [heroin] into me arm, and then the next minute I woke up in a hospital. Just, "What the fuck's going on? What's happened here?" . . . I remember the doctor coming in and saying "Did you try to kill yourself?" I said "No, I never, I was just having a hit, and I woke up here." And that was it. I got treated like a piece of shit then. He said, "Smackheads, they deserve what they get." I just got straight back into it then, and I was going out, I was robbing, shoplifting, scheming, borrowing, begging, and I wasn't getting anywhere fast. I knew what I was doing, getting back into the old routine, and I didn't want to, because I knew exactly what would happen, you know. I'd end up dead somewhere, but . . . (male, age 27)

In sports, these might be called "head games." The basketball player who internalizes a reputation as a poor free-throw shooter, for instance, not only has to manage the relatively simple shot from the foul line, she also has to wrestle with that "little voice in her head" telling her that she is going to miss. All of the participants in the sample probably heard these little voices telling them they would "screw up," telling them they do not deserve any better.

Interestingly, as in the excerpt above, this "voice" of condemnation for narrators in this sample is generally not interpreted as an internal, pleasure-seeking "id"—some internal trait leading them to commit crimes. Rather, using a victim stance narrative, the interviewees attributed the voice to the doctor who says "Smackheads don't deserve to live" or the parent who said "You're a waste of space" (male, age 26). The voice becomes the voice of a society that has largely given up on the person. After all, if the persistent offenders in this sample think they are doomed to a life of crime and punishment, they are most certainly not alone in this belief.

After a series of highly publicized reports in the 1970s that claimed to show that "nothing works" in efforts to rehabilitate offenders (e.g., Martinson, 1974), a good deal has been written about how demoralized rehabilitation professionals have become. For instance, the probation service in the United Kingdom (once thought to be in the business of helping offenders change their lives) is said to have become "uncomfortable, threatened, unsure of its role, and not at all confident of its social or political credibility" (Garland, 1997b, p. 3). Yet, if these professionals have become demoralized, imagine what messages their recidivist clients must be receiving! When offenders say that they "can't" change, they are reflecting the views of many of those around them.

THE PURSUIT OF HAPPINESS

Importantly, even when active offenders in the LDS are optimistic about their futures, they still see little personal control over this outcome:

SM: How about long term, 5 or 10 years down the road? Any vision?

Participant: I haven't got a vision to be truthful, long term. Maybe I'll win the lottery, you know. (male, age 29)

Following Emmons (1986), all LDS participants were asked to name 5 to 10 of their "personal strivings"—things they are trying to accomplish in their day-to-day lives, like "being a good husband," "doing my best at work," or "raising my kids right." One of the first active offenders I interviewed, immediately responded with "winning the lottery" as one of his daily strivings. I explained that these should be "day-to-day" goals, not ultimate dreams, but still recorded his answer. I was surprised when three other interviewees from the active offender group gave the same response.

Although all four probably misunderstood the question, this response is still telling. The myth of winning it big or making the "big score" is an internally consistent element of a passive self-narrative. If there is no connection between intentional actions and ultimate outcomes, and life is a series of chance events ("shit happens"), then why work hard or play by the rules? Success, like failure, is as randomly allocated as the daily lottery. The fact that a lottery windfall is gained through luck and not "earned" through effort, therefore, does not diminish its appeal as a life goal.

In fact, for offenders, the mythical "big score" often becomes "imbued with almost magical prospects for reversing or ending the state of discomfort" (Shover, 1996, p. 100). If only I could strike it rich, interviewees implied, everything will be all right—the hurt or indignity of a life of disrepute will vanish. Ironically, research suggests that when people do win the lottery they can become habituated to this good luck, consequently reducing the level of pleasure they experience in ordinary experiences (Brickman, Coates, & Janoff-Bulman, 1978).

During the fieldwork for this project, a probation officer joked, "You want to know what will make people give up crime? Winning the lottery." Oddly enough, several months later, I interviewed an active offender who had recently won the lottery: "Believe it or not, I won the lottery. Yea,

[I matched] five balls. Second week out [of prison] and I got five balls" (male, age 31). This unfortunately did not have the predicted rehabilitative effect: "Don't get me wrong, I've still been doing bits [of crime], doin' bits of cars and that."

Importantly, the quest for the "big score" is not about selfishness or accumulative greed in the familiar sense. Quite to the contrary, active offenders described considerable generosity in their spending patterns. Tipping extravagantly, buying gifts for others, and consistently throwing money around are all part of the experiential lifestyle that characterizes offending (Katz, 1988; Matza, 1964).

> I used to go to the meat market and rob a van full of meat, drive it out, drive it into the flats [public housing projects]. I'd take what I wanted, and then I'd say, "There y'are," and everyone would come down and help themselves, you know? I've done that all me life, yeah? I've basically done that all me life, you know. (male, age 38)

The point of winning the big score is not to horde it, but to spend it, and the path to happiness is to be found in this hyperconsumption:

> Participant: I wanted money for a solid base. I liked to party and liked a decent motor [car]. As I said before, I equated 50 grand with excitement. The money will go, of course. I'd sort my friends out, then you get stupid with it, really stupid spending, which goes with the job. That seems to be a sort of tedious, sort of boring prerequisite—being the big spender, spending more in a week than most people spend in a lifetime, and on trivia, you know.
>
> SM: Did you ever meet somebody in your line of work [drug smuggling] who would save it up and was more conservative with money?
>
> Participant: No, otherwise they'd get a job as a bank teller, because it's safe, if they want to save money. We lost bundles. It's bad business. (male, age 47)

Excessive alcohol or drug usage, often involving week-long binges, may represent the pinnacle experience in this quest for consumption according to sample members.

> One of my close friends owns a security firm. You know, it seems like everyone has done something with their lives, and it's only me that's not done nothing. I've just like, you know—it's like, I've partied! At the end of the day, I can say honestly, you know, [laughs] I can show what I've got for my money at the end of the day. (male, age 30)

In many ways, the persisting narrative, then, seems to embody Cushman's (1990) notion of the "empty self." Cushman argued that contemporary Western individuals seek "the experience of being continually filled

up by consuming goods, calories, experiences, politicians, romantic partners, and empathic therapists in an attempt to combat the growing alien-
ation and fragmentation of its era" (p. 600). The active offender seeks to
stave off this emptiness primarily with experiential thrills (drug highs, popularity, excitement).

> I used to enjoy it, the offending. I would enjoy doing what I did, just
> burgling, joy riding, shoplifting. . . . I enjoyed the rush. . . . But I used
> to buy friends as well. I've always liked attention. I've always liked to
> have a lot of people around me, and again, if I had the money I would
> take me friends out for a drink. (male, age 28)

> I was starting to enjoy the sort of fame in school, like the big car thief.
> Everyone wanted to know me and find out what I was doing and that.
> We weren't even selling [the car parts] then. It was just the sheer
> excitement. The speed of the car. (male, age 24)

Being momentary, of course, such thrills are incapable of satiating the
empty self's need, and so the quest for fulfillment carries on to the next
night's adventures (see Brickman et al.'s, 1978, lottery winners). Indeed,
considerable research suggests that extrinsically oriented goals, such as
achieving financial success or social recognition, are frequently associated
with low measures of personal well-being and self-actualization (Emmons,
1999; Kasser & Ryan, 1993). Repeat offending is only understandable if
one understands the impossibility of this quest for happiness.

> I love driving and all that like, you know, I love, you know, putting
> cars to the limits, like, putting meself to the limit in a car like, you
> know, like, it's good, like. You know what? You know what I've just
> thought about there, right? You know, like, when I used to get in stolen
> cars, like, sometimes I'd just go out on me own in it and there's these
> country lanes, like. And, you get the odd couple going at ten miles
> per hour. I was doing fucking 70 down it. And, I think, like, you know,
> I think, like, the adrenaline and all that like—I think, you know, like,
> I was saying, "I couldn't feel," you understand what I mean? Honest
> to God, I've just thought about this now: Like, [I was] doing that just
> to *feel something* inside, like, you know what I mean? Fuck me, like,
> you know, I just thought of that now. You know what I mean, 'cause
> I get a kick out of it and all that, you know what I mean? I love
> throwing cars around and that, like, it's great. D'you reckon . . . you
> know what I mean, like, trying to, you know, make yourself feel some-
> thing, like, going that fast, like, and you go 'round a bend and you,
> like, go sideways 'round it and next thing there's just this big fucking
> tree in front of you and that, and you just go, "Aaargh!" You know
> what I mean? Does that make sense, like? To me it does, like. Trying
> to sort of, like going 'round a corner and seeing a brick wall there,
> you're bound to shit yourself, like, but at least you're feeling something
> like, which is scared, isn't it? It's something, like. Like when I used to

get chased by the police, I used to feel so—honest to God—you feel so exhilarated. "Phew," but you're high as a kite on adrenaline. I got chased right, fucking from—I didn't know I was getting chased, though. I was doing 129 miles per hour, right, and when I come to the bottom of the M62 motorway, right, all of a sudden, the police surrounded me everywhere. And, this copper said, "We've been fucking chasing you for over half an hour, and we couldn't fucking catch you," and I said, "I didn't know." I didn't even know, you know what I mean? I was just flying, you know what I mean? Me and me mates were in it, like, in a 3i [sports car], and I didn't even know I was getting chased. You need to like, to like, you need sometimes just to remind yourself that you're alive, don't you, like? (male, age 26)

Again, there is no mystery regarding where this particular quest for happiness "comes from." As Matza and Sykes (1961) pointed out, "The delinquent's attachment to conspicuous consumption hardly makes him a stranger to dominant society" (p. 717). Perhaps increasingly over the past two decades (see Schor, 1998), the virtues of hyperconsumption are celebrated by the mass media, popular culture, and particularly in advertising of all sorts. Although these values compete with the popular virtues of hard work and contributing to society, the pleasures of hyperconsumption get a lot more air time (Cushman, 1990; Kasser & Ryan, 1993). Do offenders need to be reintegrated into mainstream society, then? They may be too well integrated as it is.

OFFENDING WISDOM

Persistent offenders in this sample view themselves as victims of circumstance. They claim to have a clear picture of the "good life" but do not feel they have the ability to get there using their own volition. The only refuge they can imagine is found in a bottle or behind the wheel of a stolen sports car. In the words of the participant above, "going around a corner and seeing a brick wall there, you're bound to shit yourself, like, but at least you're feeling something. It's something" (male, age 26). It is not a happy narrative.

The irony is that they just might be "right." Research on individuals suffering from depression suggests that they may actually be more realistic about their prospects for success than nondepressed people (Alloy & Abramson, 1979; Bandura, 1989). Seligman (1991) wrote,

On average, optimistic people will distort reality and pessimists, as Ambrose Bierce defined them, will "see the world aright." The pessimist seems to be at the mercy of reality, whereas the optimist has a massive defense against reality that maintains good cheer in the face of a relentlessly indifferent universe. (p. 111)

Persistent offenders, like people who are clinically depressed, might be "sadder but wiser" than their contemporaries who struggle to desist. The condemnation script the persistent offender constructs for him- or herself may or may not be an "accurate" assessment of reality, but it certainly conforms with societal wisdom about deviance, criminality, and the measure of a person's personal success.

5

MAKING GOOD:
THE RHETORIC OF REDEMPTION

Unlike active offenders, the long-time, persistent offender who tries to desist from crime has a lot to explain. The participants in the Liverpool Desistance Study (LDS) each spent around a decade selling drugs, stealing cars, and sitting in prison. Most critically, they have made repeated breaks with the life of crime and drugs (often announcing their "reform" to authorities and significant others), only to return to offending behavior. No one (including the speaker himself or herself) is going to automatically believe such a person, when they announce, "I am a new person" or "I have changed my ways."

If such an enormous life transformation is to be believed, the person needs a coherent narrative to explain and justify this turnaround. According to Lofland (1969),

> One of the most broadly and deeply held beliefs in recent Western societies is that an actor must have some consistent and special history that explains the current social object that he [she] is seen as being. . . . The present evil of current characters must be related to past evil that can be discovered in biography. (p. 150)

Similarly, the present "good" of the reformed ex-offender must also be explained somehow through biographical events. Otherwise, audiences (i.e., significant others, employers, the public) will simply not "buy" a person's claims to being reformed.

Perhaps most importantly, ex-offenders need to have a believable story of why they are going straight to convince *themselves* that this is a real change. It is easy to say one is giving up drugs and crime. Yet, when setbacks occur—and ex-convicts are likely to face many such disappointments—wanting to desist is not enough. The individual needs a logical, believable, and respectable story about who they are that "makes it impossible to engage in criminal conduct without arousing guilt reactions and feelings of shame that are incompatible with the self-conception" (Cressey, 1963, p. 158). The desisting person's self-story, therefore, not only has to allow for desistance but also has to make desistance a logical necessity.

One might imagine that if the condemnation script allows for the continuance of deviant behavior, then the desisting person's self-narrative would simply be the opposite of the active offender's script. This assumption is made all the time in correctional practice (see Fox, 1999a). If offenders make excuses for their behavior, they need to stop making excuses. If offenders see themselves as victims, then they need to stop seeing themselves as victims. The self-perspective of the desisting persons in this sample, however, did not fit this model of simple negation.

One of the overlooked difficulties of going straight (or of any comparable identity change) is what Lofland (1969) called the "horrors of identity nakedness" (p. 288). Being completely stripped of one's identity, Lofland said, is "a fate worse than death" (p. 282). Faced with the disorientation of a radical change in behavior, desisting ex-offenders may seek to maintain a consistent and coherent sense of who they are. According to Sutherland and Cressey (1978):

> Once a man has gone through the impersonal procedures necessary to processing and labeling him as a criminal and a prisoner, about all he has left in the world is his "self." No matter what that self may be, he takes elaborate steps to protect it, to guard it, to maintain it. If it should be taken away from him, even in the name of rehabilitation or treatment, he will have lost everything. (p. 558)

This is consistent with what is known about self-identity in general. Self-schemas tend to remain fairly stable over time, because individuals carefully screen and select from their experiences in an effort to maintain a structural equilibrium of the self (Caspi & Moffitt, 1995, p. 485). Although self-narratives do change, this change tends to involve incremental, internally consistent shifts rather than a wholesale overthrow of the previous self-story. Epstein and Erskine (1983) compared personal identity change to the shifting of paradigms in science. Although such a change can appear revolutionary in retrospect, it is often experienced as a more gradual evolution based on the slow accumulation of disconfirming information.

The life stories of desisting narrators in this sample maintain this equilibrium by connecting negative past experiences to the present in such a way that the present good seems an almost inevitable outcome. "Because of all that I have been through, I am now this new way." If this can be accomplished, desistance can be reshaped as a process of "maintaining one's sense of self or one's personal identity" (Waldorf et al., 1991, p. 222) rather than the "schizophrenic" process of rejecting one's old self and becoming a "new person" (Rotenberg, 1978). This secure self-identity also helps protect the person from becoming overwhelmed with shame regarding his or her past self.

A parallel can be found to the prototypical Alcoholics Anonymous (AA) narrative. O'Reilly (1997) wrote,

> Telling the story—it may be said that, in a sense, there is only one story in AA—enables the speaker to reconstrue a chaotic, absurd, or violent past as a meaningful, indeed a necessary, prelude to the structured, purposeful, and comparatively serene present. (p. 24)

Although each story is of course unique, the self-narratives of the desisting sample feature a number of key plot devices with striking regularity. This indicates that a particular identity narrative may be the most personally and culturally persuasive, meaningful, and enabling for the person who is trying to desist. This section addresses how this recovery story (or *redemption script*) "works," by outlining the elements of this particular narrative that make it especially coherent and convincing by the standards of "narrative logic" (Bruner, 1987).

The redemption script begins by establishing the goodness and conventionality of the narrator—a victim of society who gets involved with crime and drugs to achieve some sort of power over otherwise bleak circumstances. This deviance eventually becomes its own trap, however, as the narrator becomes ensnared in the vicious cycle of crime and imprisonment. Yet, with the help of some outside force, someone who "believed in" the ex-offender, the narrator is able to accomplish what he or she was "always meant to do." Newly empowered, he or she now also seeks to "give something back" to society as a display of gratitude.

This process might be characterized as "making good." Rather than "knifing off" one's troubled past (e.g., Elder, 1998), this redemption script allows the person to rewrite a shameful past into a necessary prelude to a productive and worthy life. Although the personal agency implied in the "knifing off" concept remains, "making good" involves more self-reconstruction than amputation. McAdams (1994a) divided personality into three, separate domains: Traits (the "having" aspects of the self), strivings (the "doing" aspects), and identity narratives (the "making" aspects). Desistance, perhaps like criminality, seems to exist "in the making" (my apologies to Sampson & Laub, 1993).

Thematically, the narratives that desisting interviewees make out of their lives differ from those of active offenders in three fundamental ways:

1. an establishment of the core beliefs that characterize the person's "true self"
2. an optimistic perception (some might say useful "illusion") of personal control over one's destiny
3. the desire to be productive and give something back to society, particularly the next generation.

Because similar themes can be found among samples of desisting ex-offenders as diverse as those in Burnett (1992), Hughes (1998), Leibrich (1993), and Shover (1996), these themes may form some larger construct such as *maturity* (Glueck & Glueck, 1940) or the "Reformed Self." At any rate, adapting some version of this macronarrative seems to help the desisting ex-offender find a meaning in a life filled with failure and shame.

THE "REAL ME"

Essential to every desisting narrative is the establishment of a "true self" or "real me." Turner (1976) described the "real self" as a person's subjective understanding of his or her true nature. In contemporary, Western society, Turner suggested, the individual increasingly looks for clues to the nature of this real self in what are experienced as deep, unsocialized, inner feelings and impulses and not in institutionalized roles or professional identities. Thus, one might play the part of the responsible parent, the caring nurse, or the no-nonsense drug dealer "on the outside," but one's self-perceived "real self" might be completely different.

> The judge was saying I'm no good as a mother. They don't know me as a person. They just judge me by what I've done. Other than that, they don't know me as a person. I've stood in front of the judge and said, "You are not my judge. God is my judge." (female, age 42)

In a life narrative, this core or inner self is established in recurring themes and significant episodes in the person's past, however brief or unimportant they might have seemed at the time. Filmmakers frequently use this narrative technique. Think of any generic group of "bad guys" (they are almost always "guys") in the movies. The leader will show no sign of common humanity. A handful of others will be stock character thugs: ugly, stupid, and generally disposable (their demise will precede the climactic disposal of the leader, with a fraction of the fanfare). Yet, often, there will be one bad guy who will show the occasional glimpse of redeeming personal integrity. This may be conveyed in a moment of hesitation or a lingering look back at a victim, but it will be enough to foreshadow an ending whereby this particular bad guy aids our heroes in some way, ensuring victory for the good side. Such an ending is only believable because of the use of foreshadowing scenes. If one of the other thugs were to make such a conversion at the film's end, viewers would be confused and the narrative might be lost.

Narrators in this sample carefully established their essential nature through personally significant foreshadowing episodes. Even when they were "at their worst," the desisting narrators emphasized that "deep down" they were good people. In a process with parallels to Braithwaite's (1989) restoration process, the ex-offenders look in their past to find some redeeming value and emphasize their "essential core of normalcy" (cf. Lofland, 1969, p. 214).

> I used to play truant, and there used to be a show on in the afternoon in England in the '70s, called "Crown Court," and it was like, reconstructions of court cases. And, I used to play truant to watch that because I used to want to be a lawyer. Um, because of the justice thing, you know, the world wasn't fair. And, I do believe that if I hadn't have gone the way I did [into armed robbery], um, 'cause I am quite intelligent and articulate, I would have done it. I would have actually been a lawyer now. It was me burning ambition it really was, and I'd stand about like this all day [pretends to be a barrister], with me wig on and all that. You know, righting wrongs. (male, age 30)

Even in descriptions of playing truant, protagonists emerge as moral heroes, concerned with greater truths.

Instead of discovering a "new me," the desisting ex-offender reaches back into early experiences to find and reestablish an "old me" in order to desist (see Rotenberg, 1987). In some ways, this narrative reconstruction functions in the same way as Goffman's (1961) process of "reverting to an unspoiled identity" (see Biernacki, 1986). After all, not all of the roles played by participants in this sample have been deviant ones. All of the narrators have played the role of the thief or the junkie, but they have also occasionally played the loving parent, working-class hero, loyal friend, and so forth. By falling back on these other identities, they are able to deemphasize the centrality of crime in the life history and suggest that they were just a normal people "all along." Notice the repetition in these quotes:

> I now feel as though I can achieve what I've *always wanted* to achieve, you know, which is gain some qualifications and get a job that I can, um, help other people in. (male, age 36)

> What I always saw in other people was one thing I *always wanted*, and that was integrity. . . . It's either in you or it isn't and I used to think —I knew I had integrity, but as soon as I used to pick up a drink, it just went wayward. (male, age 32)

This rebiographing also parallels what Lofland (1969) called the "well-nigh universal practice" of digging through newly discovered deviants' pasts for evidence that they were always different.

> Acts in [the deviant person's] past that were once viewed in a certain way are reinterpreted. Other acts, which had gone unnoticed or had seemed irrelevant, are brought forth and considered central, for they help others to understand that the Actor was that way all along. (p. 150)

Most likely, this consistency is retrospectively imposed on one's narrative. For instance, the same narrator who described beating up suspected homosexual men in public men's rooms as a teenager later said,

> Yeah, [getting a] job was good because like, you know it was giving me a chance to earn me money honestly, which is something I've never done before you know. Plus it was helping charity, which is something like *I've always wanted to do*. I've always liked helping people who are worse off than meself. (male, age 24)

There is no objective sense in which this claim to a lifelong charitable desire can be verified or refuted. It becomes believable, however, when there are clues or hints of this core self in the person's self-narrative. For instance, few of the participants claimed that their true self was careful with money, diligent, tender-hearted, steady, reliable, or responsible. Such a story would be completely at odds with their known histories and would require considerable evidence or explanation.

The most common strategy, therefore, is to mine even deviant episodes in one's past for positive qualities. For instance, many narrators establish their "true self" as a heroic underdog who only did what needed to be done to help family and friends.

> We used to live by a coal pit thing. . . . We had a coal fire, no one had coal fires, but we did. . . . And, I always remember, I was about, I don't know, 8 or 9 years of age, and we had no coal, so the most sensible thing to do was to steal some from the pit. But, we had to go through all these woods and forests, and it was so spooky. And, I always remember I had my other brother with me, who was crying and moaning, and I dragged him along. And, we had to go down what must have been a 40- or 50-foot embankment, get the coal in a bag, carry it all the way back, but that was the way it had to be. When I did it, I never ever told anyone, I think certain things that I did when I was young, and I was always wise enough to know it was wrong, and I felt ashamed, but some things you did because you just felt you had to. (male, age 32)

Another Hollywood trick: In any group of bad guys, if one of them is unusually intelligent, witty, or attractive, it is a safe bet that this character will be the one to change by the film's conclusion. The ugly, stupid, and brutish are rarely thought to be worth redeeming in Hollywood scripts or in rehabilitative efforts. Similarly, the desisting participants in this sample seem to have also decided that they are "better than some common criminal."

> I wasn't happy selling [drugs], you know. You're making money and whatever, it was just something that, what it was, it was the people that I'd come into contact with, selling it. I just didn't like—it took me into a world, a seedy world that I didn't like. So, um, that had a little sort of, also had a, um, I don't know what the word is, a contributing factor. . . . I didn't like the shady world that it brings with it. You know, and when I say that, I mean the low-life scum bags, low intelligence, you know. I had nothing in common. (male, age 20)

When describing their offending histories, almost all the desisting narrators frequently emphasized that they have "a good brain," "a good heart," or some other positive attributes. Even those who did admit to being "no bright spark" frequently emphasized their street smarts and understanding of how life works.

> What I used to do—this is why I've escaped jail so far, I really used to use me brain—so what I used to do is get trains and coaches out to places. I'd spend the first of the morning checking around everywhere, routes of escape, which way I could go, stuff like that. Then, I'd usually do it in the afternoon, around four, quarter past four. That's the time we used to steal the computers, too. Because, it's like a low-energy time for people. They usually aren't very alert. They usually have other things on their mind, getting dinner ready or whatever. People don't tend to take so much notice of things about quarter past four. But what I did as well, I got a mate's girl to cut off all me hair, and I super-glued the hair to the inside of me baseball cap, and wear the baseball cap, so they'd be looking for somebody with long hair. I used to take a change of clothes with me in a carrier bag. Never wear a mask. It's trouble. It's really obvious [we laugh]. But, you know, I'd bend the baseball cap down and sometimes I'd wear glasses as well. I must have done about six or seven of them [armed robberies] at various places . . . and I never got caught 'cause I used me brain, see. (male, age 30)

Interviewees use the intelligence and bravery they displayed as offenders as evidence in convincing themselves that they will be equally successful at going straight.

> Yea I always classed myself as a good thief now I want to be a good photographer. (male, age 36)

> I lived in the fast lane then, [and] I still live life in the fast lane in respect of work. I'm a highly, highly motivated sort of person. (male, age 32)

All the energy we used to have for thieving—we used to get up and rob all over the country, that's what we used to do get up hire a car we'd be all over the place just busy all the time, making money—and all that energy has just gone into all legit things, you know. (male, age 33)

THE "I," THE "ME," AND THE "IT"

While the redemption script emphasizes the socially valued aspects of deviant involvement, the other aspects of one's criminal past (selfishness, macho posturing, violence, cruelty, slothfulness) are put into a different category by participants. These are not part of the "real self," rather these are products of the environment.

It was just that, um, I realized that the entire thing had all been an act, my entire life, all me criminal offenses, all me drug taking, it was all a sham. . . . It was just like what it was, was right at the core of me, I am who I am now, who I've always been inside. I've always been intelligent, right, inside. I've always been intelligent, honest, hard working, truthful, erm, nice, you know, loving. I've always like. But it was always wrapped up in so much shit it couldn't get out. Um and it's only now that . . . I've realized that. That that wasn't who I was, I did it all to try and, to try and find out who I was. . . . That's what people I knew were doing, people I looked up to and . . . you know I was just adapting. I used to adapt to me peers, which most people do, but some people choose the right peers. (male, age 30)

The core self of the desisting ex-offender is the diamond, whereas the environment she or he lives in is described as the rough.

Then me mum found out what I was doing [heroin use and burglary]. She come to the flat and got me, um, brought me home. She knew I had a bad problem. I was a different person, psychologically. I just— *it weren't me.* (male, age 25)

Participant: I was working [at a youth apprentice scheme]. Me and me mates were also getting [legitimate] work on the side, like, through this scheme. That was the only time that I hadn't been in trouble or been robbin'. And then it finished, the scheme, it just ended. Phhhwttt. I just started to take drugs then, and it all started to go wrong.

SM: You had never taken drugs prior to that?

Participant: Didn't even smoke or nothing. It was just where you lived. As soon as you come out of your house it was there. Like everyone was on it. Every single one. Near enough every single lad was on it. Smack, all kinds, rock [crack], coke—normal cocaine.

SM: But you weren't tempted by all this when you were working?

Participant: No, didn't bother with it. *It wasn't me.* (male, age 29)

The offending came from out there, not inside. It "wasn't me," interviewees said. Frequently, when describing their past lives in crime, desisting narrators seemed to attribute their behaviors to something Petrunik and Shearing (1988) called "the It." In George Herbert Mead's framework, the self consists of an "I" (the self-as-subject, the I who acts, does, and chooses) and a "Me" (the self-as-object, the Me who is known, observed, and blamed). Petrunik and Shearing added to this conceptualization by calling attention to human behavior that agents believe to emanate not from the "I" but rather from an alien source of action, or an "It." This autonomous "not-I" force is internal (i.e., part of the self) yet is responsible for behavior considered unintentional, unpredictable, and uncontrollable.

Therefore, even though the person appears to *do* some behaviors intentionally, the behavior is experienced as something that happens *to* them (see also Bateson, 1971). Petrunik and Shearing (1988) used the example of stuttering. Stuttering is something that certain individuals feel "happens to them," whereas speech pathologists say that "stutterers *do* their stuttering" (p. 440). Individuals who stutter may acknowledge that they "have a stutter" but feel that the behavior is beyond their control. Stuttering is experienced as the product of a "mysterious, intrusive force," or the It.

Using quite similar language, participants in this sample repeatedly described heroin addiction or alcoholism as an alien force, a monkey on one's back. Frequently, this addiction itself was endowed with the ability to "do" things:

The drink was killing me by the age of 21. (male, age 32)

Heroin made me sneaky. . . . But it just become part of me life kind of thing, I had to have it. (male, age 25)

One interviewee described a period of 5 years over which he had remained abstinent from drugs, but said that one day, "You know, it just happened to lapse" (male, age 31). Rather than "I got back into drugs," or even "I had a relapse," the "It" just happened. Many sought explicitly or implicitly to separate themselves or at least their "real selves" (the I) from the addiction, suggesting that the behavior that others attribute to the Me (crime, for instance), can be caused by either the I or by the It.

This pattern was not limited to interviewees who used addictive drugs, however. The overuse of the passive voice and descriptions of being carried away by situations and circumstances were common to almost all the narratives. In a somewhat extreme example, one interviewee described how he was rearrested within a week of his release from prison:

> Mad isn't it. What it was, was, it was breach of probation but it was relatin' to cars. What happened was, you see, I've got this—I haven't got the fetish anymore, believe it or not, but I had this fetish. I could just be walking 'round town, and something would just say to me, "Go in that car and take it." And, zoom, I'd be gone. I've had like people trying to smash the windows to try and get me out of their cars. (male, age 31)

More typically, narrators used more subtle, linguistic devices to avoid directly acknowledging responsibility for extensive patterns of negative patterns:

> It just went on and on. It went on like that for about 2 or 3 years. (male, age 33)

> It started off with little things and then it got bigger you know. (male, age 40)

> You're stuck in a vicious circle. It's money, drugs, money, drugs—and it just goes round and round and round. It's like a roundabout. (male, age 27)

Even when describing the process of desistance, criminal behavior can still be passively described as an "it" that just goes away:

> It just like fizzled out. It's just been years. It just stopped. (male, age 29)

> It just stopped for some reason. I don't know why. (male, age 31)

Another linguistic strategy used by participants was to deindividuate or refer to themselves as just "one of many" (Matza, 1964, p. 90). Especially in describing their childhoods, narrators often replaced the singular "I" with the plural "we" to diffuse the blame and hence soften pangs of guilt (Festinger, Pepitone, & Newcomb, 1952):

> Me and my gang, we were like the local hard cases, and we turned into a gang of tit heads, idiots. Like real scruffy, "Give us a ciggie," [he pretends to panhandle] and that type of thing. . . . With stealing, it wasn't so much a fashion, but I would have looked odd if I didn't. As I say, the company I was in all through school, we all done exactly the same thing. All my mates were in the same gang. They're all in jail now or out and on heroin. There's no exception really—maybe one or two—but basically we are all the same. (male, age 29)

If "we" are all the same, and there is no exception to this rule, then little blame can fairly befall the "me."

> We started hanging about on street corners, we all had our heads shaved and started wearing Doc Marten's boots, stuff like that, going

'round beating people up, you know, that used to hang round public toilets—you know the type that used to hang round public toilets and that. . . . Like, we had a thing against homosexuals back then, you know. Just kids growing up. Then we started stealing more cars then —not for any reason except just to drive 'round in them and then dump them. You know, the feeling of power, having your own car. (male, age 24)

Substituting an "I" for the "we" in the preceding passages might change the meaning from almost sociological descriptions of working-class, British youths "just growing up" to admissions of essential psychopathy.

Finally, like the previous narrator, participants frequently substituted the second-person pronoun "you" for the "I," in an attempt to draw the listener into the story and emphasize the universality of the behavior.

It sounds mad, but when you're on drugs, you don't think about . . . (male, age 29)

At 19, you just think it goes hand-in-hand with being young. (male, age 32)

The compulsive, ubiquitous use of "you know" and "you know what I mean" is also a way of constantly maintaining a connection between the speaker and the audience. Phrases like "I was young, you know" and "You know yourself that if you can't find a job . . ." beg the question of the legitimacy for one's behavior. All of these largely unconscious rhetorical devices are probably best understood as being part of an impression management strategy (Goffman, 1959). By separating the actions of the "It" from the essential nature of both the "I" and the "Me," ex-offenders are also able to protect themselves from the internalization of blame and shame.

REDEEMING ONE'S "SELF"

Making good, in this framework, is not seen as a matter of being resocialized or cured, but rather becomes a process of freeing one's "real me" from these external constraints or "finding the diamond in the rough." This process of self-discovery was frequently described in terms of empowerment from some outside source.

Before I came here [to a job training program for ex-offenders], I was just looking at this brick wall. But when I came here, that brick wall moved out of the way, and it's given me a clearer view, you know, it's given me a runway. And I'm halfway up that runway. And when I get to the end of that runway: take-off. (male, age 31)

Several desisting interviewees used some variation of the following theme,

"If it weren't for X (organization, new philosophy or religion, some special individual, God, etc.), I would still be involved with crime" in their explanation of desisting.

> When I got out [of prison], you know, it's as if someone in a higher place is looking down and saying, "Right you are starting now. All the cogs are fitting together, and you are going away from that and you are going to become this sort of thing." You want to become what you want to become, set your own ambitions, don't you? (male, age 33)

In fact, the theme of empowerment was one of the most distinguishing characteristics between the two LDS samples in a test of proportions ($\chi^2 = 12.46$, $df = 1$, $p < .001$). At five times the proportion of persisting narratives, desisting narratives described scenes in which "The subject is enlarged, enhanced, empowered, ennobled, built up, or made better through his or her association with something larger and more powerful than the self" (McAdams, 1992; see appendix for a description of this coding).

Importantly, while the catalyst for the change is said to be an outside force, desistance almost always seems to come from "within." You "become what you want to become." Interviewees did not describe being passively rehabilitated or reformed by the outside force, rather they describe gaining personal power. The outside force removes the "brick wall" but it is up to the individual to "take off."

This initiation into personal initiative is frequently described in terms of a "looking-glass recovery" process. At first, the individual had no belief in himself or herself, but someone else (often a partner or a social organization) "believed in" the person and made the ex-offender realize they did in fact have personal value.

> Well, before I'd gone to college, [my girlfriend] had said that she knew that I had potential, and nobody else had ever told me that, that I could do something with me life. (male, age 28)

Following this external "certification" (Meisenhelder, 1982), however, the individual now internalizes his own self-worth and realizes his own ability to choose a destiny.

Describing Malcolm X's transformation from prisoner to civil rights leader, one ex-offender said, "Malcolm found himself, in himself" (male, 30s, *field notes*). On a less grand scale, most desisting participants said they found some buried talent or personal trait, however mundane, that they could now exploit in their new lives.

> I've *always* liked playing with wood, making things out of wood. I've *always* been good with me hands.... So I thought "woodwork."... That is just the choice I made. It's supposed to take you a year doing the NVQ [degree], and I've just finished in four and a half months!

The teacher said like, he said he doesn't believe that I haven't done [professional training] before. (male, age 33)

Another interviewee described his decision to take up truck driving as a similar process of finding a buried talent.

I don't know, like. I know fucking I'm not any bright spark [genius], you know what I mean? . . . But I love, I don't know, I'm not being big-headed or boasting, you know what I mean, but I can drive. You know what I mean, and I *know* I can. Going to jail, they give you these tests to see if you're mentally—or whether you're better with your hands or your mind. For coordination, right, out of 100 points, right, I scored 110. (male, age 26)

TRAGIC OPTIMISM: MAKING "GOOD FROM THE BAD"

As in the above examples, redemption narratives rarely involve just getting by. Reformed ex-offenders seem to always operate at "110 percent."

[Now I'm doing] a part-time diploma over 4 years or 3 years, and . . . I'm top of the class, all of me assignments are all A's. So yeah, I'm doing really well on it. This is the end of me first University year, in 3 weeks time, so I've got another 2½ to go. (male, age 30)

While sometimes measured in grades or skill, this sense of achievement is most often reflected in a person's contribution to his or her community, family, or group. The fathers I talked to were not just fathers, but super-fathers. The volunteers were super-volunteers. The counselors were super-counselors. In the redemption narrative, making good is part of a higher mission, fulfilling a role that had been inherent in the person's true self.

To test whether desisting participants tended to be more consistently optimistic in their outlooks, the LDS narratives were analyzed for occurrences of "redemption sequences" or "contamination sequences" (see McAdams et al., 1997). In a *contamination sequence*, a decidedly good event "turns sour." In a *redemption sequence*, the opposite occurs, "something good" emerges out of otherwise negative circumstances. (Of course, descriptions of giving up crime itself were not included in this coding.) In this analysis, two independent raters found that 70% of the desisting group narratives included redemption sequences in the sampled passages compared with 25% of active offender narratives ($\chi^2 = 12.39$, $df = 1$, $p < .001$).

In perhaps the most important manifestation of this positive outlook, former offenders tend to recast their lives as being "planned" or orchestrated by a higher power for a certain purpose.

It's as if [being involved with crime, going to prison] was all meant to happen now you know. (male, age 33)

> I have the philosophy that things happen when they are meant to happen. Like this [going straight] now. (male, age 30)

> I'm glad I had to go through what I had to go through. See, this is recovery for me. I'm glad I had to go what I had to go through to be where I'm at, because this is where I am supposed to be. See, I believe in predestination. Whatever's happened to you is supposed to happen to you. (female, 30s, *field notes*)

Narrators seek to find some reason or purpose for the long stretches of their lives for which they have "nothing to show." This rationalization usually takes the form of "If it weren't for X (me going to jail, my life of crime, etc.), I never would have realized Y (that there are more important things in life than money, that I was good at helping others, etc.)." The good has emerged out of the bad.

In many ways, this resembles what Frankl (1984) called "tragic optimism," or the belief that suffering can be redemptive. In this case, however, the belief is that one's *mistakes* can make one a stronger person. In fact, for many, the only thing they do have "to show for themselves" after 10 years of involvement in criminal behavior is the wisdom they gained from spending this much time on and beyond "the edge." This experience, for whatever it is worth, is turned into a strength in the redemption script.

> I can honestly say, I've ducked and dived, but I've never been crooked.
> . . . All that shit and all that rubbish and all those things I've done have been the biggest asset to where I am now. It's like, you do find yourself being a bit of a role model sometimes. (male, age 32)

Not only has the speaker effectively separated his past mistakes from his true self (he was never "crooked" deep down), he also has become a better person because of all that he has been through.

Sometimes the benefits of having experienced crime and drug use are literal. One interviewee who found work counseling young offenders said that going to prison was a "good career move" for him. More typically, interviewees said, the experience of having "been there and back" has provided them with a sense of "street cred" (credibility among young people) or else an insight into life or how the world works. Ex-offenders say they have learned from their past lives, and this knowledge has made them wiser people.

This is vividly expressed in the following excerpt from an interview with a female ex-convict from New York (Maruna et al., 1999):

> I believe that all recovering addicts are the Chosen Ones. That's my point of view. I feel we are all chosen by God, because we're loved. . . . Like, I feel addicts are lucky when they learn recovery. Because the people who are not addicts, they're not—they still have their problems. People who are in recovery and go through programs, they

learn how to live life on life's terms. . . . So I feel we're special because we're learning how to deal with the world. And, the people that aren't addicts, they don't know how to deal with the world because they were never taught. So, I just feel like we're the special ones. (female, 30s)

While rarely this explicit, the underlying suggestion in many desisting narratives is that the person who experiences crime and then goes straight is in some ways morally superior to the person who has never experienced drug use or criminal behavior. The ex-offender, after all, has tasted the euphoria of easy money, drugs, and criminal domination and has still managed to renounce these pleasures and pursue a more productive lifestyle. Rotenberg (1987) described this as the theme of "ascent through descent" and argued that such a belief is firmly rooted in Midrashic hermeneutics. Talmudic sayings such as "Repentance is so great that premeditated sins are accounted for as though they were merits" and "In a place where re-penters stand, the perfect righteous may not stand" celebrate the reformed deviant as the bearer of wisdom and hope (Rotenberg, 1987, p. 87; cf. Augustine's *Confessions*).

FINDING ONE'S PURPOSE

According to Lofland (1969), "Transformed deviants tend to become not merely moral but hypermoral. . . . They take on a relatively fervent moral purpose" (p. 283). The desisting participants in this sample indeed often claimed to have found a higher purpose and found fulfillment in "fighting the good fight" (male, age 30), defined differently by each narrator. For this Liverpool sample, this "moral purpose" often took the form of mutual-help movements or class-based identity politics. In a U.S. sample, ex-offenders may be more likely to turn to race- or faith-based social movements (e.g., Maruna, 1997). Regardless of the specific framework, ex-offenders who desist seem to find some larger cause that brings them a sense of purpose.

In many ways, desisting participants seem to have reached the revelation that "I am what survives me," described by Erik Erikson (1968, p. 141) as the essence of a construct he called *generativity*. Generativity has been defined as

The concern for and commitment to promoting the next generation, manifested through parenting, teaching, mentoring, and generating products and outcomes that aim to benefit youth and foster the development and well-being of individuals and social systems that will outlive the self. (McAdams & de St. Aubin, 1998, p. xx)

In a content analysis using Stewart et al.'s (1988) coding system, desisting narratives in the LDS scored significantly higher than persisting narratives on this theme. On a measure of overall generativity content, the median score in the desisting group was 6.71 (M = 6.9), compared with a median of 1.79 (M = 1.79) in the persisting group narratives ($p <$ .01). The details of this content analysis can be found in the appendix.

Changing the Currency

Each of us seeks to stave off meaninglessness and void by finding some life pursuit worthy of our time. As was outlined in chapter 4, for the active offenders in this sample this fulfillment is largely sought in the "big score" and other experiential thrills. Desisting interviewees, on the other hand, expressed a desire for more lasting accomplishments or "something to show" for themselves. They described newfound pleasures in creative and productive pursuits, and often expressed a special attachment or duty to some particular community, group, or cause.

> I just—I get more of a thrill out of being on my little computer at home at ten o'clock at night, writing a song, than going out earning all kinds of money. It's like, because like I say, I wanted to be recognized for my creativity, it's true. I really, at the end of the day, want nothing more than someone else to say they like my work. That's more important. Whenever I've put money first, that's been the root of my evil. (male, age 32)

One interviewee, a former drug smuggler who took up painting in a prison education course, described this eloquently as a "change of currency":

> The only thing that is going to improve a geezer [guy] is changing your currency of life, from pounds [money] to something slightly more heady: yoga or art or music or whatever. The people I know from nick [prison] that took up art, they get an equivalent buzz. When I finish a painting, I get the same buzz as I got when I landed 80 kilos on a beach in Spain. So, I don't make much money, I'm quite poor, but I altered the currency. Life's currencies can be less, you know, hard cash, basically less physical. What do you spend your money on? Having a nice time. For what? So you can enjoy life. But if I can enjoy life by painting pictures, talking to impoverished artists and getting arse-holed [drunk] every now and again, going to exhibitions, it suits me fine. (male, age 47)

This difference in motivation goes beyond realizing that crime is "wrong." In fact, few desisting ex-offenders described reaching this conclusion (see also Burnett, 1992; Irwin, 1970). The difference can be found in personal definitions of success and assessments of "what matters in life" (Leibrich, 1993).

> It's what you want out of life, isn't it? Like, I always thought I was going to be rich. I always robbed thinking I'll hit the jackpot one day, but I never did. (male, age 33)

Several desisting ex-offenders said that they have never been as financially poor as they are now that they have gone legit.

> Whereas before I wouldn't dream, wouldn't think, wouldn't bat an eyelid, do you know what I mean, to spend 200, 300, 400, even 500 pounds a day. Now I have to manage on 100 pounds [US $150] a week. Whereas I was spending up to 500 pounds a day. It's a big leap from 500 pounds a day to 100 pounds a week. I'm trying to manage it, barely, but I'm managing it. (female, age 23)

Desisting interviewees said that experiential and consumptive pleasures are no longer seen as ends in themselves that can justify any means:

> The luxuries most people think of in life are fast cars and all that, like. That's bullshit. They're not, like. Luxuries in life are fucking running water in your taps, like. Some people haven't got that. Food in your cupboard, leccy [electricity], gas, and a TV to watch, maybe. You wouldn't worry if you haven't got a TV. You've still got luxuries, you know what I mean? . . . But because, you know, nowadays there's so much of it and all that in this country, like people have forgot, you know, just like how fucking fortunate they are, like, you know what I mean? You know, [I wish] someone had've said that to me [when I was young] like, 'cause I always wanted fast cars and loads of money and that like. (male, age 26)

Several participants mentioned "learning the value of money" since going legit.

> SM: What do you think has been the high point, the best times of your life so far?
>
> Participant: Well, getting to go to Australia [on a work assignment].
>
> SM: Why that?
>
> Participant: It's just cause I've achieved it. I could have went out and robbed the money for that and went to Sydney anytime I wanted, like, but it wouldn't be the same, you know. (male, age 36)

Another participant explained:

> Participant: I'm not proud of being poor, because I am poor, but I earned what I own, and that makes me proud. (male, age 30)

A few desisting ex-offenders, in fact, blamed their offending behavior on the evils of money itself:

> Me mind's changed a bit about money, the more money I have, the more I take drugs. The less money I've got, and I'm not taking it. The money's the evil thing. (male, age 33)

Unfortunately, as a desisting interviewee explains, "It doesn't work like that" (male, age 32). In quite similar stories, two interviewees said that at one point they gave away all of their money (thousands of pounds in ill-gotten savings) in an attempt to go straight, only to find this left them in worse shape than before.

> Participant: I was just sick of it all. So, I had this crazy notion that if I made meself poor, I wouldn't be able to afford heroin or cocaine. So if I remove the money, I won't be able to score. . . . Looking back on it, it was pure idiocy. It went a lot downhill after that.
>
> SM: What happened next?
>
> Participant: I went to live with me friends. . . . Tried to do me turkey [come off heroin]. Couldn't hack it. So, I had to go out stealing. Just the shame of it, I had to go out stealing car radios, car stereos, getting 60 quid [pounds] from them. (male, age 30)

According to interviewees, for a person to desist, scaling down monetary ambitions is only half the battle. One also needs to find a new purpose in life. Generative motivations can apparently fill this void.

Degenerative Lives, Generative Stories

The prototypical example of generativity and ex-deviants might be the case of Bill Sands (1964), an ex-convict who says the only way that he could find "inner peace" and a "sense of accomplishment" was to abandon a successful entrepreneurial career and dedicate himself to helping other ex-convicts change their lives. Like Sands, several sample members assumed the generative role of the "wounded healer" or "professional ex-." Brown (1991) defined "professional exes" as individuals who "have exited their deviant careers by replacing them with occupations in professional counseling" (p. 219). This seems to be an increasingly popular path for former deviants who desist from crime and drugs. As one reintegration worker told me, "I don't know how much time you've spent around recovering addicts, but every addict who gives up drugs wants to become a drug counselor."

Although only 3 of the participants in this study had found full-time, paid work as counselors or social workers at the time of the interview, 11 others were doing volunteer work to this regard or hoped to become full-time counselors or youth workers. Two others were employed full time in different careers but were active as volunteers with young offenders. Because of the use of snowball sampling, such volunteers have likely been oversampled in the LDS. Still, the desire among reformed deviants to help others in this process is a well-documented phenomenon. Brown (1991, p. 219) reported that an estimated 72% of the professional counselors working in the over 10,000 substance abuse treatment centers in the United States are former substance abusers. In addition to such professional work, thousands of long-sober individuals freely volunteer their time to helping others in mutual-help groups like Alcoholics Anonymous (AA).

In the LDS, I purposely avoided oversampling members of any particular organization, such as AA or Phoenix House, as these groups can promote consistencies in the language of reform used by their members (Denzin, 1987). Nonetheless, the impulse toward volunteerism and mentoring could be found in almost every narrative:

> Hopefully I'll be a probation officer soon—or rather work in the probation service, not as a probation officer. I want to *give people my life* —you know, experiences—what I been through. You know, tell them what experiences they can have if they do what I done, basically. (male, age 31)

This urge to "give people my life" appears repeatedly in the interviews with desisting people, who use almost identical language in explaining this desire:

> Like, the way I see it, if I could stop even one person taking drugs again, it would be enough. I don't want to be a drug counselor or nothing like that, but if you can learn off what I'm telling you and *stop one person going through the life that I've gone through*, that's an achievement, isn't it? A big achievement, 'cause I wouldn't like anyone to go through what I've gone through and what I've put me family through as well, you know what I mean? (male, age 33)

> I now feel as though I can achieve what I've always wanted to achieve, you know, which is gain some qualifications and get a job that I can, um, help other people in, you know. Train and get some full-time employment where I can contribute, you know, and maybe help save —*even if I only saved one out of a hundred*, you know, um. I know there's people out there, they'll trust me, once they gain my trust and I can tell them things about me. There's things that I haven't told you yet—things I'm just remembering now. Like, I've had fights while under the influence of alcohol, lots of bad things. You know, just try and make the connections, just try and get through to them. (male, age 36)

Participant: I just woke up one morning and said, "I've got to put this to use now." You know, I can actually tell youngsters where I'm coming from and basically what jail's about. And that's what I want to do. That's me aim. It's gonna take me a couple years to get settled in, 'cause I'm actually starting some work now for probation. It's gonna take me six or seven months before I actually start. I'm gonna be buzzin' with that, you know what I mean?

SM: Why do you think that's something you want to do?

Participant: Well, basically, I'm sick of jail, you know, and I know what jail's about. And I know a lot of these youngsters wouldn't want to go to jail. They need guidance. Do you get me? So, I feel as if I can give the guidance. Maybe *if I had ten lads in a room and I could stop one of them going to jail*, I'd have done a job, and that's basically what I want to try and do. If I get one to listen to me, and think, "Well fuckin' hell, look where he's been all his life." I'm talking like ten years in jail, basically half of my life gone. . . . You total all my sentences up, it's over eleven and a half years and I could have done a life sentence. I just want to get through to them. (male, age 30)

A lifetime that is deemed a "waste" or a shame can be "put to use" by saving one—"even just one"—other life from repeating the same mistakes. This cautionary story is intended in particular as a gift for the next generation.

> I was saying to [my brother's] kids the other day. I'd sat both of them down the other day, and I said, "Listen, me and your dad have wasted our lives. I don't want yous to do what we've done. For 15 or 16 years, me and your dad wasted our lives, and now we want you to take a leaf out of our book." (male, age 33)

Ironically, although the speaker says that his life has been wasted, by living to tell the tale, he has in fact found a social purpose or meaning for this part of his life: It has produced a "book" that he can pass on to the next generation.

Indeed the desire among inmates and ex-offenders to convert their life stories into actual book form seems to be quite common. "For whatever reason, a great many former offenders believe their life history would make an entertaining and perhaps useful contribution to understanding crime and those who commit it" (Shover, 1996, p. 190). This phenomenon may be rooted in the same underlying motivation that is behind the "professional ex-" phenomenon—the desire to make a lasting contribution or leave a positive legacy ("something to show") with one's life.

The professional ex-, according to Lofland (1969), essentially has two "selves": the deviant person that he or she was and the normal person that he or she is now. "The deviant person that he was is kept very much alive through the practice of relating, even ad nauseam, the character of the deviant person he used to be" (p. 232).

> Hopefully, I'll be something to other people. To a few people down by ours, I already am. I know people coming in here [to a voluntary re- integration program] now, and they've found out about it because they've seen me. I led through example. I get a lot of people now, everyone else's ma's whose on drugs, have got me harassed all the time, saying "Can you help our boy, Joe, or whatever?" "What if you just come round for a couple of nights and spend time?" (male, age 36)

The construction or reconstruction of one's life story into a moral tale might therefore, itself, be an important element of sustaining significant behavioral reform.

RECOVERING WISDOM

The moral heroism of the redemption script "serves to make accept- able, explicable and even meritorious the guilt-laden, 'wasted' portions of an Actor's life" (Lofland, 1969, p. 287). This reconstruction also allows the ex-offender to "unabashedly and proudly" announce his or her past, instead of having to run from it (Irwin, 1980, p. 94). Essentially, the de- sisting ex-offender has found a meaning in his or her otherwise shame- filled past.

The transition from being a model of degeneracy and vice to being a generative role model for the next generation may seem like an extreme shift. Indeed, some may be troubled that long-term ex-offenders could feel so positive about their lives. Yet, this sense of optimism and self-efficacy might be useful for sustaining desistance. For all of its problems, being a criminal provides individuals with at least momentary escapes into excite- ment, power, and notoriety. If going straight means accepting docility, self- hatred, and stigma, there is little reason to desist from such escapes.

Making good in the face of all the obstacles and risk factors detailed in chapter 3 is hard work. It is far easier to allow oneself to slip back into familiar behavior patterns than face such challenges without one's usual comforting defenses. (As one active offender liked to say, "Better the devil you know.") According to Bandura (1989),

> There is a growing body of evidence that human attainments and pos- itive well-being require an optimistic sense of personal efficacy. This is because ordinary social realities are strewn with difficulties. They are full of impediments, failures, adversities, setbacks, frustrations and in- equities. People must have a robust sense of personal efficacy to sustain the perseverant effort needed to succeed. (p. 1176)

As such, it is the desisting sample members who seem to be distorters of reality (see Seligman, 1991). Yet, rather than criminogenic cognitive distortions, in Bandura's (1989) words, "They exhibit self-enhancing biases that distort appraisals in the positive direction" (p. 1177).

The major components of the redemption script are also largely consistent with what is known about how individuals rationalize different types of life traumas. When individuals suffering from illnesses or other life traumas find some "silver lining" or convince themselves that some benefits have emerged out of their adversity, they tend to adjust better to their situation (e.g. Taylor, 1983; Tedeschi & Calhoun, 1995). People who construct these "positive illusions" also seem to suffer less psychological distress and are less prone to depression (Taylor, 1989).

The difficulty, in the case of ex-offenders, of course, is that transforming a deviant life story into "an inordinately worthwhile personal identity" (Lofland, 1969, p. 283) carries an implicit (and sometimes explicit) attitude toward mainstream morality and justice.

> I want to go into some kind of counseling work, because I know I'd be good at it, because I've been there. A lot of the problem with probation is they're just, they're pen pushers, you know, they just sit in the college for a few years, read a book about psychology and they think they know it all, and they don't. They just haven't got a clue. (male, age 24)

> [An ex-con] can empathize with you, because he's been there. He knows what it's like to need it [heroin], to be standing there in the rain and the cold for hours waiting for your dealer. He knows what it is like to feel that, you know, humiliated and worthless and just have no respect for yourself at all, like. If someone hasn't been there . . . why should I listen to them [talk about rehabilitation]? Why should anybody? (male, age 31)

The confession that conventional authorities had it "right all along," while seemingly implicit in the act of choosing to desist, does not come easily to the lips of many reformed ex-offenders.

One interviewee explained that he has not become a volunteer with probation because he now supports "The System." Quite to the contrary, he is entering the probation service because he was "so bloody fed up with The System, that I wanted to get in here and try to change some things" (male, age 31). This reformist approach is common to many of the desisting narratives:

> SM: Why (would you want a career in) social work?
>
> Participant: I always said that I'd like to work with kids my age, and just the amount of things I've seen done to children by social workers, who are out of hand. . . . There are social

workers who are qualified, but are idiots. You can't tell me about social work! (male, age 28)

I'd love to actually go and work within the system, the prison system. Find out what is really happening in the system, find the faults, and write a report. (female, age 26)

Another participant explained:

The main reason I do this job [working with other ex-cons] isn't because it's easy for me because I've been there and I speak the language. I do this because I still believe in justice. A lot of the people I work with have been shunned by society. They're seen as scum. A lot of people would just as soon kill them. They really would. But I see the diamond [in the rough]. (male, age 30)

In the desisting self-story, the "System" may need more reform than the recovering individual himself or herself. While the ex-offenders in this sample are playing by the rules of mainstream society, they often emphasized their dissatisfaction with the culture that "led" them to offending in the first place (see also Irwin, 1970, p. 156). In fact, rather than overcoming a "criminal value system," the interviewees saw themselves as recovering from *society's* value system in some sense.

Well, at least I've got food in the cupboard you know. You've got to be grateful for the little things in life. People who have everything don't appreciate what they've got. They take things and people for granted. They treat people like shit. They've got money and they think they're better than you. (female, age 42)

This critique is reflected in the well-known monologue of a desisting ex-offender in the film *Trainspotting*:

Choose Life. Choose a job. Choose a career. Choose a family. Choose a fucking big television. Choose washing machines, cars, compact disc players, and electrical tin openers. Choose good health, low cholesterol, and dental insurance. Choose fixed interest mortgage repayments. Choose a starter home. Choose your friends. Choose leisurewear and matching luggage. Choose a three-piece suite on hire purchase in a range of fucking fabrics. Choose DIY and wondering who the fuck you are on a Sunday morning. Choose sitting on that couch watching mind-numbing, spirit-crushing game shows, stuffing junk food into your mouth. Choose rotting away at the end of it all, pishing your last in a miserable home, nothing more than an embarrassment to the selfish, fucked up brats you spawned to replace yourself. Choose your future. Choose Life.

While the speaker, Renton, does eventually go straight by the end of the film, "choosing life" as it were, the antiestablishment message is quite clear:

Before you judge my past choices as deviant, take a long look at your own life, mate.

This long monologue, quite remarkably, became something of a pop culture mantra among teenagers and university students throughout the United Kingdom. In 1996–1997, the ubiquitous "Choose Life" monologue could be found on T-shirts, coffee mugs, and posters, and a pop song even set the speech to dance music. Although few of these legions of *Trainspotting* fans are themselves former heroin addicts or burglars like the character of Renton in the film, discomfort regarding the transition away from deviance might be somewhat universal among young people. Like the ex-offenders in this sample, many youths may seek to balance this tension by trying to transform the mainstream even while they are joining it. Idealistic passion, overconfidence, and even a touch of self-righteousness may be traits shared by both successful ex-offenders and successful young people as members of both groups seek to make a place for themselves in the world of conventional adults.

III

APPLIED MYTHOLOGY

Leslie Wilkins once described the field of corrections as "applied mythology" (cited in Fogel, 1975). By this, he meant that very little of what is done in the name of offender treatment is based on grounded evidence about how people change. Likewise, Ross and Fabiano (1983) suggested that "Corrections appears to be functioning in a 'conceptual vacuum'" (p. 2). Indeed, even the most highly regarded rehabilitation researchers admit that the field "is not viewed as a professional area of practice, replete with a growing body of core psychological knowledge and opinion with which practitioners and managers should be familiar before 'innovative' programs are introduced" (Andrews, Bonta, & Hoge, 1990, p. 45).

In the absence of such a conceptual framework for rehabilitation practice, faddish all-purpose "cures" have flourished in what has been called an epidemic of "panacea-philia" (Gendreau, 1996). In fact, the dominant philosophy in the corrections field has been described as "anything goes," with many interventions drawing from an "ill-digested mixture of behaviorism and neo-Freudian psychologies" (Cohen, 1985, p. 154). As Cohen pointed out, "It is easy to find a single agency which lists as its 'methods': role playing, transactional analysis, problem solving, task setting, reality therapy, behavior modification, operant reinforcement, video game skills, remedial education and camping trips" (p. 154).

In an effort to rectify this situation, academic researchers have struggled to develop a science of corrections. The best of this genre, frequently dubbed "what works" research, seeks to identify "empirically based best practices" with the help of standardized evaluation techniques, controlled quasi-experiments, and meta-analysis. This "what works" literature has played an essential role in challenging the notion that "nothing works" in corrections (Martinson, 1974).

Although this evaluation-based research is very useful in answering the question, "Does this type of program work (on average, overall)?," it tells us little about *how* rehabilitation works, *why* it works with some clients, or why it fails with others (Chen, 1990; Palmer, 1994; Pawson & Tilley, 1997). The answers to such questions have been generally locked away in the "black box" of program evaluation research, treated as unknowable—or else unimportant in the face of challenges like Martinson's "nothing works."[22]

---

[22]Prior to being put on the defensive following the "nothing works" attack, rehabilitation research frequently asked these more micro-level questions about how the process of reform

Yet, the individual client does not experience some undifferentiated "program," like behavioral therapy or Alcoholics Anonymous (AA). Every individual experiences and interprets unique social interactions within a program setting (D. A. Lewis, 1990). The long tradition of change process research in psychotherapy (e.g., Rice & Greenberg, 1984; Toukmanian & Rennie, 1992) has taught us that every intervention or program actually consists of thousands of different micromechanisms of change (e.g., confrontation, learning to trust, and self-reevaluation). Whereas macrolevel research asks, "Does rehabilitation work?" or "Does group therapy with offenders work?" this microlevel research starts a few thousand steps back and asks, for instance, "How do different individuals tend to respond to direct confrontations of their behavior?" By gradually accumulating knowledge about these micromechanisms of change (hence opening the black box), researchers may be able to develop a more theory-driven agenda on effective programming (Pawson & Tilley, 1997). Unfortunately, this sort of science of rehabilitation is a long way off.

THE ROOTS OF CORRECTIONS

A few implications for correctional practice might be inferred from the Liverpool Desistance Study (LDS). The highly subjective data collected for the LDS are not well suited for arguing for or against the effectiveness of particular programs or interventions. However, they may provide some insight into the process of maintaining behavioral change.

Cressey (1963), for instance, argued that if criminal behavior is dependent on the neutralizations or verbalizations that make deviance possible, then "Attempts to change that conduct should concentrate on processes for avoiding some verbalizations and acquiring others . . . the words utilized in acquiring what is called a 'self conception' must be changed" (p. 152). This is an idea worth repeating: If the cognitive neutralization techniques play an important role in allowing for deviant behavior, then rehabilitation probably involves a reworking of these self-narratives.

Certainly, the construction, deconstruction, and reconstruction of self-stories are at the very core of traditional correctional interventions. Thune (1977) and O'Reilly (1997) suggested that the power of storytelling may account for the success of twelve-step programs like Alcoholics Anonymous, which can be found in prisons and correctional settings across the United States (and indeed are the only form of "therapeutic support" offered in many prisons). The edited volume *Alcoholics Anonymous* (1939), the primary text (or "Big Book") that has introduced millions of people to

---

worked (e.g., Grant & Grant, 1959; Palmer, 1965; Sealy & Banks, 1971; Warren, 1971). In the post-Martinson (1974) era, however, such work clearly made less sense. Why study how rehabilitation works, if we have not even agreed that anything works to begin with?

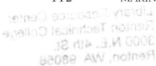

the twelve-step philosophy, is itself a collection of 29 life stories of the original members of the organization. AA founder Bill Wilson has said, "The 400 pages of Alcoholics Anonymous contain no theory; they narrate experience. . . . Being laymen, we have naught but a story to tell" (O'Reilly, 1997, p. 129).

Recovery stories continue to be told at twelve-step fellowships around the world. "Rarely is any point made in AA meetings or publications without at least a few fragments of some individual's life history being presented to support it" (Thune, 1977, p. 79). AA members implicitly model their own life stories on the stories in the Big Book and those told by more experienced members of the fellowship (O'Reilly, 1997). Far from mere mimicry, this reworking of one's self-story according to the AA model is itself the recovery process used in twelve-step programs (Thune, 1977, p. 80). Regarding Narcotics Anonymous (NA), for instance, Ronel (1998) wrote,

> NA's accumulated biography, expressed as members' sharings, functions as raw material for the process of re-biography. It gives communal meaning, direction and structure to an individual life story. Individuals can therefore fashion their life stories to conform with those of the sub-culture, and live according to them. (p. 194)

Rebiographing is also essential to the practice of reintegrative shaming in the restorative justice model (e.g., Clear & Karp, 1999). Victim-offender mediation and other forms of conferencing involve a mutual retelling of the events leading up to and including the immediate offense. All sides describe their interpretation of the event and how it made them feel. Mediation practitioners refer to this as "telling their stories" (Zehr, 1990, p. 161). This storytelling is intended to humanize victims, offenders, and the family members of both. It is also an ideal method for deconstructing offender neutralizations. The denial of injury or denial of victim, in particular, becomes immediately implausible in such a circumstance.

Similar examples of storytelling and self-story analysis can be found in the group therapy (E. M. Scott, 1998) and in cognitive self-change interventions (Bush, 1995) conducted in innovative correctional environments. As such, narrative reconstruction might even be seen as a "root metaphor" (Sarbin, 1986) for correctional practice itself. Essentially, when the black box of correctional programming is pried open, one may find that it contains a complex web of discourse—organizational narratives, reformer narratives, personal narratives, and the interaction therein (Cooren, 2000). According to O'Reilly (1997), "Narrative is not a cure, but it is a method, a path toward redemption. Redemption lies in . . . a better understanding—an improved epistemology" (p. 65).

If this is the case, phenomenological research may have a contribution to make to the science of corrections as a supplement to controlled evaluation experiments (Lovejoy et al., 1995; McCorkle, Harrison, & Inciardi, 1998). According to Brickman and his colleagues (Brickman et al., 1982), "If either helping or coping is to be understood, the two processes must be studied together rather than separately" (p. 370). If one knows what personal myths seem most appealing to desisting persons, one can better direct the narrative reconstruction implicit in the rehabilitative efforts. This is certainly not what Wilkins meant by "applied mythology," but the phrase is an apt description of this vision of correctional research.

SUPPORTING MAINTENANCE

Frequently, discussions about correctional policy get caught up in the pendulous debate between deterrence and treatment. The question is what is the best way to change a wrong-doer's behavior, the "carrot" or the "stick"? Perhaps fortunately, the LDS data have little to say about this controversy, so I will not be entering this dialogue. After all, it is not clear what "caused" the LDS interviewees to decide to make good—the turning point could have been a form of deterrence or else some helpful intervention (or both). I cannot say for sure because they were already desisting "when I found them."

On the other hand, although little in the LDS can answer the question of how to "turn the bad into the good," the findings can provide some suggestions about how people who have *already decided to stop offending* can maintain this desistance. This is no small thing. If personal change is a long-term, cyclical process of trial and error (Hser, Anglin, Grella, Longshore, & Prendergast, 1997; Prochaska & DiClemente, 1992), treatment interventions should probably focus less on changing committed offenders and more on providing support for those who make initial efforts to change (see Marlatt & Gordon, 1985).

In an irony noted by several interviewees, although considerable resources are spent encouraging individuals to stop offending, once the ex-offender does make this break, he or she is generally abandoned by social support networks. This might be precisely the period when the ex-offender needs the most support.

> Participant: It's funny, when you are on drugs there are a million places you can go and have people help you, but when you are clean and not into crime and all that, then suddenly there isn't anyone that will help you. . . . When you're into crime and drugs and stuff, you've got drugs help lines. You've got drugs counselors, drug units. You've got the probation that'll help you. There's NACRO [National Association for the Care and Resettlement of Offenders], sort of thing, that'll help you

along the way. There was like, the [probation] hostel staff. . . . But, once you turn the corner, there's nothing really. There's no sort of organizations that can help you out. . . . There's nothing like counseling or anything like that, or people that can help you manage your money, stuff like that.

SM: What sort of help would you like to see?

Participant: Well, you know, counselors, people to give you the encouragement to stay on the straight and narrow. (male, age 24)

Another interviewee explained why she relapsed soon after leaving a 30-day detoxification program for people with heroin addictions.

Within like two months [after starting the program], they'd forgotten about us. We were just left . . . and when you leave, you haven't finished [the change process], and we were just left. I know they had—they didn't have that much time because new residents were coming in, and they had to help them. But . . . we shouldn't have been left on the hardest part [of the recovery process]. The easy part's getting off [drugs], it's staying off that's the hard part, and we were just left to fend for ourselves. (female, age 26)

For this reason, a group of former drug users, all of whom completed a Liverpool detoxification program, formed a weekly support group to give and receive this necessary follow-through assistance. Augmenting such efforts at relapse prevention may be as important a goal of correctional practice as convincing those who do not want to desist to contemplate it.

In the following chapters, I explore in greater depth the three key themes that characterized the desisting narratives in this study (generative motivations, the core self, and a sense of agency). In doing so, I make tentative suggestions how each of these self-understandings might be encouraged in correctional practice. I claim no experimental evidence for the effectiveness of such practices, only offer them as possibilities on the basis of the narrative testimonies. Finally, as narratives are cultural artifacts, I take the opportunity at the end of each of the following chapters to speculate about where these story lines are "coming from" and what purposes they might serve. This speculation is based in theory (e.g., my own metanarrative for interpreting the world). This perspective need not be shared to appreciate the findings from the research, nor, I hope, has it colored my own interpretation of the data any more than it does the perspective of any other researcher.

6

WORK, GENERATIVITY, AND REFORM

The link between work and the rehabilitation of offenders has been assumed for at least the past century. According to Simon (1993), "Wherever you look in the development of modernist penality you will find labor. Exhort the offenders with religious tracts, but make them work. . . . Educate them as citizens, but make them work. Treat their pathological features, but make them work" (p. 39). As such, the finding that desisting sample members in the Liverpool Desistance Study (LDS) derived meaning from a variety of productive pursuits should be comforting to those in the offender reintegration business. The specific nature of the productive motivations and their role in the sample members' identity narratives, however, need to be emphasized and understood.

In particular, the desisting self-narrative frequently involves reworking a delinquent history into a source of wisdom to be drawn from while acting as a drug counselor, youth worker, community volunteer, or mutual-help group participant. Although this generative phenomenon is well documented among persons in recovery (Brown, 1991; Green, Thompson, & Fullilove, 1998; Hughes, 1998), such efforts are often questioned or considered insincere. For instance, in a favorable review of reformed ex-offender Bob Turney's (1997) book, Sir Stephen Tumin is quoted as saying, "I have always been rather against the idea of prisoners after discharge becoming professional former prisoners. They should, it seems to me, learn the lessons of imprisonment and move on to fresh lives with new occupations and new interests" (back cover). Similarly, during the LDS field-work, a critic of the "professional ex-" phenomenon said, "Sometimes, these cons misunderstand and sort of want to become one of the therapists themselves, instead of going out and finding real jobs." In some cases, ex-offenders are even prohibited from pursuing work that would put them in contact with young people or other offenders.

> When I was on me diploma in social work [course], I was paid by my local authority [city government] as an outreach worker for the youth justice team, working with young offenders. And when they saw that I was on the course and could become qualified [as a social worker], they withdrew the placement and said that I couldn't be employed by them because I was an ex-offender. (male, age 28)

Part of this resistance may be based on class-based, territorial interests. As Leary (1962) wrote, "Allowing criminals to take over responsibility and authority and prestige as experts on 'crime and rehabilitation' brings [them] into competition with the professional middle class" (p. 66). However, some of this resistance can be attributed to the lack of a theoretical un-derstanding for why ex-offenders seem to be drawn toward generative roles and activities. In this chapter, I try to analyze the reformative aspects of generative pursuits and, on the basis of interview testimony, I speculate as to the origins of these motivations.

HOW GENERATIVE SCRIPTS "WORK"

Generativity is a product of both inner drives and social demands (McAdams, Hart, & Maruna, 1998). As humans age, the adults face so-cietal expectations—encoded in normative, age-graded standards and but-tressed by economic and structural opportunities and constraints—to take responsibility for the next generation (Neugarten & Hagestad, 1976). For-mer offenders, however, may face unique personal and cultural demands for developing generative goals and plans.

Interviews with active offenders suggested that criminal behavior might be used as a way of filling a void or emptiness in a person's life. Additionally, external stigma and an internalized sense of shame also led to feelings of being "doomed to deviance." Generative pursuits seem to address all of these needs in the lives of desisting interviewees:

- *Fulfillment:* Generative roles can provide an alternative source of meaning and achievement in one's life.
- *Exoneration:* By helping others, one relieves his or her own sense of guilt and shame.
- *Legitimacy:* The penitent ex-offender who tries to persuade

others not to offend is a well-known and established role in society.

- *Therapy:* Helping others actually helps the ex-offender maintain his or her own reform efforts.

Each aspect of generativity's appeal is developed in this chapter.

Generativity as Fulfillment

One of the struggles described by interviewees in this sample was the creeping sense that one's existence was meaningless or useless.

> We always had a lot of money and a lot of gear [drugs] and that. It wasn't really a problem to us, 'cause we always had it. But it was a problem like. I just wasn't happy with me life at any stage. About 18 months ago, I just had enough like, so I took 100 tablets just to kill meself. (male, age 36)

> I had nothing to do so I just lapsed back into it [burglary] but I still had it in me mind that I wanted to leave it alone like. It had come to a time where I'd had enough of it you know. I'd had enough of prison and all the lifestyle that goes with it you know, and just the uselessness of everything. You know, just feeling useless. I would still go out robbing and making money and spending it on something else, but it was still not fulfilling to me and still felt like I was wasting meself. (male, age 33)

Waldorf et al. (1991) compared this experience to Kierkegaard's (1843/1941) concept of despair. In the state of despair, a life of meaningless hedonism leads an individual to a choice between either death or conversion to a religious life. Although organized religion played a primary role in only a few of the LDS narratives, the interviewees often showed a similar sense of newfound purpose in some larger community. Like the recovering drug abusers in Baskin and Sommers's (1998) research, many "were like religious converts in terms of the fervor with which they attempted to establish and maintain support networks that validated their new sense of self" (p. 136; see also Lofland, 1969).

Perhaps most importantly, other-centered pursuits provide socially excluded offenders with a feeling of connection to or "embeddedness" in the world around them (Singer, 1997). By providing a supportive community and a network of people with shared experiences, these organizations can transform a seemingly individual process like desistance or recovery into a social movement of sorts (Hamm, 1997; Sands, 1964). This connection to something larger than the self (even in the name of *self*-help) appears to be a vital part of the desistance process (see Baskin & Sommers, 1998, p. 137).

Additionally, although they may be likely to fail in many legitimate careers, ex-offenders often discover that they are quite good at counseling other ex-offenders. They find that this is a field in which they can achieve and even excel. Like the ex-convict in O. Henry's (1953) "A Retrieved Reformation," who uses his safe-cracking skills to free a trapped child, wounded healers are able to use their wealth of criminal experience for prosocial ends.

> SM: How have you found working with kids in your new job?
>
> Participant: It's been brilliant. The times I've been out and the kids have started battling, and the social worker just flaps, "Uh, oh." I was picked specially to work with [a particularly difficult young person]. I have earrings, long hair. I don't give a shit. That's the bottom line. I told him, "It's my job. I will allow you to tell me to fuck off once, but it's your loss. I'm here to help you." And I was in for nearly an hour and he asked me to come back, and I built up a very, very strong relationship with him—so much so that we got him out of the Secure Unit [of the prison]. . . . I had a lot of response. (male, age 29)

Indeed, numerous observers have outlined the theoretical and practical reasons why former deviants should be recruited to work as rehabilitation practitioners (e.g., Cressey, 1965; Lofland, 1969).

> With such backgrounds, [wounded healers] are living examples of the transformation that is possible. . . . When the [going] gets tough, it is possible to say, "He did it, so can I." A would-be identity model derives legitimacy from his [or her] having traversed the same route. To expect deviants to have affective bonds for—to take as identity models— others who have not had that career is to expect an atypical, unusual and treacherous identification. Perhaps only deviants are expected to be so unusually responsive to persons different from themselves. (Lofland, 1969, p. 268)

Ex-offenders are, after all, experts on the subject of deviance and desistance, and each has the wisdom (or what one interviewee described as "insight") that comes with having "been there and back." One interviewee, who had expressed considerable criticism for social workers (who had, among other things, taken her children away from her at one point), surprised me by announcing at the end of the interview that she wanted to become a social worker herself:

> I want to show people the positive side of social work. When they [social workers] come around, they don't do that. . . . I want to show people that I've been there, I've been through this stuff, so I can relate to what they're going through. (female, age 26)

Interviewees also described the fulfillment they derive from being able to contribute to a social control establishment that had long been seen as their adversary. One wounded healer, a volunteer reintegration worker, said that he realized just how far he had come when a client asked him to write a letter of support to a parole officer on the client's behalf. "Writing to a parole officer as if he were a peer, rather than my superior, like" (male, age 30).

Most of the other occupations available to ex-offenders ("thankless, stinking work in dog food factories," according to one) do not provide this same sense of achievement.

> I used to work for a local supermarket, stacking the shelves and things. No problem with the [criminal] record, I didn't declare [the convictions]. But I just gave it all up. I just got bored. It was dead boring. Ended up on the dole. Didn't have enough money to live off, and again the easy option was to start offending again. (male, age 28)

The dispositional traits of LDS sample members (low conscientiousness, high need for excitement) make them rather poor fits for low-status, repetitive work. Like the active offenders interviewed in this study, if faced with a choice between such work or criminal involvement, they are likely to choose the latter (and, of course, they did for many years). One active offender explained,

> I can't explain it. . . . It's just that when you see people with nice things, you say "That's where I want to be." Then you see this lot working hard, real struggle, going to work everyday, and still with nothing to show for it. Then you see this other group [criminals] out having a good time, never bored, and they got the nice things that the posh people have. (male, age 27)

Fortunately, desisting sample members were able to find leadership roles in community groups, in voluntary organizations, or in their families that could provide them with a source of personal satisfaction. Going straight, therefore, does not seem to be about defiant rebels turning into diligent working stiffs. Instead, defiant rebels are able to find social roles or occupations that can provide them with the same sense of empowerment and potency they were seeking (unsuccessfully) through criminal behavior.

Generativity as Restitution

All of the interviewees in this sample had to manage the shame and guilt that accompany involvement in criminal behavior. Generative activities seem to help a person come to terms with past mistakes and "move on."

> I feel tremendously guilty for what I've done, and that really is a big thing, because I'm waiting to go now and train as a Victim Support

Worker. I'm going to go and work with the victims of crime. D'you know what I mean? I'm human. (male, age 28)

Another participant explained:

> But I owe [my children] a lot, you see. Like I told you, she had me son when I was in jail. So, I haven't even paid him back for that. I've been in [prison] twice since. I haven't actually paid them back to say I'm sorry. I want to do it in a nice way. I want to leave them something. I want to give them something back. But that's hard to do, 'cause I got nothing to give them. (male, age 40)

Braithwaite and Mugford (1994) wrote, "The gesture of restoration to both community and victim, even if it is modest in comparison to the enormity of the crime, enables the offender to seize back pride and reassume a law-respecting, other-respecting and self-respecting identity" (p. 148). One of the interviewees described his experiences doing woodwork projects at a reintegration program in much the same terms:

> I mean, since I've been here, I've made three big playhouses, like eight-foot wide by ten-foot with an upstairs and all. Gettin' a buzz. I mean, I took so much out of the community, but the first one we made, we donated that to the children's home. So we took that much out of the community, [but] now we're putting something back in. It's not much compared to what we took out, but we put something back. I mean, it helped the kids, it helped the parents. Me kids are always asking me when am I going to build something for them. Every house I've built, my kids have seen it. That's a buzz, that. (male, age 31)

Some interviewees described wanting to help less fortunate others as a reciprocal gesture, because they themselves had received so much help from volunteers, counselors, or reintegration workers. "I try to give people respect. What people gave to me, I try to give back" (male, age 33). Other times, the atonement is directed at family members or significant others who have stuck by the person.

SM: So you gave up the smack [heroin]. How about stealing cars and that?

Participant: I don't bother with cars and all that now, like. I've had a legit car, like, you know to drive me mum around. Like, that's what I do now, like. That's why I've got me shit together now, like. Me ma, like, she's had four strokes, you know, and as I said before, me ma is me world, you know what I mean, seriously like. I do believe that, like. So I, like, I look after me ma and all that, like, you know. I try to do good things for her—for meself, you know what I mean, but for her too, you know. I've done bad things to them in the past and that, like, you know. I wasn't the ideal fucking son and all that, was I? You know what I mean, so I do try now, though. (male, age 26)

Another participant explained:

I mean, my kids are starting to call me "Dad" now, whereas years ago, they used to just say, "Who's he?"—'cause I used to just come in, get something to eat, then go out. Now they're calling me Dad. I feel like a dad. I'm backin' them, I'm dressing them, taking them to school. That's things I've never done. They're two brilliant kids. I'm just sick I missed out on the early part of their life. I'm making up for it now. (male, age 31)

Significantly, though, the debt that desisting offenders describe is often an abstract, rather than a specific, one. The "score" that some interviewees feel they need to settle is generally with society, the community, or God. It is not a direct debt to the individuals whom they have harmed along the way. As one desisting participant, now a drug counselor and social activist, said,

If I were to approach every person I ever ripped off and tell them I was sorry or whatever, one of them is going to go and call the police, and I'll get thrown in the nick. . . . I think I can do the universe a bit more good out here. (male, age 30)

Perhaps the greatest debt most of the sample described was a debt to themselves. They felt that they wasted their own lives and their own potential by behaving stupidly, sitting in prison cells, and messing around. Perhaps this is why saving "just one" other life is seen as enough to provide a sense of redemption.

Generativity as Legitimacy

Lofland (1969, p. 210) wrote, "Long years of truly exemplary conformity or even hyperconformity and stellar service to society may be required" before an actor publicly identified as deviant can achieve the status of a "pivotal normal." This is probably well known by participants in this sample, who uniformly tried to underscore the magnitude of their newly found morality with statements such as the following: "I don't even litter anymore" (male, age 30) or "I don't smoke. I don't even drink" (male, age 26) or "I won't even pay the wrong fare on a bus" (male, age 25).

In addition to this aggressive piety, the pursuit of full-time generative roles can expedite the process of obtaining public acceptance. When a person becomes a probation officer or an antidrugs campaigner, they need not constantly remind and convince others that they have changed. Their acceptance of conventional values is embedded in their new role in society (Cressey, 1965). However, nothing inherent in becoming a factory worker or day laborer openly advertises that a person has given up crime. Indeed, many active offenders in the sample described doing such jobs occasionally.

Finally, the "penitent rebel" has for centuries played a highly useful, symbolic role in the upholding of societal values (Faller, 1987). In the Victorian era, Ignatieff (1983) argued, the "drama of repentance" symbolized "the triumph of good over evil in all men and women. If there was a social message in the ideal of reform it was that the institutional salvation of the deviant acted out the salvation of all men and women, rich and poor alike" (p. 92).

Such repentance rituals continue to play an important role in societies like contemporary Japan (Haley, 1996), yet the cultural apparatuses that institutionalize the repentant role (e.g., the sacrament of penance) have "withered or disappeared in the West," according to Braithwaite (1989, p. 162).

Although this seems to be true on an institutional scale, sporadic examples of the penitent role remain in Western culture. The moralistic confessionals of Alcoholics Anonymous (AA), for instance, may be the primary reason for the widespread public acceptance of such self-help organizations:

> This success appears to be accounted for largely by AA's use of the repentant role available in American society, constructing a "comeback" for "repentant" alcoholics based on their apparently intense adherence to middle-class ideals coupled with their repudiation of the "hedonistic underworld" to which they "traveled" as alcoholics. (Trice & Roman, 1970, p. 538)

Although we may not hold out much hope for deviants, members of mainstream society are still generally comforted when deviants say they want to be like us (see Faller, 1987). It is on some level reassuring to know that we are not missing out on some great party by not using heroin or joining gangs.

Generativity as Therapy

Perhaps the most important appeal of pursuing generative goals is the rehabilitative aspects of such activities. It is a well-known irony that help-givers are often helped more than help-receivers in a helping relationship (Brickman et al., 1982). Cressey (1955) referred to this as "retroflexive reformation": "A group in which criminal A joins with some noncriminals to change criminal B is probably most effective in changing criminal A, not B; in order to change criminal B, criminal A must necessarily share the values of the anticriminal members" (p. 119). Counseling similar others can also provide a constant reminder of the purpose of reform.

> Working here [at a reintegration program], I meet people every day who are still stealing, still using drugs, and I look at them, and it is a

real reminder of how far I've come. . . . So, I use these reminders to keep me honest, keep me from being depressed. (male, age 30)

Indeed, the therapeutic value of helping others is well known by rehabilitation organizations. The explicit service orientation of AA, codified in the Twelfth Step and the Fifth Tradition, serves to "engender . . . an involvement in the human community and foster an aspiration to participate usefully" in life on life's terms (O'Reilly, 1997, p. 23). AA members who have been sober for many years may remain with the organization, not just because they need to receive ongoing support but because the act of supporting others can itself be empowering and therapeutic (Brickman et al., 1982). In fact, AA's cofounder Bill Wilson said that he felt that his own sobriety was dependent on his assisting other alcoholics. According to O'Reilly (1997), "next to avoiding intoxicants," the therapeutic power of helping is "the major premise upon which [AA] is built" (p. 128). According to Mimi Silbert, coordinator of Delancey Street Project, an ex-offender reintegration program in San Francisco, "People will change simply by 'doing' for somebody else" (Whittmore, 1992, p. 5).

EXPERIENCING ONE'S SELF AS A CAUSE

As useful as they are, generative aspirations do not appear magically in the hearts and minds of ex-offenders. In fact, the interviewees' stories indicate that a person might be initiated into generative behavior in much the same way that one is thought to be initiated into deviant behavior. For instance, in Becker's (1963) classic model of "becoming a marijuana user," a person first has to learn the proper techniques for using the drug, then has to learn to recognize and enjoy the sensations that the drug brings through a process of modeling more experienced users. Desisting ex-offenders describe a similar process through which they learn that they are capable of creative, productive work, and *then* learn how to find pleasure in these pursuits. As Tocqueville (1835/1956) argued, "By dint of working for one's fellow-citizens, the habit and the taste for serving them is at length acquired" (p. 197).

Learning to Be Straight

To make good, a person may need "not only motive but also method" (Leibrich, 1993, p. 51). An ex-offender may need to experience some level of personal success in the straight world before they realize that they do not need to offend to regain a sense of personal agency. As one desisting ex-con explained, he had known he wanted to go legit for a long time, but he "just couldn't picture it" (male, age 29). Rotenberg (1978) wrote,

"It seems unlikely that one would label himself a 'soldier' just by reading about army life. . . . In order for self-relabeling to occur, one has to be organismically involved in the new role carrying that label" (p. 90).

Although most of us learned the pleasures of learning and creative thought as children, most of the participants in this research said their memories of school are almost entirely negative. Even achieving the most basic accomplishments in the classroom can therefore be a revelation to the ex-offender.

> Like, from when I first started [a computer training course] like I must have had me ma harassed, going home with little things that I'd done on the computer. Looking back now, a 10-year-old kid could do them, but it was *that I'd never done anything before*. I'm starting to do things, and I'm getting good reports. It just makes you feel good in yourself. I think it builds your confidence more than anything. I've got no short-age of confidence now like. (male, age 36)

The interviewee's mother, interviewed separately, said,

> I mean, I didn't know [he] could do all this. He's even doing written work. He was never any good at school. He never ever went to school. He was hopeless at school. He just wasn't any good at all. Whereas his brother was quite good at school, but [he], no, he just wasn't any good. He didn't take any notice to anybody. But, then, he started doing all this [through a reintegration program for ex-offenders], and I thought, "This is brilliant." And, he puts himself out you know. The only thing he does now, he has a few bevvies [drinks] and that's not harming anybody but himself you know what I mean? I am so de-lighted. (tape-recorded interview)

As with one's first exposure to deviance, there is "nothing even ap-proximating a guarantee of conversion" involved in this initiation phase (Matza, 1969, p. 117). Exposure to productive roles is probably necessary, but not sufficient, for the conversion experience. This taste of productivity, like one's first taste of deviance, brings the person to the "invitational edge" requiring a "leap" (or, optimistically, a push). The ex-offender who has been initiated into productive activity can still decide she or he is not interested. Yet, the decision now is made from inside. Relapsing back into crime is no longer a matter of simply going back to "the devil you know," because the ex-offender has been introduced to more than one option. The person has tasted productivity and tasted hyperconsumption and now can choose between the two on slightly more equal terms.

Learning to Enjoy Generativity

The next step in becoming a marijuana user, according to Becker (1963), is learning to enjoy the effects one has just learned to experience.

Like getting high, sensitivity is a "socially acquired taste" not different in kind from "tastes for oysters or dry martinis" (p. 53). The initial experiences of such behavior may at first be perceived as unpleasant or at least ambiguous. After all, there is nothing obviously or inherently pleasurable in learning a trade, painting, raising children, or building a house. One has to learn to redefine these difficult activities as rewarding and pleasurable.

Four participants, all describing different productive pursuits, used the cliché, "It's like I'm addicted to this now, instead of being addicted to drugs." Enjoying productivity is such a novel experience, apparently, that desisting ex-offenders need to ground the experience in a construct that they are more familiar with—being "addicted" to some behavior.

> You know, the way you've got into a routine of sitting in the house, watching the telly, you seem to get into the routine of coming to work as well, it's good. It feels good like. It's better. You feel like you're doing something. You're made up [pleased] to say to someone, "Yeah, I'm going to work." It feels good like. (male, age 28)

> Every penny I get now—where every penny used to go on drugs— now it goes on buying new tools and equipment like. It's as if I'm addicted to joinery. I must have an addictive personality. If there's something I get into, I get into it, you know, full hog. It's never in half measures. I'll go to the hilt whatever I do and that's what I've done. . . . I just haven't stopped doing jobs for all the family and that. It's just nice to be able to go back to them and say, you know, "Here's your brother—this is me now, no fucking zombie. And, I've got me uses, you know, and I'll help yous anyway I can now." Not that I've ever done wrong by me family, but just being on the drugs has hurt them a lot. (male, age 33)

As with Becker's (1963) marijuana smokers, this redefinition may occur in interaction with more experienced "users" (straights) who have "been there" and can relate to the frustrations inherent in productive pursuits and help them reinterpret these feelings of initial discomfort as rewarding.

INSTITUTIONALIZING GENERATIVE INITIATION

"Work" covers a broad range of activities, spanning from stigmatized "dirty work" (Shover, 1996) to leadership careers in the managerial class. Almost always, when policy makers talk about ex-offenders needing to "work," they are implicitly referring to the former—the jobs that the rest of society does not want to do. The cartoonist Barbara Brandon captured this unspoken intent in a comic strip that was deemed too controversial for a special "Black Issue" of the *New Yorker* magazine. In the cartoon's first panel, a White woman enjoins an African American woman to "Get off your butt and get a job." In the next panel, we see the African American woman sitting behind a large desk in an office. The White woman now says, "Hey, wait a minute, I wanted *that* job!"

Work can be found punishing and work can be found rewarding. If it is found rewarding, then it seems likely to help support desistance. If it is found punishing, then it may provide an individual with an excuse ("victim stance") to return to criminal behavior. And, of course, all work is not created equal—some jobs are far more likely to be experienced as punishing. As in the cartoon, the unspoken purpose behind such labor may in fact be the "disciplining" of the poor (Foucault, 1988c; Simon, 1993). Hard work will be "good for them" (with an emphasis, always, on the "them"). As Irwin (1970) wrote, the "model ex-convict" should be "penitent, puritanical, respectful of authority and industrious, but *not* ambitious" (p. 175).

For many, the psychological lesson of coerced, hard labor may be that work is punishment and something to be avoided.

> They say, "We're taking you to this ugly old detention center for five days." I'm like, "No," you know, "I've done 28 days [in jail]. You've just given me 28 days [as a sentence], I'm free to go." Apparently, there's a rule in English law that says that no sentence can be reduced by remission to less than five days. They call it, "Having to do five days for the Queen." So apparently if you're on remand for six months and you go to jail and you get [sentenced to] one month of jail, you still have to do five days for the Queen. Which I was pretty irritated about, because I'm sure the Queen wouldn't do five days for me. So I had to go to this detention center. The first thing that happened to me when I got there was I got me nose broke by a screw, that's why it's over to the right [shows me]. Punches me full in the face, when I had my arms handcuffed behind me back for not saying, "Sir." Um, it was 6 in the morning to 6 in the evening scrubbing floors, hands and knees. . . . So, . . . after that, I just went back down to London and just carried on [with crime] . . . just see what kind of scams I can work. (male, age 30)

No cult or social movement would use these tactics to recruit new members, and indeed few ex-cons leave the chain gang or labor camp as passionate adherents of the values of hard work. Shover (1996) wrote,

> Not all types of employment are equally likely to moderate offenders' criminal involvement, but there is little surprise about the kinds that do. They return a decent income, enable the individual to exercise intelligence and creativity, and allow for some autonomy in structuring the day's activities. (p. 127)

Requiring offenders to pick up garbage along the highway probably will not create many environmentalists. Yet, giving convicted offenders the option to volunteer at homeless shelters, build houses with Habitat for

Humanity, or counsel juvenile offenders (as alternatives to sitting in a cell) just might help "turn on" a few individuals to something besides criminal consumption (see Van Voorhis, 1985). This hypothesis has been bolstered by research indicating the effectiveness of community service and volunteer work as a socializing force (McIvor, 1992; Nirel, Landau, Sebba, & Sagiv, 1997; Uggen & Janikula, 1999). If this aspect of the "punishment" process is found enjoyable and rewarding by the offender (like it was for participants in this research), then so much the better for society.

One important rehabilitative innovation designed to provide opportunities for learning the rewards of generative behavior in the U.S. was the "New Careers" movement. Under New Careers programs, inmates and ex-convicts could earn the privilege of working as counselors, teachers, and rehabilitators for other inmates or offenders under community supervision. The key principle of the movement was the idea of reciprocity or complementarity—in a program in which one person helps another, both parties benefit (Cressey, 1955, 1963, 1965). While most New Careers programs disappeared along with other Great Society-era programs in the 1980's, the therapeutic power of reciprocity is recognized by many contemporary self-help and reintegration programs. Indeed, the seventh step of the ex-offender self-help group called "The Seventh Step" involves the mission to help "lift up" other ex-offenders.

Frequently, ex-offenders experience their first tastes of success in reintegration programs run by charities and nonprofit groups. Often kept fairly low profile, these organizations can achieve an almost religious adherence among their clients:

> Believe me. Never in my life have I ever asked for help, but I asked NACRO [the National Association for the Care and Resettlement of Offenders] for help and they saved my life. They saved me, and they won't accept that. They say I helped myself, but I couldn't do it without them. They saved me and I feel an obligation to them for that. (male, 40s, *field notes*)

The ex-offenders who self-select into these organizations want to change but have little idea of any other sort of life besides the life of drugs and crime. These reintegration programs are frequently the only avenue such individuals have to gain exposure to and experience in productive activities.

> You can't just give [ex-users], "Just say No," you have to offer something to say "Yes" to, some real alternative.... You have to make it so [ex-offenders] don't have time for drugs—make it so drugs would get in the way of what they really want to do.... One of our clients once said, "Drugs used to be the answer for me, now they are the problem." ... To get to that stage, they need to find something of value in themselves. (Keith Midgley, Alternatives to Drugs Programme, Liverpool, *field notes*)

Unfortunately, under the current funding policies in the United Kingdom and elsewhere, support programs for ex-offenders (often innovative, grassroots organizations) tend to disappear as quickly as they appear, sometimes leaving clients disappointed and embittered. Every reintegration group I worked with, including an organization that has been in existence for over three decades, was surviving year to year, competing for 9- and 12-month contracts to do a job (ex-offender reintegration) that requires a far more long-term vision. Without a more permanent investment and commitment to community-based reintegration, it is nearly impossible to develop program integrity and provide the continuity that people undergoing a life change need.

Research is also lacking on the topic of reintegration. Compared with the amount of research on punitive, deterrent policies like boot camps or shock incarceration, surprisingly little empirical research has focused on social programs that provide criminal offenders with material assistance, employment opportunities, or other general assistance. In a fascinating aside, Uggen and Piliavin (1998) have subtly implied that the reason for this academic oversight might be a political one—federal funders of research may fear that the results will be too positive.

> If these [opportunity-based] programs are shown to increase the probability of desistance from crime among offenders, policy makers face a potential dilemma. Should they support full implementation of these programs they may face accusations that they reward the unworthy for their criminal behavior; conversely, should they oppose implementation, they may be criticized for withholding proven crime control measures. (pp. 1421–1422)

7

MEA CULPA: SHAME, BLAME, AND THE CORE SELF

Central to the redemption script used by desisting interviewees is the notion of a "core self" or "real me" that is explicitly distinct from the party responsible for committing the bulk of crimes in the narrator's past. This sense of self-protection seems to contradict one of the fundamental tenets of rehabilitation practice—the need to "own up" to one's past. Indeed, many rehabilitation philosophies might view such a belief as evidence of denial, criminal thinking, or a cognitive error (see Samenow, 1984). In my favorite phrase, Alcoholics Anonymous (AA) members refer to the use of such excuses and justifications as "stinking thinking."

Perhaps second only to work, "owning up" to the immorality of one's past behaviors is consistently held up as a key first step toward reform (Garland, 1997a). Indeed, a considerable amount of contemporary therapeutic work with offenders is intended to break through an offender's hardened shell of rationalizations and coerce the person to accept responsibility for past actions (for two divergent perspectives on this theme, see Galaway & Hudson, 1996; Walters, 1998). In particular, the shaming of offenders has reemerged as a leading paradigm in correctional practice and theory. Occasionally these calls for shaming reflect the "reintegrative" approach proposed by Braithwaite (1989), but more commonly, the desire is for the "good, old-fashioned" practice of stigmatizing wrong-doers (Abraria, 1994). "Shame has become in the 1990s what self-esteem was in the 1980s: a blurry psychological phenomenon that is ill understood, but that nevertheless has become a catch word for sweeping social diagnoses and prescriptions" (Massaro, 1997, p. 646).

Shame-based "technologies of the self" seek to "subjectify" or "responsibilize" offenders through the ritual of confession (Foucault, 1988c; Garland, 1997a). In this framework, the only acceptable confession is one in which the person accepts complete and unmediated blame for an event. As Fox (1999b) illustrated in her field work inside a correctional program, a "good core self" story would not be well received in such counseling. In one scenario described by Fox, for instance,

> The inmate . . . believed he was a good person [and] he did not perceive this to be an error. . . . Clinging to this belief that he was essentially a decent person was deemed erroneous and further evidence of how deeply ingrained his criminal thinking was. (p. 448)

In the case of sex offenders, those who refuse to accept responsibility for an offense during therapy can be terminated from treatment and punished with probation revocation or extended stays of imprisonment (Kaden, 1999). Self-incrimination, in these circumstances, is seen as a necessary part of the recovery process, and therefore in the best interests of the accused offender. Nelson (1996) compared this coercion of therapeutic confessions with the practice of the ecclesiastical courts, in which compulsory confessions were allegedly justified for an equally charitable reason —to save the accused's soul from eternal damnation. Indeed, although the push for cognitive therapy and therapeutic shaming is relatively new, there is nothing new about the emphasis on confession in rehabilitation. The two have been intimately linked throughout the history of corrections (Foucault, 1988c; Rose, 1996).

Unfortunately, little empirical evidence can either confirm or refute the claim that the internalization of shame is a necessary prerequisite for successful offender reform (Northey, 1999). On the one hand, Leibrich (1993) found that a sense of shame for one's criminal behavior was "the most commonly mentioned reason for going straight" (p. 67). On the other hand, Irwin (1970) found that even among reformed ex-offenders "there is no denial of, or regret for, the past. In fact, the past criminal life is looked back upon with pleasure and excitement" (p. 202). In this chapter, I further explain the way the Liverpool Desistance Study (LDS) sample members view their past lives and discuss the possible implications for therapeutic work with ex-offenders.

ACCOUNTING FOR CRIMINAL CAREERS

Every narrative in the LDS sample was coded for the use of excuses and justifications—as well as concessions of guilt, shame, and remorse—

using an adapted version of Schonbach's (1990) comprehensive coding framework (see the appendix for a description and representative examples from the LDS analysis). Coded episodes included not only discussions of criminal behavior but also any *failure event*. Defined by M. B. Scott and Lyman (1968), failure events include both deviant behavior (dropping out of school, running away from home, infidelity, etc.) and neglected obligations (quitting or losing a job, leaving one's children, etc.). Speakers use justifications, excuses, and other explanations for past shortcomings of all types, and it was hypothesized that patterns in the use of these rhetorical devices might extend to all aspects of the way a person sees his or her past behavior.

In our analysis, over 1,400 such failure episodes (an average of around 30 per interview) were coded for occurrences of one of the 29 subcategories of attribution types. We compared the frequencies of each category across sample-member narratives, controlling for the number in the other categories, and no differences were found between persisting and desisting narratives. Overall, when describing failure episodes, interviewees across the two samples were most likely to use neutral reporting (about one third of each participant's failure episodes) or else made excuses for the behavior (also one third). The most common excuses involved blaming one's behavior on the difficulties of one's situation or else blaming the effects of drugs or alcohol (see Maruna, 1998 for a detailed analysis).

Justifications were used less frequently, with the most commonly used being the denial of injury ("No one was really hurt by it"). Research suggests that justifications of violence and deviance are most commonly used among peers, whereas exculpatory excuses are most commonly used when presenting one's story to strangers or outsiders (Harvey et al., 1990). Toch (1993) gave the example of the hockey player, who might plead with officials that his actions were accidental but would never say to his peers, "You can imagine my chagrin when I misjudged the distance between Big Pierre and myself and knocked his teeth out with my stick" (p. 195). One's peers better understand justifications like "the bastard had it coming" or "I did it for us" than the outsider would. In fact, the most common excuse used by interviewees in this sample—"It is all down to the situation I was in"—implies that the listener is not in the same situation and so probably cannot empathize with the behavior out of its context.

Although explicit expressions of shame were relatively uncommon overall (see Irwin, 1970), all of the interviewees in the present sample frequently conceded the negativity of their behavior when describing failure episodes. Concessions or admissions of wrongdoing were used in almost a quarter of the account episodes across the two groups. Usually, these involved statements such as "That was really stupid of me" or "That was the worst mistake I ever made."

Accepting responsibility for one's behavior in the self-narratives of this sample, then, is certainly not an all-or-nothing affair. Sample members in both groups seem to have a shifting or conflicted sense of responsibility for past actions. Like most people, they feel worthy of blame for certain behaviors but feel that many others are largely outside of their control. Participants in both groups seem to feel obliged to take responsibility for their past behavior. Yet, they also appear to want to align themselves with conventional moral values. As Sykes and Matza (1957) suggested, doing so often means developing some sort of neutralization for the offense.

The result is often a chaotic jumble of excuses and justifications mixed in with concessions and admissions of shame:

> Em, yea, I was selling drugs, so I got done for supplying. I've been done for possession, shoplifting, stolen check books, social security books, but I can still put me hand on me heart and say I never walked into anyone's house and took their money [*justification*]. So there's still some morals. I mean, I did go to me mum and take £25 out of her purse. I phoned her up two days later. She did know already, but it had to come from me. I wouldn't have phoned me dad up if I'd took it off him, 'cause he's got money [*justification*], but me mum was always there for me standing in the way and taking a hiding. So she was always there and it did cut me up robbing the money off her [*concession*], but I needed it [*excuse*]. . . . So I've done lots of bad things [*concession*]. (female, age 35)

These complicated accounts indicate the complexity of the individuals' sense of control or responsibility over their past lives:

> . . . because I do, I blow the money. I mean, I'll get me money and I'll sneak out the door with it at times and blow it. And, [my girlfriend]'s got nothing there to buy the kids clothes and that. I mean, don't get me wrong, me kids don't go without food. I've never—I'll suffer, I'll die for me kids, and that is straight. But there's times when I know we're up a bit on the money and I'll take that money, and it's—I feel bad doing it, but I have to do it. You don't understand all that, you know, I *have* to do it. I mean, I could say the drug makes me do it, but I'm not going to blame the drug. It's me that does it, but I do it for the drug. (male, age 28)

In other words, "I won't say the drug does it, yet I can't say that I do it either." Participants in both groups suffer from this conflicted locus of control, sometimes using a bewildering mixture of the passive voice, the third person, and the conditional verb tense. All along, an effort is made to obligingly "take responsibility."

> I had no money . . . even to do things that a normal lad my age with a job could do. . . . So I was turned to reoffend. Obviously, I'm not making excuses, but . . . (male, age 28)

"Obviously" none of the desisting narrators want to make excuses, "but . . ." they do.

Interviewees, often literally, did not like the way their stories sounded during the interview process. On several occasions, the interviewee would use some sort of excuse ("everybody was doing it" or "the drugs made me do it"), which I would repeat to them in sincere affirmation ("Sure, in that situation, you didn't really have much of a choice"). Surprisingly, the interviewee would very often become defensive when he or she heard such statements, and would say something like, "Well, I had a choice. You always have a choice." In some ways, this resembles the deviant's dilemma identified by Sagarin (1990):

> If they claim that [deviant impulses] arose spontaneously and are beyond their control, they then relinquish any semblance of free choice.... If they claim that the feelings are those that they wish to have and would have chosen had there been a free choice, they must take responsibility for and explain the rationale of making a choice contrary to the advantages offered by an alternative path. (p. 808)

The participants in this sample seem to want to have it both ways.

Judging from their narratives, participants in both groups seem to subscribe to conventional moral values (see also Kornhauser, 1978; Sykes & Matza, 1957). None of the interviewees expressed any acceptance or tolerance for lying, cheating, stealing, or hurting others—without reason. In general, interviewees viewed crime as an evil, if at times a necessary evil. When discussing crime in the abstract, interviewees sounded almost conservative in their views.

> Oh, I know. It is getting bad. The guns and the drugs are just out of control and it's just going to get worse. They can build all the prisons they like, but nobody is going to be able to do anything about [growing crime rates]. (male, age 37, formerly involved in armed robbery)

In the specific contexts of the interviewees' lives, some, but not all, criminal behaviors are made to sound permissible or excusable. Yet, conventional moral values are also generally conditional. Although research indicates that there is widespread disapproval of predatory crime across social groups (Glaser, 1978), for instance, even the most explicit moral prohibitions, like "Thou shalt not kill," are largely excused in cases of war or self-defense. During the interviews, participants tried to fit their past behaviors into this contingent value system and often told their life stories as "morality tales," casting themselves as the protagonist or moral hero (see Toch, 1993).

Samenow (1984) wrote, "[Offenders] will acknowledge that, from society's point of view, they are criminals. But not one really regards himself that way. Every [offender] believes that he is basically a decent human being" (p. 160). Survey research has generally confirmed this clinical observation, with only a small percentage of prison inmates identifying themselves primarily or even secondarily as "criminals" on a variety of surveys

(Burnett, 1992; Shover, 1996). Participants in the current research fit this pattern, emphasizing throughout the interviews that, despite some stupid mistakes, they are not really bad people.

Importantly, interviewees rarely attributed negative behaviors to underlying personality defects or character weaknesses. During the life story interviews, participants only described themselves in negative terms ("I am just stupid sometimes")—even in the past tense ("I was really stupid back then")—in about 2% of the descriptions of failure episodes. More typically, the concessions used by interviewees regarded bad behaviors, but not bad selves:

> I weren't thick [stupid] at school. Like, I got like an O-level and 5 GCSEs [qualifications] at school, so I don't know why I went off the rails like I did. Cause I was educated and that. (male, age 28)

"REAL" CRIMINALS

Concessions of guilt were often tempered with comparisons to other, worse offenders to reinforce the speaker's alignment with traditional values (see Blanton, in press).

> I have done some things in me life, but I haven't stooped to the levels a lot of people have. Everyone in our area says, "You know, even though you have been on drugs, you've never burgled houses, you've never robbed old people, you've never robbed people's handbags and things like that. Yous have still got respect." But a lot of people on drugs, you know yourself, they'll beat a granny and rob her purse. They will stoop to any levels. [My group] still had our morals about us. We were still committing crime and it's still costing people money, the taxpayer and what have ya, but we never hurt anyone. . . . Say, if we are not going to get money today, "Tough shit, it's hard shite." We're not going to go out and murder anyone just to get it, which is a good thing in a way. (male, age 33)

These spontaneous downward social comparisons (Taylor, 1989) often reflected what Rotenberg (1978) called the "myth of the psychopath" or the idea of the natural-born criminal. The interviewees simply insisted that they were not one of them. Desisting ex-offenders, for instance, frequently said that real criminals probably could not change their behavior and make good. After explaining my research to one interviewee, he said, "I bet you won't find too many others [who have reformed]. I mean, all the people I grew up with who were, like, into crime and that, they're either in jail or dead, like" (male, age 25). Another ex-convict explained that he would be a good probation officer, because he knows "a lot about how criminals think and behave":

> Criminals have a familiar pattern don't they? I mean they have the track suit [a working-class fashion statement in Liverpool], but also

they have, you know, certain mannerisms, you know, a certain walk [he demonstrates]. Especially those in the drugs, you know. (male, age 36)

Desisting interviewees frequently differentiated themselves even from their "partners in crime," seeing their friends as the natural or "real" criminals while setting themselves apart as never quite fitting in:

How I started? It was just me mates and all that, you know. Like, I wasn't like, I know I used to fight and all that like, but, you know. And like I'm not saying I was different in that sense, but I was in a sense, I was different. But like the way I was brought up, you know what I mean, like. And the lads who I started hanging around with were great lads, really was, but they'd been brought up around robbing and all that like, you know what I mean, so obviously they *naturally* progressed into that. I wasn't, you know what I mean. And like even they used to say that, you know what I mean. Like I just started getting into this and that like, you know, robbing car stereos, briefcases out of cars, stuff like that then. Then I started robbing cars like, that was me thing. I've never robbed a house, I've never robbed a house in me life like, no and anyone who does rob a house, I've got no regard for them whatsoever. I think they're the lowest on the earth to be honest with you. Alright, I know I did steal and all that, but I can honestly say I did steal off people who had it like, you know. And um, I done all big shops and big warehouses and all that like, you know. Ram raids, smash and grabs, whatever. I done ram raiding, smash and grabs and robberies, you know stuff like that. (male, age 26)

These interviewees have committed plenty of serious crime (in a "ram raid," one drives a usually stolen vehicle through a storefront window, runs in the store, steals whatever they can, then escapes in a second vehicle). But, they were never themselves *real* criminals like the "lowest of the earth."

Frequently, this point is expressed in explicit, typological terms. An active armed robber, who had never used drugs of any sort, explained that there are "two types" of robbers: the Old School (the "ultimate criminals" of which he included himself) and junkies, who fail to follow any of the established rules of the Old School: "Junkies are a whole different thing. They're nuts. The junkies will stick together just to get gear [drugs], but that's all. The Old School will stick together out of a common bond" (male, age 28). Interestingly, in a different interview, a heroin user explained that there are "two types" of heroin addicts as well. The first group (his type) consists of the generally good people who happen to be addicted to the drug. The second group, as always, consists of "the nuts."

There's the likes of us that had a normal everyday home and, like, we were living just a normal life, weren't we? [He looks to his wife.] And still are now. We're still living a normal life, even though we are in me Dad's and have no property and everything. . . . The other type, the house robbers, they will do basically anything you know or take anything. . . . They're the ones that get the smackheads the bad names. (male, age 38)

Again, this dichotomy is directly borrowed from conventional wisdom: All of us have committed occasional crimes and misdemeanors ("We were just kids" or "We all did it back then"), but there are a small number out there who are the "true" criminals. The essential irony of sample members accepting this belief, of course, is that conventional society would likely include most of them among the psychopaths. Yet, instead of outwardly accepting this stigma, the interviewees are actually able to use this cultural belief as a way of protecting themselves against shame. After all, according to society, real criminals are "less than human" (Goffman, 1963). Because all of the interviewees are certain that they are fully human, they use the idea of the "real criminal" to reassure themselves that they are not among the "real" bad guys. How can they be, after all, when they live in "normal everyday homes" and do not have that "certain walk?"

LOVING THE SINNER, BUT HATING THE SIN

Several observers have noted that, although appearing irrational to outsiders, deviance has its own internal logic (e.g., Canter, 1994; Shover, 1996). For instance, if a person views success as a matter of fate and luck, rather than hard work, pursuing the "big score" or lottery lifestyle makes intuitive sense. Similarly, if people believe that they have consistently been punished for no reason by authority figures, it makes sense that arrests and convictions have no great shaming effect on them. Indeed, in many ways, this logic can perpetuate itself. Perhaps in the most obvious example, if people believe that society is against them, they might logically decide to disregard that society's laws. The more crimes they commit, of course, the more society will turn against them in a self-fulfilling cycle.

Nonetheless, the storied identity of the persistent offender also seems to be based on a great number of glaring contradictions and discrepancies. The belief in the "good core self" among active offenders is probably chief among these. This belief, where it exists, might be seen as an ideal "opening" for rehabilitation. Desisting ex-offenders explained:

I always thought myself to be a bit of a hippie at heart, and all this violence just didn't sit too well with that picture of myself. (male, age 30)

I couldn't believe I was doing it, but I still did it, . . . I hated it. I used to think "I'm worth more than this." I really thought I was worth more than this. . . . I didn't want to do it but I did. Booze crippled me. It made me into someone that I never liked being, stripped me of everything I had, and it took me to the depths of—it took me down to doing check card fraud. And, I always said I never wanted to do that. Lots of the things I did [as a con man], I was chuffed [pleased] with, but check cards? And, I used to think, especially at Christmas time, I thought, someone's had their check card stolen, and I'm out spending it. I don't know, that's the one thing. (male, age 32)

When the essential inconsistency between feeling one is a good person and yet doing bad things is thrust to the foreground by "disorienting episodes" (Lofland, 1969), deviant identities may begin to deconstruct. According to Lofland (1969), "Human identities and human meanings are arbitrary constructs imposed on a reality that is essentially without meaning. As such, all systems of meaning, of human reality, are continuously subject to breakdown and rupture" (p. 290).

In the LDS interviewees, this deconstruction often seemed to occur organically in interactions with other deviants. In several instances, interviewees said that they looked around and asked, "If I am such a clever bloke, what am I doing in here with this bunch of losers?"

I'd always wanted to be clean. Even being around drug addicts all the time, I've always thought meself to be above it. It weren't me, kind of thing. I've always thought that even though I was on it—I mean, I didn't look down on anyone but, I mean, I used to look down on meself kind of thing. I put meself down. I hated it. (male, age 25)

That was when I just decided, um, I'd give it a shot at doing something else rather than crime, you know. The borstal, it didn't rehabilitate me, but it just seemed, it showed me how many negative and stupid people there are in the world. And, I just looked at meself and them and the way they, they carry on. I just knew. . . . I had a little bit more than them, in respect of intelligence you know . . . I just knew I wasn't as stupid as 90 percent of those fellas in jail, you know. (male, age 36)

The experience of arrest and conviction, it seems, provides an ideal opportunity for this sort of existential realization. As one interviewee explained, "That's the hard thing about prison—prison breeds out the truth" (male, age 47). Unfortunately, correctional experiences frequently have the effect of strengthening, rather than disorienting, deviant identities. The degradation ceremonies of conviction and imprisonment often serve to reinforce a person's antagonistic worldview and disconnection from mainstream society.

According to Lofland (1969), correctional counseling can take two approaches: "deviant-smithing" and "normal-smithing." In deviant-smithing, the offender is stigmatized and made to feel he or she has a disease or inner pathology. Although sometimes unintentional, deviant-smithing is common in correctional practice, according to LDS interviewees:

I've been on probation all me life. I've been to all these organizations that are supposed to help you out and no one's ever done nothing. Usually, you go through the door and they are looking down at you as if, like straight away, you're a drug addict and you're a low life, sort of thing. (male, age 36)

In normal-smithing, the message is the opposite. "Communicate to him the message that, despite what Actor thinks of himself, despite what normal and deviant others think of him, there lurks within him—underneath, after all, essentially—a core of being that is normal" (Lofland, 1969, p. 213). This is parallel to Braithwaite's notion of reintegrative shaming. In this framework, although an accused offender will be expected to admit to his or her crime, he or she will also be provided with a "way out"—or, more accurately, a way back into the moral mainstream. According to Braithwaite and Mugford (1994),

> The self of the perpetrator is sustained as sacred rather than profane. This is accomplished by comprehending: (a) how essentially good people have a pluralistic self that accounts for their occasional lapse into profane acts; and (b) that the profane act of a perpetrator occurs in a social context for which many actors may bear some shared responsibility. (p. 146)

The LDS findings indicate that this image of the "good lad who has strayed into bad ways" (Braitwaite & Mugford, 1994, p. 141) is an adaptive identity that can facilitate reintegration.

Advocates of narrative therapy or rebiographing have suggested that ex-offenders be formally taught ways to reconstruct these "more liberating life narratives" for themselves (Henry & Milovanovic, 1996, p. 224). In what is being called the "archaeology of hope" (Monk, Winslade, Crocket, & Epston, 1996), narrative therapy encourages clients to reconstruct "new" life histories for themselves with the help and guidance of therapy (see especially Parry & Doan, 1994; White & Epston, 1990). For instance, beginning with the seemingly paradoxical statement "I hope to have a good past," Rotenberg (1987) asked, "Why must Western people 'hide' their old, failing, 'Mr. Hyde' self? Why shouldn't one be able to *correct one's past* [italics added] in order to bridge the cognitive gap that separates . . . one's failing past from one's . . . rebirth" (p. 49). He argued,

> If there is some truth in what Thomas (1928) wrote, that situations become real in their consequences if people define them as real, then people [can be taught] to descend into their past in order to reread it so that they may ascend. . . . Therapy must teach people to write the scripts of their future instead of reading it as an unchangeable blueprint of life plans. (p. 198)

As Thune (1977) wrote, this sort of rebiographing is "not so much a falsification of the past, any more than any other autobiographical creation is a falsification, as simply the application of a new model for conceptualizing it" (p. 84). In this framework, individuals are not coerced into accepting "prepackaged realities" (Fox, 1999b), but rather are encouraged to develop their own stories in a more natural, gradual rearranging of their past lives.

> [T]he attainment of usable truths in psychoanalysis, as in AA, is not the shedding of some superannuated "identity" in preference for a newer, brighter one, but an act of purposeful conservation and cultivation, employing native materials: the formed precipitate of character, the patterns of irrevocable past actions, the transformations of guilt, shame and error, not repudiated, but reconstrued. (O'Reilly, 1997, p. 165)

Although the average correctional facility might not be ready for this sort of radical therapy (but see E. M. Scott, 1998), parallels to narrative therapy can be found in the prison-based Cognitive Self-Change Program in Vermont (Bush, 1995), in AA, and elsewhere. Of course, almost all forms of therapy focus on helping individuals change their self-stories. Newer interventions including narrative therapy and cognitive self-change are deeply rooted in more traditional therapeutic traditions such as psychoanalysis, existential analysis, rational–emotive therapy, Gestalt therapy, transactional analysis, and other humanistic approaches. Indeed, for the LDS sample, normal-smithing frequently took place during fairly traditional therapeutic programs, which most said they had been coerced to enter.

To be most effective, interventions geared toward this sort of historical deconstruction should use a discourse that is meaningful to the offender. If enforced therapy can be written off as "psychobabble" or middle-class nonsense, as it definitely was by some interviewees,[23] these interventions are unlikely to break through offender self-defenses. The best

---

[23]Reliance on therapy techniques designed for work-a-day overachievers or middle-class neurotics tends to reinforce the impression among a few ex-offenders that counseling is essentially "a load of bollocks" and unrelated to their own lives. For instance, in one of the group therapy sessions I observed, a guest facilitator was brought in to help teach the group to deal with their anger. I was aware, from regular involvement with the group, that everyone in the room besides the social worker and myself was a regular heroin user and had probably taken heroin that morning prior to the workshop. The facilitator never mentioned the physiological symptoms that accompany heroin withdrawal. Instead, the focus was on not letting stress build up in our lives without any release.

"The speaker recommended taking 'a timeout away from everything,' and asked, 'Do any of you do that? Have a little place where you can go to be by yourself and take the weight of the world off your backs, just get away from the stress all around you?' I looked around the room to see if anyone else in the room was hearing what I was hearing. One of the clients saved me the trouble of having to explain. 'Sure, but don't we have the gear [heroin], like?' he asked. Several participants had to laugh at the irony of someone telling a group of heroin addicts that they needed a way to chill out and 'escape.' Undaunted, the instructor asked us to practice a more socially acceptable 'timeout' or stress buster. 'This might seem a little silly,' we were forewarned, as she turned on a tape-recording of ocean sounds and soft music, and asked us all to close our eyes and take deep breaths. Realizing I was the only one meditating who was not currently enjoying an opiate high, I felt distinctly left out of the full stress-busting experience." (7/31/97, *field notes*) "therapists," therefore, are often fellow recovering (or desisting) offenders or else the friends and family members of desisting offenders. "Therapeutic effects seem to be obtained through the sharing of problems among persons who have them, on a scale which makes professional therapy an extremely puny enterprise by comparison" (Toch, 1963, p. 119).

The well-known professional ex- Bill Sands uses a normal-smithing approach when counseling young offenders as part of his Seven Steps outreach work.

> I said, "Hello. My name is Bill Sands. A friend of yours told me you were here. When I was about your age I sat in a cell like this, only it wasn't in jail—it was in San Quentin prison. I was fighting mad at the whole world, just like you are. I hear you have been doing a lot of fighting. But I understand that along with all that brawn you have a pretty high I.Q. Why don't you try using it to get yourself straightened out—out of here." (Sands, 1964, p. 190)

Using a classic "hate the sin, love the sinner" strategy, Sands exposed the young person's neutralization (the world hates me), while coupling this with an attempt to find some redeeming value in the individual (a high IQ). Essentially, Sands offered the young person a story—a self-story that worked for Sands himself. The three-part plot structure of Sands's self-concept can also be found in many of the desisting narratives in this sample:

1. Like a lot of young people in troubled circumstances, I was full of anger, so my offending was justified.
2. But I am also too smart to let this passion be my downfall.
3. So, once I saw where I was heading, I applied my energy and smarts toward more positive and rewarding pursuits.

The young person in Sands's example is under no obligation to rework his self-narrative in this way but is allowed that opportunity. Doing so will let him preserve his positive self-concept (in the same way that his previous neutralization did), but it will also obligate him to desist (in a way that his old story did not).

Sands's outreach effort is also buttressed by the fact that he himself shares the self-story that he offers to the active offender. The wounded healer stands in direct contradiction to the deviant neutralization (repeated constantly in interviews with active offenders) that "anyone from my background, addicted to this stuff, with a criminal record, etc. would do exactly what I'm doing." The professional ex-, for one, does not. This contradictory information has to be either rejected ("He's not really straight") or else assimilated into the person's narrative. Faced with this disorientation, a likely concession or amendment to the person's self-story might be, "OK, not everyone in my situation commits crime, but it takes a lot of skill to succeed in the straight world, and I don't have any straight skills." Although still excusing criminal involvement, this new self-story provides an opening, a window of opportunity, that was not there in the previous narrative.

Rehabilitation maverick Father Peter Young, who founded the HIT (Housing, Industry and Treatment) Program in New York, similarly likes to say that his job is to "take away an offender's excuses." By this, he does not mean that he forbids the use of justifications or exculpatory language, however. Instead, if an offender claims he cannot desist because he or she has no skills, HIT trains the individual. If clients blame their addiction, HIT provides drug counseling. This goes on and on until eventually, the client either has to admit to simply being criminal or else desist.

EXCUSES AND US

What then, of "good, old fashioned shame" (Abraria, 1994, p. 1) in the midst of all this loving of sinners? Although Leibrich (1993, 1996) found shame to be a key reason for individuals to give when abandoning crime, there is an important difference between the desisting ex-offenders in Leibrich's sample and the LDS sample. Over half of the individuals in Leibrich's sample had two convictions or less, and only an eighth of her sample had ever been to prison. Shaming may indeed be an effective strategy for encouraging desistance for first-time offenders, or individuals beginning to experiment with crime or drugs. In these cases, as Leibrich (1993) suggested, the trauma of just going to court or having a conviction on one's record can be a significant deterrent (p. 70).

However, in cases in which offending becomes a lifestyle, as it did in the lives of the LDS sample, shame may create as many problems as it solves. In other words, being ashamed of an isolated act or two is one thing, but it is a quite different thing to be ashamed of one's entire past identity, of *who* one used to be (for stretches sometimes lasting as long as 10 years or more). According to research on attributions and mental health, internalizing self-blame can have both positive and negative consequences (Weiner, 1991; Weiner et al., 1987). If a person dwells on a stable or permanent attribute ("If only I weren't . . ."), then self-blame may be maladaptive. Yet, accepting blame for unstable past behavior ("If only I hadn't . . .") may be adaptive (Niedenthal, Tangney, & Gavanski, 1994). Social psychologists describe this as the difference between shame and guilt. Whereas, guilt concerns discrete misdemeanors or transgressions, Giddens (1991, p. 67) wrote, shame is "concerned with the overall tissue of self-identity" and the "exposure of hidden traits which compromise the narrative of self-identity." Whereas guilt involves regretting one's behavior, shame is about the "whole self" (H. B. Lewis, 1971).

Thus, instead of being seen as "evidence of extraordinary pathology"

(Fox, 1999b, p. 436), the use of neutralizations and excuses might be interpreted as an adaptive, ego defense mechanism that actually helps to restore the speaker's bonds to society. After all, Sykes and Matza (1957) originally argued that neutralizations are necessary because the person using them *subscribes* to conventional morality. Similarly, in the attribution literature, excuses and justifications are seen as "a type of aligning action indicating to the audience that the actor is aligned with the social order even though he or she has violated it" (Felson & Ribner, 1981, p. 138). By making an excuse or justification for one's behavior, a person is able to make a claim for his or her status as a normal person. Without such a story, "there exists no means to locate their identity in a shared narrative of common experience" (Singer, 1997, p. 284).

Therefore, instead of a hardening process (e.g., Hirschi, 1969), the acceptance of neutralizations might even be the first step in a *softening* process. The deviant who feels no compulsion to make excuses for illegal behavior—the offender who says, "Nobody made me do it; I did it for the money!" or "I just enjoy it" (see Akerstrom, 1985)—may be the least likely to reform. Offenders who use neutralizations, however, seem less comfortable with their behaviors and more in line with conventional morality.

Although these are means of avoiding responsibility, these accounts also help to protect self-esteem, increase one's sense of personal worth, and reduce anxiety (A. Beck, 1979; Harvey et al., 1990; Northey, 1999). Such self-protection may be necessary for offenders to desist (Rotenberg, 1987). Indeed, Meisenhelder (1982) wrote, "The plan to exit from crime is in large part founded on the sense of the self as noncriminal" (p. 140).

Most importantly, in Western society, if individuals admit that they willfully and purposefully stole a person's purse, they would also be admitting that they are the "type of person" who could commit this sort of crime. Therefore, they admit to being fundamentally different from the rest of society. Western culture provides very few acceptable ways of saying, "I did some bad things. What can I say? I was a prick. But I'm not a prick anymore." A story like that will not fly in a society that believes, crudely, "Once a prick, always a prick" (less crudely, see Rotenberg, 1978).

In fact, Felson and Ribner (1981) wrote, "There is evidence that when actors fail to provide accounts [i.e. excuses and justifications] for their deviant behavior they are likely to be sanctioned more severely by the audience" (p. 138; see also Schonbach, 1990).

> When [my mother] found out [about my drug use] it made things worse
> I suppose. Because, that was when all the lying and all that starts,
> because they're going to ask you, "Have you been taking drugs?" and
> you're going to say, "No." And, it's not because you're being a con
> [that] you're lying. It's because you don't want to hurt her feelings. The
> same if your mum asks you if you've been taking drugs and you're
> stoned off your fucking head, you'd say "No." You don't want them to

think you're that kind of person. So that's where all the lying starts. (male, age 24)

The participants in this sample do not want to admit to significant others, or to themselves, that they are "the kind of person" who uses drugs or commits crime, possibly because such an admission in Western culture would be tantamount to admitting they are irredeemable.

Different cultures might expect and accept quite different narratives from wrongdoers (cf. Allen, 1981; Rotenberg, 1978). In Japan, for instance, noncontingent admissions of guilt, rather than explanations and excuses, are expected and rewarded by juries and other listeners (Haley, 1996). To illustrate this contrast in accepted accounting styles, Braithwaite (1989) provided the example of a Japanese woman who had made a mistake in declaring the amount of currency she was carrying when she entered the United States:

> After the woman left the airport, she wrote the Customs Service acknowledging her violation of the law, raising none of the excuses or explanations available to her, apologizing profusely, and seeking forgiveness. In a case that would not normally merit prosecution, the prosecution went forward *because* she had confessed and apologized; the U.S. Justice Department felt it was obliged to proceed in the face of a bald admission of guilt. (p. 165)

In Western society, we demand a "sad tale" of some sort from deviants to make them forgivable (Goffman, 1961). Apology and repentance, while institutionalized in cultures like Japan, play an increasingly insignificant role in Western societies, where the belief that deviants can change has allegedly been discredited (Braithwaite, 1989). The purpose of personal narratives is to make sense out of one's life (not to achieve some vague "truth"), and sense-making is a distinctly culture-bound process. As Goffman (1961) suggested, there are no true stories or false stories, only good stories (convincing, coherent, acceptable) and bad stories (unbelievable, illogical, unpopular). Therefore, if making an excuse (even if it is a "lie" of sorts) about one's past is required to explain one's present behavior, then this might be an important part of the desistance process. In other words, Western societies may prefer pleasant lies ("it wasn't my fault") to the painful truth that good people often do bad things.

8

THE RITUALS OF REDEMPTION

The third essential characteristic of the redemption script is the narrator's strong sense that he or she is in control of his or her destiny. Whereas active offenders in the Liverpool Desistance Study (LDS) seemed to have little vision of what the future might hold, desisting interviewees had a plan and were optimistic that they could make it work.

This strong belief in self-determination seems at first to contradict these interviewees' use of excuses like "it wasn't my fault" to account for past wrongdoing. Nonetheless, the peculiar combination of making excuses for past failures and yet taking responsibility for present and future accomplishments is a well-established characteristic of another group of interest to social psychologists—healthy adults (see Alloy & Abramson, 1979; Bandura, 1989). In *Learned Optimism*, Seligman (1991) wrote,

> For nondepressives, failure events tend to be external, temporary, and specific, but good events are personal, permanent, and pervasive. "If it's bad, you did it to me, it'll be over soon, and it's only this situation. But if it's good, I did it, it's going to last forever, and it's going to help me in many situations." (p. 110)

Brickman et al. (1982) provided an interesting framework for understanding and modeling this shift in locus of control. Unlike their predecessors in the attribution literature, Brickman et al. divided the concept of personal responsibility into two dimensions: blame and control. In other words, they distinguished between taking responsibility for the *origin* of a

147

problem and taking responsibility for the *solution* to that problem (see also Weiner et al., 1987). Instead of dividing personality types into "Pawns" and "Origins," therefore, this framework allows for the identification of four orientations that a person can have toward his or her behavior: a moral model, an enlightenment model, a medical model, or a compensatory model. In a *moral model*, people hold themselves responsible for their problems and for the solutions to those problems. In an *enlightenment model*, people hold themselves responsible for their problems but not for the solutions to those problems. In a *medical model*, people do not hold themselves responsible for their problems or for the solutions to those problems. Finally, in the *compensatory model*, people do not blame themselves for their problems but hold themselves responsible for the solution to their own problems.

THE COMEBACK OF THE "I"

The compensatory model seems to characterize the general pattern of the redemption script. Brickman et al. (1982, p. 372) quoted the Reverend Jesse Jackson's various slogans as being representative of this model of responsibility (e.g., "You are not responsible for being down, but you are responsible for getting up" and "Both tears and sweat are wet and salty, but they render a different result. Tears will get you sympathy, but sweat will get you change"). A compensatory model ex-offender might say, "I only got into crime and drugs because of my disadvantaged childhood, but now I am working hard to go straight." For instance, one desisting ex-offender began his life narrative with the following excuse (which we coded as "blaming family background"):

> When I was about 13 or 14, my mother and father were going through a bit of a rotten patch and me dad used to come in and belt me ma and all that. It emotionally affected me, you know what I mean? Then I like just turned to [drugs] just as a way of getting out, just getting out of a situation I found myself in, you know.

Much later in the interview, in describing how he decided to go straight, the same narrator said,

> I just said, look, I've been on [heroin] 10 years. I can't blame [others] for giving me my first go. There must be another reason why I'm still on it. I mean for years and years, I blamed what me mam and dad went through, and then it got to last year when I got out [of prison] and I thought, "This is stupid. It was like 18 years ago me mam and dad got divorced and I'm still blaming it on that today!" (male, age 36)

His story of the past has not apparently changed much. He still attributes the onset of his drug use on his family troubles. Yet, although this past cannot be changed, he realizes that no one is controlling his present except him.

Although it may be therapeutic for a person to locate the roots of his or her problems in the social environment (disadvantage, inequality, victimization), successfully desisting people seem to internalize complete responsibility for overcoming these obstacles. Notice how the following interviewee's sense of subjectivity and control makes a comeback at the end of the following narrative passage. I have used italics to highlight some of the key words that emphasize an external blame and passive explanation for past mistakes, but, later, the triumphant emergence of the "first-person singular" when the story gets good.

> Just shoplifting, robbing cars, we were just out robbing constantly, every day. No matter what we'd do, we'd go out and rob.... Even robbing some lady's handbag which I am disgusted with, but at the time, *when you're in that situation* and you're having them drugs, you don't think about nothing else but your money for your drugs. Um, I couldn't go on with it and I thought, "I don't want this." And as we were trying to stop one of the drugs, [my boyfriend] got nicked for a car offense and he went to jail again. And I couldn't handle it ... I *ended up* going to jail again, *getting the kids taken off me*.... So then I was in jail, he was in jail. We fell out 'cause we wasn't with each other, so then his family no longer wanted to know me, after all these years.... I came home ... and a week later he came home. I was in a hostel 'cause I didn't have a house, I didn't have nothing. I lost everything, everything. My mum and stepdad had the kids.... [My boyfriend] came looking for me, he wanted to get back with me and I said "If we get back together I don't want no more drugs, no nothing." He said "OK." ... I still didn't have me kids, so it was just me and him for like about 6 months. I got pregnant again, then I got this other house.... And I thought, "Right, this is going to be a new start for us." I was going to court, back and forth to the courts fighting for me kids. And, the condition they wanted was for me to get meself off the drugs, get meself a house, everything I needed, get a house livable for the children so they could come and live with me and make sure I was able to manage with me money. So *I done it all. I got me house.* But, before that, *I came off the drugs,* the actual day we moved into the house.... The next morning—he said, "Well, I'll just give it [crime] this one last day, and we won't go out and do nothing else." And, I said "Well I'm not going with you" and he went on his own and got arrested and 2 years for burglary. I ended up being on me own, fighting everything on me own. *I fought for the kids* for 13 months. And in that 13 months I got the house sorted. I got meself off the drugs. I got meself on a [detox] course. I had me daughter, me third daughter, on me own. I went into the hospital and had her on me own. Nobody

> there to hold me hand. I fought for the kids and March this year I got
> me kids back for good. (female, age 23)

Once the going gets good, the "you," the "it," and the passive descriptions (how does one "end up going to jail" after all?) fade away, and the "I" reappears, assuming almost hypercontrol. Moreover, the "fight" against a potentially hostile environment can become an all-encompassing passion.

Whereas the "I" is granted a minor role throughout most of the compensatory story, almost everything in the future is within one's personal control. Hanninen and Koski-Jannes (1999) called this transformation of the person "from a victim or a puppet to a consciously acting independent subject" a "growth story": "In the moral sense the growth story releases the protagonist from guilt by seeing oppressive relations as the cause of problems. The responsibility of one's life required for staying sober is seen to emerge as part of the personal growth process" (p. 1843).

Others incorporate generative aspirations for their children as a part of this compensation. In other words, it may be too late for me, but I can still make a difference for the next generation.

> I used to be bad, bad on the whiskey. I think meself it was to try and
> hide my childhood, but you can't. I still can't. All my friends had a
> mother and father, they all had everything and I had nothing. . . . You
> can't live your life over [but] I think *my* kids can say they had a good
> time. (male, age 40)

In these narratives, making good involves taking control over one's life and using that life to contribute, accomplish something, and leave a positive legacy.

> I mean, most people who get off drugs just sit there with nothing to
> do, and you get bored, and start taking drugs. You have to occupy your
> time. That's what it's all about. There's no good just sitting there.
> What's the point of getting off drugs if you're only going to sit there
> like a zombie? Get off drugs and sit there like a fucking straight zombie?
> You might as well still be on them. You get off them to do whatever
> you want to do. You know what I mean? If you are going to go to
> college and learn whatever you are good at, then get there. (male,
> age 33)

There is a paradox in some spirituality-based conversion narratives whereby one gains personal control by explicitly "giving up" personal control to the will of a higher spirit. Although this narrative was not common to the Liverpool narratives, it is frequently found in U.S. samples of reformed ex-offenders (e.g., Johnson & Toch, 2000; Maruna, 1997). This apparent contradiction (giving up control in order to be free) should still be seen as agentic in nature—the person freely chooses to give over his or her life to God. According to O'Reilly (1997), the "surrender" of control involved in the twelve-step movement signifies "less a relinquishment of 'power' than a clarification of personal power's finiteness. . . . [Surrender is] a marshaling of what is available rather than a wholesale abnegation of control or initiative" (pp. 23–24).

The optimistic sense of personal control in the LDS of the desistance narratives bordered on overconfidence and brimmed with optimism. I asked each narrator whether they thought they would reoffend in the future. Considering the fact that they frequently accounted for past offending as being out of their control, one might assume that they would have difficulty answering this. Perhaps, one might expect an answer like, "Depending on the circumstances, I might." None of them did. Most likely, leaving the door to future offending even slightly open is too dangerous. Instead, the desisting person convinces himself or herself of complete control of the future.

BURNING OUT OR FIRING UP?

This image of the agentic desister contradicts the better known figure of the "burnt-out" ex-convict. In this model, defiant rebels eventually lose the youthful spirit and passion required to maintain a deviant lifestyle in the face of repeated failure. A strict ontological or maturational reform position implies that this burnout is largely due to physical reasons. They lose the youthful energy, strength, and stamina necessary to play the role of crazy armed robber, nimble thief, or intimidating drug dealer.

To examine these physical dimensions of the burnout hypothesis, I asked each research participant, "Are you in worse physical condition now than you were 5 years ago?" Whereas over half of the active offenders said, "yes," less than one fifth of the desisting participants of roughly the same age agreed that they were in worse physical shape now. In fact, those who had overcome heroin addictions frequently laughed at the question. "Look at me, mate. I'm fit as shit. Five years ago I was a bag of bones" (male, age 31). I asked one desisting participant where he channels all the energy he once used as an armed robber:

> I run 5 miles a day [laughs]. And do, em, [wind surfing], mountain climbing, em, endurance walks as well. . . . Em, I did 14 mountains in one day, the 14 mountains in Snowdonia over 3,000 feet, in one go, like 29 miles. (male, age 30)

Instead of physically burning out, career criminals might actually have to charge themselves up emotionally, psychologically, and possibly even physically in order to desist.

Indeed, members of the active offender sample seemed far more burnt out with their lives than the desisting sample did.

> There comes a time right, when you really get pissed off with [taking heroin]. I mean, like, I've been on it nearly 8 years, something like that. And, your first couple of years it's a novelty, you know what I

mean, and you going out scoring with your mates and all that. And, then you realize . . . "Look what it's done to me. Me life is just in bits." And I'm sick of it, just purely sick. You know when you're sick of something and you just want it to go away and leave you alone, and that's what I'm like now. I just want it to go away and leave me alone. But it's hard. You know what I mean. (female, age 26)

This is not to imply that desisting interviewees did not mention having become sick of criminal behavior. Quite to the contrary, most said that criminal pursuits become intolerably boring,[24] repetitive, and unfulfilling —all consistent with the burnout hypothesis. The point is that, at least in the LDS sample, the experience of burnout did not have anything like a perfect correlation with desistance. A person can, apparently, burn out, hit rock bottom, and yet carry on with criminal behavior. This, of course, is consistent with the way that the term *burnout* is used in other roles. For instance, just because a parole officer is burnt out with her job, this does not mean that she will necessarily resign and begin a new career. In fact, the burnt-out individual may become so despondent that he or she lacks the energy required for such a career move.

Equally, ex-offender narratives provide little support for the familiar picture that shows offenders as passively reformed by social mechanisms. In a fascinating variation of attribution bias, Mischkowitz (1994) found that while social workers attributed ex-offenders' change to outside factors (wives, jobs, or changing geographic locations), desisting ex-offenders attributed their ability to desist to their own "free will." While significant others are thanked for their help, participants in the LDS took full credit for changing, as well. The following speaker describes a girlfriend who stuck with him even after finding out about his criminal record:

Like, I was expecting, "See ya, mate," but she hung in there. And I thought, "well, here y'are! You know what I mean? Someone's giving me a try here. I might as well repay the favor." But something I want to stress, though, I didn't just do it for her. I done it for meself as well, you know what I mean, 'cause it was there all the time. I wanted to change and that was just the little push I needed. (Male, age 25, *field notes*)

---

[24]This "routinization of adventure" (Lofland, 1969) and the dull monotony of the persistent offender's lifestyle are generally lost on conventional others, who tend to glorify and romanticize criminal pursuits. For instance, one desisting interviewee told me that I was not the first academic to show an interest in his life. Another researcher had apparently contacted him when he was involved in crime, and asked if he could observe the interviewee and his mates for a few weeks to learn about life in the gang. The interviewee said that he got the impression that the researcher was "disappointed" by the boys' rather repetitive lifestyle. "I think it wasn't as exciting, not as glamorous as he thought it'd be. He'd say, like, "Are you sure that's all you do?" I think he expected us to be more sort of glamorous, you know, gangsters and that." (male, age 26)

Deviance, for those who first experience it, can be a thrilling adventure (Katz, 1988), yet once one does the same activity long enough, whether it is taking cocaine, robbing grocery stores, or riding roller coasters, the sneaky thrills fade.

Similarly, some desisting participants expressed disdain for the well-known notion of the "geographic cure," which suggests that ex-offenders are best able to desist when they move away from their neighborhoods.

> I never trust anyone who says they are off of drugs, but yet they can't go back into their old neighborhood. I say, "Then you're not really cured are you?" (female, 30s, *field notes*)

> A lot of people, when I was in that rehab in the prison, a lot of people were saying I couldn't go back to my own neighborhood [and not be tempted to relapse]. But I said, that's one thing I want—to stay there to prove I'm off drugs. I wouldn't like to move away and everyone would think "he's just living somewhere out of the way." I want to stay and walk round with my head held high and say, "Look, it's the same me." (male, age 33)

Interestingly, several active offenders did mention the need to "just get out of this neighborhood":

> You can be down in like London or Coventry or Birmingham, wherever, and [heroin] doesn't even enter your mind. And when you get on the train, and you're coming back to Liverpool and you get to Runcorn train station right, it's horrible, 'cause you start sweating and you start feeling withdrawal symptoms, even though you haven't had it for like 6 months. It's horrible, it's dead psychological like as well, you know. And as soon as you get off the bus, I've got to find, I've got to go and find gear [drugs]. I have thought about moving out and all that, but if I did move what would I do? I wouldn't have no one to turn to, I'd have no family, I'd have no friends you know, it would just be too hard. (male, age 33)

> It's the environment I live in. I keep crying to these probation officers —that's why I don't give a shit for them—I keep telling them to get me a flat in a different area. And, what do they do? They put me right in the same, damn neighborhood. And in a few days, you get the same people back at your door. If I want to change, I have to change my area. The same environment will breed the same behavior. I've been screaming at them [probation officers] since day one. . . . I think I'd like to move into some "sticks" area, and just get a total fresh start. Get me head together. It sounds funny, but I just want to start something different. I mean, I'm 27, and I've spent 7 years in different prisons. I got to change something. (male, age 27)

This is the most frequent excuse for criminal behavior among active offenders in this sample—"it is not me, it is my environment." Therefore, the geographic cure may be part of a medical model framework of understanding deviance as outside of one's control.

Subscribing more to a compensatory model of responsibility, desisting interviewees sometimes resented the implication that they were "weak-willed" and saw the geographic cure in part as trying to "make lepers" out of them by casting them from their homes (male, 40s, *field notes*). Similarly, I asked a desisting interviewee who described himself as a recovered alcoholic if he was "able to" walk into a pub without having a drink.

> Yeah, no problem at all. I'm one of the lucky ones. Yeah, lots of people in AA [Alcoholic Anonymous], well, lots of people in general say you shouldn't [go into pubs]. . . . [To me] the whole idea of coming off the booze is so that you can go back out there in the big, wide world. That's all I wanted. If I—I'd go back out drinking if I didn't think I could hack it in life, because the whole idea of coming off the booze is so that you can hack it every day. . . . I have to face everything head on. (male, age 32)

Going straight, according to the interviewees, is in no way about accepting defeat. Desistance was uniformly described as an active, rewarding, and even defiant process.

> Like, I am proud of myself, because I know I've done it. I've gotten over the worst of it, and I'm there now. (male, age 31)

> You know like, I'm going to college and all that now, and do brilliant and I'm the best one on the course. The teacher's wrote a note [hands me note from teacher addressed to me]. You can read that later if you want. And, em, it's just amazing the turnaround you know what I mean? I just can't believe. I'm buzzing with it. It's not as if I'm doing it 'cause other people want me to do it. I'm doing it 'cause I want to do it. (male, age 33)

> The amount of respect I had, when old friends and associates would see [my girlfriend] and say "How's he going on?" They would all ask, they would go and ask, and they were really proud of me because I'd gone against the grain. (male, age 28)

Interviewees described desistance as "going against the grain," "beating the odds," or simply "going straight," not as quitting, burning out, or giving up. Their vision of desistance is one of renewal, gaining strength, finding who they really are, or bettering themselves.

Above all, making good is not described as merely giving in to the power of the criminal justice system. Indeed, desisting people make the opposite claim. "The System," as they explain it, does everything it can to keep ex-offenders trapped in the cycle of crime and prison. Otherwise, "All them screws [prison guards] and all the bizzies [police detectives] would be out of jobs" (male, age 26). Desisting interviewees frequently insisted that they were not in the least bit "afraid of prison." For the antiauthoritarian rebel, desisting is framed as just another adventure consistent with their lifelong personality, not as a change of heart. Again, this allows the individual to frame his or her desistance as a case of personality continuity rather than change.

This evidence seems to support the use of *motivational* rather than *confrontational* approaches in offender treatment (Foote et al., 1994). After all, it seems clear that the active offenders in this sample lack hope and self-efficacy more than they lack shame (see also Kantzian et al., 1990). Motivation, however, involves more than just cajoling offenders to believe in themselves or to "take responsibility" for their futures. I am haunted by an image of ex-convicts being encouraged to spew platitudes like, "I'm good enough, I'm smart enough and, gosh darn it, I deserve it." Equally ridiculous is the image of a prison counselor encouraging inmates to "take responsibility for your behavior" while they are kept in an environment that essentially takes all responsibility and choice away from them. Research and common sense suggest that the isolation and disempowerment of the incapacitation experience can exacerbate an individual's felt lack of personal control (Blatier, 2000).

The LDS narratives support the idea that empowerment is probably about "learning through doing, and becoming transformed as a result" (Henry, 1994, p. 299). According to one of the reintegration programmers I worked with,

> You can't teach people self-esteem. These pine shelves and cabinets [made by ex-offenders in a reintegration program's woodwork training] are the vehicles for self-esteem. . . . If I had a piece of chalk in my hand and tried to lecture these guys about self-esteem all day, they'd turn and run the other way. They associate that with school, and they hated school. We teach them self-esteem by letting them prove something to themselves, challenge themselves, learn that they have the talent to accomplish something besides sitting around the house all day getting high. (Keith Midgely, Alternatives to Drugs Programme, *field notes*)

Simply put, the way to learn initiative is to "do well": "Performance accomplishments are likely to increase a person's sense of self-efficacy and appraisal of internal control" (Caspi, 1993, p. 366).

RECOGNIZING REDEMPTION

As Shover (1996) insisted, "Despite the individualistic bias and tone of [explanations for desistance], the change process, like the process of juvenile involvement in crime, is a social and interactional one" (pp. 143–144). Not only must a person accept conventional society in order to go straight, but conventional society must accept that person as well (Meisenhelder, 1982). In the narratives of desisting interviewees, this reintegration into a straight life was frequently formalized in the form of a social ritual.

The most difficult obstacle ex-offenders face in the effort to make good is one that they have partially created for themselves. Ex-offenders zigzag between crime and noncrime, and they frequently make the claim that they are going straight "for sure this time, I really mean it," only to relapse into crime and drugs. Like the boy who cried wolf, the drifting deviant eventually loses credibility, even with himself or herself. Because employers, agents of social control, and other community members have little confidence in their own ability to discern between legitimate and illegitimate claims to personal reform, the safest option is to interpret any ex-offender's claim to going straight as "phony, feigning, unbelievable or implausible" (Lofland, 1969, p. 210). To do otherwise would be to "open oneself to the perceived possibility of being hurt, taken in, suckered, abused, put down or in some other way being made to seem a less-than-competent player of the social game" (p. 212).

Knowing this well, the LDS interviewees seemed almost obsessed with establishing the authenticity of their reform (see also Weinberg, 1996).

> I try to do good things. You know what I mean, and I do try. But me old fella [father] doesn't recognize, you know what I mean. And he calls me, like just the other night he started calling me a "waste of space" and all that, you know what I mean, an idiot and all that. Me old fella's run after me with shotguns, handguns, machetes, knives, baseball bats, you know, when I was on heroin. You know what I mean, but, you know, it is getting better slowly like, you know. I've been off it for three years now like, but me old fella just refuses to recognize the positive things. You know what I mean, he just keeps on, he just keeps on bringing up the bad things I've done, and you know, he says "You were on heroin" and all that, and you know what I mean, and he really does, honest to God you know. I even said this to him, "Back then and now are—I'm not the same person!" I'm really not. I can feel it in me soul. You know what I mean. I'm not the same person. I'm not violent in any way like. I'm not. I do lose me temper and all that you know what I mean, but like, I think if someone walked up and hit me I wouldn't be bothered you know what I mean? I wouldn't. (male, age 26)

At that point in the conversation, I felt that the speaker actually wanted me to hit him—or probably more to the point, he wants his father to hit him—just to prove the authenticity of his reform. In his case, 3 years without taking any drugs or committing crime is still not enough to convince others that he has changed. "Even outstanding conformity is likely always to be greeted by . . . suspicion and fear," according to Lofland (1969, p. 210). Therefore, desisting persons often describe passing "authenticity tests" like the "turn the other cheek" test proposed by the interviewee above.

> Me mum has told [others], "I can see a change in [him]." At one time me mum couldn't leave 20 pounds [U.S. $30] or 10 pounds or 5 pounds

on the fire [heater] without me taking it, and now she just leaves her purse there. The first time she done it, I thought it was a trick. I thought she left it there to see if I'd take it. And, she told me, she said, "I left that there with money hanging out to see if you'd take it." And I hadn't took any. I mean, she sends me to the shops now with 10 pound notes [bills]. I mean. (male, age 31)

Presuming, legitimately, that the interviewer they were going to meet might be skeptical about their claims to successful desistance, interview participants often had supporting documents ready on hand at our interviews to establish their credentials as truly reformed. One showed me a letter from his community college teacher, testifying to his hard work and capability. Two had letters from their former probation or parole officers ready when I arrived. Three produced copies of their offense record that included the date of last convictions. Most interviewees urged me to "go ask me ma," or "talk to my bird [girlfriend], she'll tell you," which I tried to do whenever this was appropriate. "Merely individual claims of privately accomplished change carry little weight" according to Lofland (1969, p. 289). Interviewees' life stories were constantly interspersed with testimonies from those whose views have not been discredited:

> You'll see it in my file. Or [the manager of the drug treatment clinic] will tell you. Have you been to the clinic? Well, they've got this receptionist, she used to be terrified of me. Now, she says she can really see the change in me. She said, "I used to be terrified of you." I am, like, proud of myself. (male, age 31)

> Me ma's made up [pleased] with me, she can see the change in me and all that. She says I'm a "new person." (male, age 26)

While the testimony of any conventional other will do, the best certification of reform involves a public or official endorsement from media outlets, community leaders, and members of the social control establishment:

> The one policeman who stopped me was saying he was happy with me progress. He said, "I'm made up [pleased] to see you doing what you're doing." Most of them [cops] don't give a shit. They'd stitch you up [frame you] and have you back in jail sooner than have you out. Even if you were doing nothing. But this was the first genuine policeman I'd met for years. He said, "You're doing well, keep it up," and you know, it put a little spring in me step. Buzzing you know. For a policeman to be saying it to you, I must be doing something right, you know? (male, age 33)

> The paper did a story on me like a few months ago. We've got copies of it here. They were just saying how much I've achieved in the short amount of time I've been doing photography. (male, age 36)

> It's like, this Monday I'm giving a talk for the Probation [Service], you

know to the local magistrates, and that's the first step like, hopefully 'cause I want to go into something like that [as a career], you know probation or drug counseling or something, or youth counselor. It's . . . , you see, in four years the Probation have never had anyone who's done so well as me, but like 'cause I've done that well the Chief of Probation has asked me if I'll go to this meeting—every few months they have a meeting with the magistrates—and she's asked me if I'll go and like, you know talk. You know, like as a success story sort of thing. (male, age 24)

My life story? My life story has been in the papers and stuff. I was in [names three different magazines] and on the news and everything. (male, age 31)

Reformation is not something that is visible or objective in the sense it can be "proven." It is, instead, a construct that is negotiated through interaction between an individual and significant others in a process of "looking-glass rehabilitation." Until ex-offenders are formally and symbolically recognized as "success stories," their conversion may remain suspect to significant others, and most importantly to themselves. After all, only a few years ago, each participant had been officially and publicly labeled a "criminal" in the media and by social control authorities as high as judges.

I would say that four years ago, the judge's comments, "You are a menace and a danger to society. Society should be protected from the likes of you," it didn't go down well. (male, age 28)

Critical Elements of the Redemption Ritual

Building on Garfinkel's (1956) "Conditions of Successful Degradation Ceremonies," Braithwaite and Mugford (1994) described what they called "reintegration ceremonies." Whereas in the *degradation ceremony*, an actor's social identity is publicly lowered to that of deviant or outsider, in a *reintegration ceremony*, "disapproval of a bad act is communicated while sustaining the identity of the actor as good" (p. 142). These ceremonies, most frequently used with juveniles or with individuals in the early stages of a deviant career, are meant to ensure that "a deviant identity . . . does not become a master status trait that overwhelms other identities" (p. 142)

The long-term offenders in this sample, however, have long been branded with the master status of the deviant. Being publicly shamed and offering an apology, as described by Braithwaite and Mugford (1994), will probably not suffice to redeem the reputation of such individuals. Instead, they may need to undergo some sort of "elevation ceremony" (Lofland, 1969), "certification process" (Meisenhelder, 1977, 1982), or "delabeling process" (Trice & Roman, 1970). Lofland (1969) suggested that elevation ceremonies "serve publicly and formally to announce, sell and spread the fact of Actor's new kind of being" (p. 227). These include the ex-offender's "public appearance before a formally assembled group, [and] the public profession of one's personal transformation" (p. 228). Similarly, in Meisenhelder's (1977) certification stage of desistance, "Some recognized member(s) of the conventional community must publicly announce and certify that the offender has changed and that he [she] is now to be considered essentially noncriminal" (p. 329).

For desisting participants in the LDS, these redemption rituals often emerged out of *unsuccessful* degradation ceremonies. Groups of friends, intimates, and conventional others publicly testified on the desisting person's behalf, leading an agent of social control to formally acknowledge the ex-offender's change in behavior. In almost all the cases in which this ritual occurred, the interaction was perceived as:

- *Unprecedented and unanticipated:* Narrators often said "no one had ever taken this sort of chance on me."
- *Merited:* Narrators perceived the event as long-awaited justice, not as a lucky break.
- *Formal:* Rituals involved respected community members and frequently took place under the auspices of the social control establishment. Narrators sometimes interpret the judgment as being the judgment of all of society.

Compare the following examples from desisting narratives. In all three excerpts, desisting ex-offenders, who were experiencing and enjoying productive behavior for the first time, all happened to wind up back in court. Analogous phrases in the three passages have been italicized to emphasize the uniformity of these descriptions in the narratives.

> Here's one for you: I got caught in '94. *Although I was off the bottle and I'm trying to go straight*, I'd been caught for driving while disqualified [without a license] again. When I was inside [the jail], I got a visit from the police, and they'd got my prints on a [forged] check [from several months previous]. So when I was in prison I got charged with check card fraud. So I came out for the driving offense and all of a sudden, I've now got to face going to court over the check card fraud, and I was looking at 2 years [in prison]. Worst nightmare, especially when you're trying to go straight. And you think, "Oh my God, I can't believe this!" And, I've got the baby, 6 months old, at home. And I went to court and I went in, I was in and out of court, and it came to the crunch, and I went to Crown Court. Oh, I thought "I'm going to get 2 years [in prison] here." And I'm trying so hard in my life, and I just—and, anyway. The judge, everyone, I couldn't believe it. I burst into tears. *I couldn't believe it.* I'm very high on emotions by this stage in my life, and I burst into tears, because people must have seen something in me then. *Someone must have seen some good in me*, and all these people wanted to help. And they all came to court, and anyway, he [the judge] gave me Community Service. He didn't have to. He

could have, he said, "I could send you to prison." But he said, "I don't think it will do you any good." He said "And these people here, they seem to believe in you." And he, well, I got community service. (male, age 32)

In the second redemption ritual, the narrator is explaining how a roommate at a halfway house was caught possessing drugs, leading to the arrest of all the residents on suspicion of conspiracy to distribute narcotics:

To cut a long story short, . . . all of a sudden like the house gets busted and all that like, you know. I got arrested eventually in the end. Goes to court back up in Blackpool and all that. And [my priest] give a letter [on my behalf], and [John], the manager of the hostel came and put a good word in for me. And, you know, by the time it went to Crown Court in Preston you know, honest to God, *I've never seen anything like it* in me life. I goes up in court, and I said to John, "I'm getting off [running away]," I wasn't going to turn up, right? . . . [But] I goes in court, and the judge says, "Name," you know. I could see I was going to get sent away then 'cause it was happening dead quickly, you know. "Name," and then, "Address," and all this. And then me solicitor said, "There's this man, John S ———, who'd like to say a few words on the defendant's behalf." And they started telling each other jokes! Honest to God, so I'm like that to me solicitor, "What's going on here? What's going on here?" Right? All of a sudden I just turned round like that and, "Alright Mr. A ———," and all that, "You done your training and all that. That's fine," and all that. "I'm releasing you into this man's custody. Keep up the good work." I was like that, "Whoah! What's going on here?" you know. That man turning up like that, the judge changed his mind, you know. I'd never seen anything like it in me life. You know the way they just started talking and all that like, you know. And, I had letters of you know, sort of support, off priests and, you know, people who I'd made contact with. I had one off NACRO [the National Association for the Care and Resettlement of Offenders], you know, 'cause *I was doing good you know.* It wasn't just bullshit like. I was doing good. I was trying, you know, so *they give me a chance like.* And I know it's been a slow progress and all that. You know what I mean like, as I say like, Rome weren't built in a day like. (male, age 26)

Finally, in this last example, an old crime came back to haunt the desisting interviewee:

So I gets took to Walton Prison. For the first time in my life, like, I was really upset like. *Things were going right.* For the first time in a long time, things were going right, and it was just a total kick in the balls. So I was there for about a week. . . . So this morning the screws [prison guards] come to me door and say, "Come on mate, you're in the Crown Court." So I goes to the Crown Court and me solicitor stands up and says, this is for me Crown Court appeal which I was expecting. And, the fella from the day training [reintegration] program is also there, and he explained to the judge that I only had a couple of days left to do, and then I would have finished the Program. Well, they told him about me girlfriend and how well everything was going, and he let me go. He deferred me sentence for 6 months and that was *the best chance anyone's ever took on me*, because I paid him back with interest. You know, in that 6 month period we moved into a flat, I got a job working for a charity—that was before the job that I'm in at the moment—I got a job working for a charity and you know, everything was great. The probation officer that I got, he was like, *the first time ever that a probation officer has believed in me*, you know, was willing to give me a chance. He wrote me a brilliant, brilliant report, and all that. . . . When I went back to the court like, you know, they were made up [pleased] with me basically, because I'd stayed out of trouble, I'd completed the probation [rehabilitation] course, I'd managed to get a job, plus we had a flat, we were living in a flat together. We'd done everything required. And so, you know, it's given me the chance that I wanted basically. That's all I'd ever wanted was someone to sit there and believe in me, which like [my girlfriend] done. Like, you know, she was sent by God basically like, because without her, I'd still be in that hostel now, or in jail or dead. (male, age 24)

While the courtroom provides an ideal backdrop for recasting judgment on all three narrators' lives, the essential aspect of the ritual is the unexpected testimony of "normal-smiths" (Lofland, 1969) or conventional others who impute normality on the ex-offenders. All three narrators knew that they were "trying." They were making some progress toward staying straight. Yet, none of them had any confidence that this effort would aid them in any way in the eyes of society. Recall that desisting ex-offenders still generally view the world as unfair and assume the deck is always stacked against them. Suddenly and unexpectedly, though, there is justice. They have done well, and someone actually "believes in them."

The social impact of the redemption ritual is undoubtedly significant. In the above examples, the ex-offenders were allowed to remain in society instead of going to prison. Yet, the psychological impact of the rituals might be even more important. They realize, for what they claim is the "first time" in their lives, that they have some control over their own destinies. As in Brickman et al.'s (1982) compensation model ("It is not my fault, but it is my responsibility"), this is a newfound control, and one that carries on to other aspects of their lives.

Almost all of the narrators described "getting off" from criminal charges in the past. Yet, these were always interpreted as "lucky breaks" or random events. Under such interpretations, there is no reason not to continue offending. In fact, one might as well celebrate the good fortune. Throughout the narratives, criminal trials are described as something like a "game," based on the luck of the draw. Outcomes were decided because the judge "was dead easy" or a "real bastard." Sometimes, the defense attorney "didn't have a fucking clue what she was doing" or else the prosecution failed to get any witnesses to testify. The difference in the redemption ritual is that there is no "cock up." Someone has finally "seen something" in the ex-offender, and now the ex-offender can see the same thing. They have the ability to act positively and be rewarded for it. As such, the redemption ritual may be ultimate authenticity test desired by desisting ex-offenders.

> [After] certification, individuals convince themselves that they have convinced others to view them as conventional members of the community. . . . They begin to feel trusted; that is, they feel their contemporaries are likely to see them as normal and noncriminal. They no longer feel suspect. Certification, then, completes the exiting, or change, process by solidifying the self-concept of the ex-offender. (Meisenhelder, 1982, p. 138)

Institutionalizing the Redemption Ritual

Importantly, in the narratives of the LDS sample, most of the redemption rituals were entirely serendipitous. As such, more formalized and systematic mechanisms for recognizing reform efforts might be worth considering.

Positive acknowledgment or recognition of rehabilitation is a rare thing in the criminal justice system. By its nature, criminal justice is almost entirely negative. When ex-offenders are "rewarded," they are generally rewarded for what they do *not* do. Additionally, their reward is *not* having something done to them. If a parolee avoids arrest, stays out of fights, passes drug tests, and shuns shady characters, they might earn the reward of getting off parole for "good behavior." Yet, this is not good behavior as much as it is "not-bad behavior." Rarely does the criminal justice system reward the *positive* things that ex-offenders accomplish. Efforts in employment settings, neighborhood groups, job training programs, family matters, self-help groups, college classes, and volunteer placements generally go officially unrecognized by the system.

There are some exceptions of course. The graduation ceremonies in correctional boot camps and in ex-offender job training programs certainly qualify as redemption rituals. Yet, it is questionable just how widely recognized or appreciated these accomplishments are once one leaves the confines of the program itself. Similarly, in prison, inmates can be credited for "program time" or even moved to an "honor wing." These distinctions serve a very important purpose in encouraging rehabilitation, but the recognition is not very meaningful for those outside of the institutional setting. In some ways, earning the distinction of "good behavior" in a prison is tantamount to being named "most likely to succeed" in Hell. It is not something many will put on a résumé. The prison environment is simply too different from conventional society. As many inmates insist, "It doesn't matter what you do and say in here—what matters is how you act out there" (male, 20s, *field notes*).

The best existing precedent for an institutionalized system of redemption might be found outside corrections—the academic "honor roll." Teenagers, like ex-offenders, after all, are an automatically "suspect" population (Matza, 1969). When an urban teenager is shot, for instance, it is immediately assumed that he or she was probably up to no good. Yet, if the media and social control establishment report that the shooting victim was "an honor roll student," the story changes. Suddenly, the (hardly subtle) implication becomes, "This was a good kid, who did not deserve to get hurt." The identity of "honor roll student" appears to have become synonymous with innocence, just as the identity of "gang member" presupposes guilt.

The correctional system might need to adopt its own version of an "honor roll" (metaphorically, of course). Any such distinction would need to be made highly exclusive. Like the academic honor roll, the distinction would need uniform, agreed-on standards at a high enough level that only a small percentage of paroled ex-offenders can achieve them. The recognition (in whatever form it takes) would have to be a meaningful achievement not only in the eyes of the public but also to the ex-offenders themselves in order to be the "authenticity test" that desisting ex-offenders so badly want. If ex-offenders perceive that "anybody" can get this credit, it will become meaningless.[25]

Redemption rituals, especially those certified by the State, can provide a psychological turning point for ex-offenders. If police officers, judges, and wardens were to shake the hand of the desisting ex-offender, and say, "Well done" (as the judges did in the three rituals in the last section), the ex-offender would have to acknowledge some level of *justice* in the "justice system." This would take away a crucial neutralization (condemnation of the condemners) and would pull ex-offenders more deeply into mainstream society. Sincere recognition from the same authorities that certify individ-

---

[25]In fact, ex-offenders who make a concerted effort to go straight often express considerable concern about the authenticity (or lack thereof) of other ex-convicts' alleged conversions (see Weinberg, 1996). Frequently, during fieldwork, ex-offenders would pull me aside to explain who among a group of reintegration clients were "really" making a go at changing their lives and who were just conning the staff at the intervention. "I think this [reintegration project] is good, aye. Like, a few people who come in here don't really give a fuck, you know what I mean, one way or the other. Like, I don't want to mess, you know what I mean. There's people here who just come in here and get their money [bus fare or compensation for child care] and go home, and go and score [drugs] with the money. And it's not right 'cause it's taking the piss [making a mockery]." (male, 20s, field notes)

If the "fakers" get the same acknowledgment and status rewards that the authentic changers receive, any honor roll status will be without value.

uals as deviants could have a lasting effect on the way ex-offenders perceive the social control establishment *and vice versa*.

In the United States, the federal government is currently revisiting the idea of ex-offender reentry (Travis, 2000) and is experimenting with a variety of "reentry courts" and other innovations (Reno, 2000; Talucci & Solomon, 2000). It is hoped that one of the lessons from the turbulent history of parole in the United States that will inform these reforms is that reentry requires a sincere commitment to reward positive behaviors, as well as punish negative ones. A reentry court should therefore be empowered not only to reimprison ex-felons but also to officially recognize their efforts toward reform.

Rebiographing as Policy

Perhaps the best (and most useful) recognition an offender could receive from the system is the chance to change his or her past. The British legal system, for instance, has institutionalized a form of state-sanctioned "rebiographing" for ex-offenders. Under the 1974 Rehabilitation of Offenders Act, an individual's criminal history actually "expires" after a given number of years (depending on the length of one's sentence), and the person is no longer required by law to declare his or her criminal convictions to most prospective employers. Even when asked directly, "Have you been convicted of a crime?" the law allows the desisting ex-offender to say, "No." In this liberating model, an ex-offender is therefore legally enabled to rewrite his or her history to make it more in line with his or her present, reformed identity. After several years of good behavior, the State essentially says, "You don't appear to be the sort of person who has a criminal record, therefore you needn't have one."

Parallels, of course, can be found in the U.S. juvenile justice system, in which juvenile records are destroyed upon one's transition to adulthood, and also in the law on bankruptcy, in which credit histories can be redeemed after a set number of years. For that matter, a parallel can be found in American politicians' responses to questions about illegal drug use. Apparently, the United States permits more than a little selective amnesia or autobiographical creativity if the individual is a member of a class of people we believe in—a juvenile, a debtor, or a political animal. "Common criminals," on the other hand, often are not even allowed to vote in an election because of their criminal past, let alone run for office. This selective application of the "forgive and forget" doctrine can recreate the supposed dichotomy between Us and Them.

Of course, legal rebiographing probably should not be granted easily or automatically to *any* population. Under British law, an ex-convict might have to stay out of trouble for as many as 10 years to earn this privilege. Moreover, perhaps ex-offenders should even be required to do more than stay out of the reach of the law. An unlikely trio of New Yorkers, Ed Koch, Al Sharpton, and Charles Ogletree, are currently circulating a "second-chance" pardon plan for nonviolent drug felons that would expunge their felonies only on the condition that they complete their sentences, receive a high school equivalency diploma, and pass their drug tests after release (Alter, 1999). A "repentant role" might also be built into the deal (Trice & Roman, 1970). Maybe an ex-offender should be expected to literally pay his or her debt to society, through community service or restitution (see Bazemore's 1998 proposal for instituting "earned redemption" into criminal justice).

Whatever the requirements, the ultimate reward for this (proactive) "good behavior" should be permission to legally move on from the past. If not "forgive and forget," at least "remember and forgive." Without this right, ex-offenders will always be ex-offenders, hence outsiders, or the Other. A *correctional* system that does not institutionalize such opportunities at redemption is at best an Orwellian euphemism for the reproduction of more of the same.[26]

CONCLUDING REMARKS

Both narrative therapy and Britain's 1974 Rehabilitation Act recognize the importance of providing ex-offenders an escape route from repeating their pasts. The persistent offenders interviewed for this project said that they wanted to make good but did not think they were capable of doing so. They felt they were "doomed" to deviance.

Not coincidentally, the reigning popular and professional discourse about offenders in Western culture suggests that criminality is probably a permanent and inescapable trait of individuals (Irwin & Austin, 1994, p. 84).

> I wanted a house, I wanted a life, stability and a future, and that [going straight] was the only way I could do it. . . . My probation officer told me that I'd never do it [make good]. In fact, to say that, the inmates around me were saying I would never, ever do it, like. (male, age 28)

Paraphrasing Martin Luther King, Jr., Sagarin (1975) called this pro-

---

[26]In 1910, when he was Home Secretary, Winston Churchill made a famous speech along these lines to the British Parliament, "The mood and temper of the public in regard to the treatment of crime and criminals is one of the most unfailing tests of the civilization of any country. A calm and dispassionate recognition of the rights of the accused against the State, and even of convicted criminals against the State, a constant heart searching by all charged with the duty of punishment, a desire and eagerness to rehabilitate in the world of industry all those who have paid their dues in the hard coinage of punishment, tireless efforts towards the discovery of curative and regenerating processes, and an unfaltering faith that there is a treasure, if you can only find it, in the heart of every man—these are the symbols which in the treatment of crime and criminals mark and measure the stored-up strength of a nation, and are the sign and proof of the living virtue in it." (cited in Gorringe, 1996, p. 226)

cess the "tyranny of isness" (p. 144). "The sense of helplessness and hopelessness surrounding people locked into certain deviant identities may well be derived from, or fortified by, the implicit connotation that some statuses constitute essence or isness, rather than behavior or feeling" (Sagarin, 1990, p. 808). Essentially, societies that do not believe that offenders can change will get offenders who do not believe that they can change.

Every culture has a limited range of grand narratives or meta-narratives expressed in mythology, proverbs, and folk sayings. Cultures with few models of redemption may be the cultures with more doomed deviants. At the least, in cultures like that of Israel (Rotenberg, 1978, 1987) and Japan (Braithwaite, 1989; Haley, 1996), where the idea of criminal essentialism does not seem to be as dominant, rehabilitation efforts seem to be greeted with less hostility than in the West (see also Allen, 1981). According to Braithwaite (1989),

> Japanese idiom frequently accounts for wrongdoing with possession by a "mushi" (worm or bug). Criminals are therefore not acting according to their true selves; they are victims of a "mushi" which can be "sealed off," "thus permitting people to be restored to the community without guilt" (Wagatsuma & Rosett, 1986, p. 476). The cultural assumption of basic goodness and belief in each individual's capacity for eventual self-correction means that "nurturant acceptance" ("amayakashi") is the appropriate response to deviance once shame has been projected to and accepted by the deviant. (pp. 64–65)

Although the West has its own redemption stories, "the Prodigal Son is hardly one of our leading folk heroes" (Braithwaite, 1989, p. 162). As one reintegration worker said,

> People believe that God used to be able to turn sinners into saints. He could save Saul of Tarsus on the Road to Damascus, but it's like they don't seem to think He can do that anymore. Like today's criminals are just so bad that even God can't touch them. It's sad. (male, 50s, *field notes*)

Indeed, over the past two decades, hardly anyone in the field of corrections has espoused or endorsed "Kennedyan" type idealism. (Cullen and Gilbert, 1982, may have been the last of this breed in the United States; more recent rays of hope have shone mainly from Australia and Canada.) At least since Martinson's (1974) paradigm-shifting attack on rehabilitation, a hard-nosed, cynical "realism" has characterized the study of crime and social science in general. Of course, we know where this realism led Dr. Martinson: The author of the "nothing works" thesis committed suicide soon after writing an apologetic retraction of his controversial report. American criminal justice policy has also seen this pessimistic version of "reality therapy" to its logical consequences, incarcerating 2 million American citizens and transporting them to maximum security prisons often hundreds of miles from their families and home communities.

A generalized disbelief in change is apparent even in the narratives of those people who have gone straight. Like Shover's (1996) interviewees, LDS interviewees often struggled to explain their own change in behavior.

> [I am going straight] just cause I know what it [drugs and crime] leads to like, but I always knew that. I don't know. I don't know what's happened to me. I don't know why. I can't believe it myself sometimes. (male, age 33)

Most insisted that they have not changed at all. They were good people "all along" (they simply behaved badly for a decade or so). Several of these interviewees expressed views about the essential nature of "real criminals" (people they met in prison, for instance) no less conservative than the views of police officers I spoke with. Finally, when interviewees did try to describe the change they experienced, their descriptions often dwelled in artificial-sounding clichés ("I saw the light" or "It just hit me one morning") that seemed to have little connection to the long-term change process they were describing. Not only are there few change stories readily available to ex-offenders therefore, there may not even be a language or discourse available for describing this change. The words may simply not be there.

The creation and promotion of a "replacement discourse" (Henry & Milovanovic, 1996) for the language of criminal essentialism may help ex-offenders write redemption scripts for themselves. Of course, essential to the development of this new language of reform is the sharing of success stories (see Coles, 1989). Braithwaite (1989), for instance, called for

> a culture, or rehabilitative subcultures as in Alcoholics Anonymous, where those who perform remarkable feats of rehabilitation are held up as role models—the pop star who kicked the heroin habit, the football hero who repented from wanton acts of violence—where ceremonies to decertify deviance are widely understood and easily accessible. (p. 163)

The transformative power of stories, proverbs, slogans, and folk sayings may be a neglected area of study for social scientists (Bassin, 1984; Shoham & Seis, 1993), but the power of these meta-narratives is well known to rehabilitation practitioners—and, most importantly, to desisting ex-offenders. When reformed ex-offenders share their stories with others, as the interviewees in this research have done, they are leading the effort to transform public discourse regarding crime and criminality.

By paying attention to these stories, we can learn not only about offenders but also about ourselves. According to Cressey (1963), the rationale behind involving reformed ex-offenders in the counseling of other offenders is that "the persons who are to be changed and the persons doing the changing must have a strong sense of belonging to one group" (p. 155). This is a telling quote. In this case, the "one group" refers to ex-convicts, recovering addicts, or former offenders. Yet, on some level, we are certainly all one group. When ex-offenders share their stories with non-offenders, they are working to "actively repudiate their alien status and acknowledge membership in the same world to which the rest of us belong" (Singer, 1997, p. 295).

After all, the "myth of the bogeyman" is a narrative. Like a self-narrative, this sort of cultural narrative serves a distinct psychological purpose. This bogeyman myth allows nonbogeymen (the "Us") to relieve ourselves of the shame we feel for our shared responsibility in creating the "Them."

> The myth of pure evil confers a kind of moral immunity on people who believe it. . . . Belief in the myth is itself one recipe for evil, because it allows people to justify violent and oppressive actions. It allows evil to masquerade as good. (Baumeister, 2000, p. 96)

Indeed, maybe the myth is too entrenched to change. Perhaps, we really are too cynical, too hateful, or too "realistic" to change our thinking about deviants. Then again, as a wise man once said, "Hey, I was the worst of the worst. If I can change, anyone can" (male, age 31).

APPENDIX:
ADDITIONAL
METHODOLOGICAL NOTES

CONTENT ANALYSIS METHODOLOGY

Unlike most in-depth, qualitative studies, the Liverpool Desistance Study (LDS) included the use of well-validated, content-analysis systems for analyzing complex narrative data, deriving qualitative scores, and testing differences among individuals and between groups. Thematic content analysis involves "coding" or "scoring" verbal material for manifest (rather than latent) content or style to infer or assess the psychosocial and cognitive characteristics of a sample of individuals (Smith, 1992). Murray (1943) described this process of assessing characteristic thought patterns and personality from selected verbal material as "thought sampling." Our objective was to preserve the richness, spontaneity, and meaning of participants' life narratives while rendering the data comparable across individual cases and amenable to nomothetic research.

Four content dictionaries were chosen on the basis of the initial qualitative findings, the findings from a pilot research project, and existing phenomenological research on desistance. To establish the reliability of this coding, I asked pairs of graduate students to learn each of the coding schemes (see Acknowledgments). This coding was "blind" in the sense that the coding was done independently and the coders were rating episodes or phrases that were extracted from the body of the larger text. As such, they had no way of knowing whether the passage they were coding belonged to a desisting or persisting group member or anything else about the speaker. Importantly, any passage that mentioned desistance specifically (e.g., "That is what has kept me straight these last few years . . .") was either amended or excluded from the coding.

In measures of agreement, the two independent scorers achieved Cohen's kappas between .61 and .68 on the four coding schemes. Fleiss (1981) suggested that kappas between .40 and .60 are fair, those between .60 and .75 are good, and those over .75 are excellent. Considering the complexity of the coding frameworks and the subjective nature of the data in this project, these agreement scores were considered more than adequate indications of the reliability of the coding.

Generativity Content Analysis

Stewart et al.'s (1988) coding scheme measures five primary generative themes: (a) caring for others, (b) the general desire to make a lasting contribution to society, (c) concern for one's children, (d) a need to be needed, and (e) productivity/growth (see Exhibit A.1). To correct for correlations with verbal fluency, I expressed the scores in terms of themes per thousand words of text.

Following Stewart et al. (1988), the unit of analysis was the *meaningful phrase*, with only one content category possible for each phrase. Coded passages included all hypothetical statements regarding future goals (e.g., "I want to begin spending more time with my kids, helping them out") and statements regarding the present (e.g., "I enjoy teaching my kids to read"). Prototypical examples of these themes from the interviews are listed in Exhibit A.2. When coding, descriptions of current or future involvement in criminal behavior were not coded. Although these might be examples of self-absorption or lack of caring, including such descriptions in the coding would make any proposed association between measures of generativity and desistance tautological. The two independent coders achieved a moderate Cohen's kappa of .61 ($p < .001$) in a test of interrater reliability.

Comparisons between groups revealed robust differences in the frequency with which such themes appeared in individual narratives. Although a few statistical outliers exaggerated the comparison of means, statistically significant differences were also found in comparisons of the median scores, as well as in a proportional analysis of the percentage of narrators with scores over two in each sample. Additionally, neither individual nor overall measures of generativity correlate significantly to measures of basic personality traits. According to the adult development lit-

EXHIBIT A.1
Generative Content Categories Paraphrased from Stewart et al. (1988)

1. *Caring Versus Self-Absorption and Failures of Caring*
   Expressions of concern with the capacity to care for others ("a sense that includes 'to care to do' something, to 'care for' somebody or something, to 'take care of' that which needs protection and attention, and to 'take care not to do' something destructive" [E. Erikson, as quoted from Evans, 1967, p. 53]). Its absence (scored *minus*) is reflected in overt failures of caring and in self-absorption.

2. *General Concerns With Generativity*
   Expressions of concerns about making a lasting contribution, especially to future generations (including through creative products) or to care for them, should score *plus*; aversions to such contributions should score *minus* whenever more specific themes cannot be scored.

3. *Children*
   The care and nurturance (positive, scored a *plus*; negative scored a *minus*) for one's child. Also, sheer desires to have children score *plus*, whereas aversions to having children should score *minus*.

4. *Need to Be Needed*
   Expression of an inner need to be needed by another or by others in general ("a gradual expansion of ego-interests and a libidinal investment in that which is being generated" [Erikson, 1968, p. 138]) scored *plus*. Denials of this need are scored *minus*.

5. *Productivity Versus Stagnation*
   Expressions of developing and growing through generative outlets (it "encompasses procreativity, productivity, and creativity, and thus the generation of new products and ideas" [Erikson, 1982, p. 67]). Rather than simply the performance of an occupation-related task, clear emotional investment and commitment must be involved. (For example, the mere reporting of working on a product is not scored here; however, if the statement includes expressions of affect regarding the work in progress, it becomes clear that there is personal and emotional investment in the task.) Productivity also involves the further growth and development of the formulated adult self (scored *plus*) rather than stagnation (*minus*) (e.g., premature fixation with no desire for further challenge or growth).

erature, developmental concerns are not mere extensions of underlying personality traits but instead are part of a separate, more dynamic domain of personality (McAdams, 1994a).

Agency Content Analysis

To explore the theme of agency in the interview, I asked participants to describe any "important turning points" in their lives. The descriptions of these turning point episodes, as well as all other descriptions of the individual's present life situation and future plans, were scored using McAdams's (1992) coding framework for themes of agency (or control) in

1. *Care Versus Self-Absorption*
   Plus: Top of the list, I want to provide a secure future for me mum. She's had it rough, so it's time for her to sit down and have me look after her (desisting group, male, age 20). *Plus two.*
   Minus: I don't give a fuck about junkies. If some junkie dies [because of heroin], I say, "Good, another dead junkie" (active group, male, age 40). *Minus two.*

2. *General Concerns With Generativity*
   Plus: I'd been wanting to do something positive for quite some time. I've always wanted to get a job that I can help other people in. You know, train and get some full-time employment where I can contribute, you know, and maybe help save, even if I only saved one out of a hundred, you know (desisting group, male, age 36). *Plus three.*

3. *Children*
   Plus: I just live for me kids now, you know what I mean? I live for them kids, man (active group, male, age 33).
   Minus: I didn't think I'd have a kid this early. I wanted, I've always wanted to be a nurse, like, so when I had the baby, I just had to pack it all in then though. Not just that, it's just totally different when you have your own kid, you know what I mean? (active group, female, age 22). *Minus two.*

4. *Need to Be Needed*
   Plus: It's nice now and again to be told that you're married to them, you're loved by them, they love you and care for you. But it's nice to be able to share that with someone, to tell them, "You're all right as well" (desisting group, male, age 28).
   Minus: Anyway, I got rid of my wife. One thing I learned about women is that they're a total pain in the ass (active group, male, age 28).

5. *Productivity Versus Stagnation*
   Plus: I thought, "I'm always on the go." I work seven days a week, I love it, I love my work—I love being out there, giving life my best shot (desisting group, male, age 32). *Plus one.*
   Minus: She said, like, "If you got off heroin now, I'd come back," you know, but I'm happy the way I am. I'm just happy to plod along, and I know I've got a habit. I'm at the stage now where I'm resigned to the fact that I'm an addict and I'm going to be an addict to the day I die, and nothing's going to change that (active group, male, age 33). *Minus three*

life narratives. This coding scheme measures the occurrence of four agentic themes: (a) self mastery, (b) status/victory, (c) achievement/responsibility, and empowerment. Exhibit A.3 provides abbreviated definitions of these content categories and prototypical examples of each theme drawn from the interview data. Two independent raters achieved a Cohen's kappa of .62 in a test of agreement. Narratives were scored either a 1 or a 0 for the occurrence of these themes. Repeated themes were not scored twice. Therefore, the maximum total score would be 4, if the narrative contained all four themes.

EXHIBIT A.3
Themes of Agency in Turning Point Episodes

1. *Self-Mastery*: The participant strives successfully to master, control, enlarge, or perfect the self. A relatively common expression of the theme involves the participant's attaining a dramatic insight into the meaning of his or her own life. The participant may also experience a greatly enhanced sense of control over his or her destiny, in the wake of an important life event.

> At first it was just to like, I didn't dream of going to college or nothing like that. I [just wanted to] get meself busy . . . and give myself time to think about what I wanted to do. [But] after doing the warm-up courses like, I found I was good at photography and . . . I started at [a community college]. And, since then I just haven't looked back. It's just gotten brilliant. (male, age 36)

2. *Status/Victory:* The participants attains a heightened status or prestige among his or her peers, through receiving a special recognition or honor or winning a contest or competition.

> Winning the [prison art competition], because I originally just painted to kill time in prison and to learn about art, and I would have done the art degree even if I couldn't paint, but as it happened, I did both and won the [competition]. Basically, the first picture I ever completed was exhibited, hung up in a frame and won a prize. (male, age 47)

3. *Achievement/Responsibility*: The participant reports substantial success in the achievement of tasks, jobs, or instrumental goals or in the assumption of important responsibilities. The participant feels proud, confident, masterful, accomplished, or successful in (a) meeting significant challenges or overcoming important obstacles or (b) taking on major responsibilities for other people and assuming roles that require the person to be in charge of things and/or people.

> When, mainly when the kids got taken off me . . . I ended up being on me own, fighting everything on me own. I fought for the kids for 13 months, and in that 13 months I got the house sorted . . . I got meself on a methadone course. I had me daughter, me third daughter, on me own . . . nobody there to hold me hand. I fought for the kids and March this year I got me kids back for good. (female, age 23)

4. *Empowerment:* The subject is enlarged, enhanced, empowered, ennobled, built up, or made better through his or her association with something larger and more powerful than the self. The self is made even more agentic by virtue of its involvement with an even more powerful agent of some sort. The empowering force is usually either (a) God, nature, the cosmos, and so on or (b) a highly influential teacher, mentor, minister, therapist, or authority figure.

> Working [for a reintegration program] has been a turning point. It's helped me get a lot of confidence back. The confidence I got given here off the people who are here, I'd never had that in school or anything. And I thought, "Hold on, these people are telling me I can do this." I've never been told I could do this. . . . They've helped me out a lot, you know, it's done a lot for me and I've been more confident since I've been here. (male, age 28)

Note. Definitions from McAdams (1992), used with written permission of the author.

Attribution Content Analysis

To measure the use of concessions, excuses, justifications, and refusals in interviewees' accounts, Laurence Alison, Louise Porter, and I adapted a condensed version of Schonbach's (1990) comprehensive coding framework for first-person attributions. The complete coding system and content dictionary used in the LDS analysis can be found in Maruna (1998). Exhibit A.4 explains each of these constructs and provides an example from the LDS narratives. In total, over 1,400 such failure episodes (an average of around 30 per interview) were coded for occurrences of one of the 29 subcategories of attribution types. In a test of interrater agreement, two coders achieved a Cohen's kappa of .68.

Redemption/Contamination Sequence Coding

McAdams et al. (1997) identified two narrative strategies that appear with some regularity in self-narratives. In *contamination sequences*, a decidedly good event "turns sour." In *redemption sequences*, the opposite occurs, "something good" emerges out of otherwise negative circumstances. For examples from the narratives, see Exhibit A.5. On the basis of the findings in Maruna (1997), it was hypothesized that the stories of desisting ex-offenders would contain more of the redemptive storytelling strategies, whereas active offender stories would instead dwell on the negative consequences that follow from previously positive story sequences.

Three sections of the interview protocol were selected for examining the use hypotheses: the "peak experience" or self-described highest point of the informant's life, the "nadir experience" or lowest point, and the informants' "turning point" episodes. Again, descriptions of giving up crime itself were not included in this coding. Two independent raters coded these three episodes across all 50 interviews for the occurrence of contamination or redemption sequences. Summing scores across the two episodes, the interscorer reliability was $r = .74$.

SAMPLING CONSIDERATIONS

An effort was made to oversample female ex-offenders for this project. Whereas women made up only 5% of the adults released from British prisons in 1993 (Kershaw & Renshaw, 1997), they made up one fifth, or 20%, of the present sample. Female participants in the sample met the same criteria for being "career criminals" used for the male participants, although they tended to spend less time in prison. All 10 female participants had regularly engaged in theft, 4 primarily sold drugs for a living, 2 had stolen

Major Content Categories for Attributions

1. *Reports*: A neutral admission of a failure event without describing the negative aspects of the action or offering any excuse/justification. Examples include straightforward explanations such as "We did it for the money" or "We did it because it was fun."

   > I'd just walk up and hit somebody under the chin, you know, their brain bounces off the back of their heads. Pick up the laptop [computer] and walk away, because laptops at the time were like 1,500 quid [pounds]. Got into that. And then, um, I decided to go to Amsterdam . . . (male, age 30)

2. *Concessions*: Any admission of guilt or offending behavior in which the speaker takes full or partial responsibility for his or her behavior and acknowledges it as a moral or social wrong. Examples include expressions of shame, guilt, or remorse for past activities.

   > My biggest regret in life was I stooped to check fraud, kiting, again. . . . I hated that, and that's a turning point in my life. . . . How can I put it, I thought, you know when you know you can make it, but you've stooped to check fraud, and it is, it's frowned upon, it's like breaking into someone's house, check fraud. I couldn't believe I was doing it. (male, age 32)

3. *Excuse*: A speaker acknowledges a failure or offense but blames extenuating circumstances. Therefore, the person recognizes the behavior as negative but denies responsibility for the event. Examples include blaming drugs or alcohol, blaming one's friends, or blaming circumstances.

   > When I was about 13 or 14, my mother and father were going through a bit of a rotten patch and me dad used to come in and belt me ma and all that. It emotionally affected me you know what I mean? Then I like just turned to drugs just as a way of getting out, just getting out of a situation I found myself in, you know. (male, age 36)

4. *Justification:* A speaker admits responsibility but denies that the behavior is negative. To justify something is to make that behavior legitimate. Examples include denials of injury (no one got hurt), denials of the victim (they deserved it), and appeals to loyalty (I did it for the kids).

   > We played by the book—we've never hurt anyone and we stole off the likes of shops, who can afford it, you know. (male, age 33)

5. *Refusals*: In a refusal, a person evades questions regarding offending. Examples include outright refusals to describe or account for offending behavior or else more subtle evasion tactics.

   > SM: How were you affording this (consumption of $500 of heroin a week)?
   > Participant: You get the money. You just get it, you get me? You have to.
   > SM: So, you were involved in what, dealing? Burglary? That sort of thing?
   > Participant: You just get the money. Leave it at that, yeah? (male, age 38)

---

cars, and 3 had burgled houses. Other reported offenses ranged from check fraud to arson.

Few differences could be found between the narratives of men and women in this sample. This of course could be due to the very small number of women in the sample. Nonetheless, the best existing research on

Contamination Sequence

> As I said I won 10 fights [boxing] on the trot [quickly]. . . . I won 10 on the trot. Then I started smoking [marijuana] and then I lost a fight about 3 weeks after I started smoking. I wasn't fit enough, I started feeling fucked at the end of the 2nd round, and that was it. It was fatigue that I lost the fight. So I packed [boxing] in myself. (male, age 29, persisting group)

Redemption Sequence

> SM: Is there a time in your life that you consider your "lowest point"?
> Participant: Having to sleep rough, in the snow in the winter. That was the only time I was homeless. I'd always managed to find somewhere, but yeah, that was rough. I was almost glad—well I was glad—when I was arrested. It was the winter and the police thought I was dead when they found me, and I was actually glad to be put into a police cell because it was warm [laughs]. (male, age 28, desisting group)

women who desist from crime (Baskin & Sommers, 1998) has uncovered subjective changes very similar to the findings in studies of male ex-offenders (see also Eaton, 1993; Graham & Bowling, 1995; Sommers, Baskin, & Fagan, 1994). Women's stories have been included in this sample primarily in an effort to uncover the universal, rather than the gender-specific, aspects of making good. It is likely that there are both.

The stigma attached to female offenders and drug addicts, especially those with children, is probably greater than that for male offenders (many of whom have children themselves). Yet, society also probably holds out greater hope that more female offenders can be reformed. In popular and media accounts, for instance, women offenders are much more often portrayed as victims of circumstances. An example of this was seen in Texas recently, when traditional death penalty supporters fought against the execution of Karla Faye Tucker. Although the alleged rationale for this unexpected compassion was that Tucker was a born-again Christian, surely she was not the first inmate on death row to accept God into his or her life. This example hardly suggests that female ex-offenders have an easier time proving their reform, however. After all, Tucker was executed, despite the efforts of the Christian Right, in 1998.

Although a similar effort was made to locate desisting ex-offenders from ethnic minority groups, only 3 of the 65 persons interviewed in this research project identified themselves as Black, and only one of those interviews was included in the quantitative comparison. According to the 1991 census, less than one half of 1% of Merseyside residents identify themselves as "Black Caribbean," "Black African," or "Black Other" (I particularly like this last one, "the Black Other"). Moreover, minorities in the United Kingdom are notoriously underrepresented in voluntary reintegration programs (Awiah, Butt, & Dorn, 1992), through which I made several contacts. Additionally, when applied to a population as segregated as Liverpool, snowball sampling tends to produce highly segregated samples (e.g., Miller, 1998).

Hughes (1998) has done excellent research on the phenomenology of desistance in minority communities that largely corroborates and strengthens the key conclusions of the LDS. Among other generative factors, for instance, she found that desisting African American and Latino men are strongly motivated by "the development of a deep-seated respect and concern for children" (p. 146).

I purposely avoided oversampling individuals who were active members in any one particular therapeutic organization, like Alcoholics Anonymous or Phoenix House, which can provide their members with an overarching language of reform and somewhat prepackaged narratives and interpretations (Denzin, 1987). Still, unlike Biernacki's (1986) sample, many of the individuals in this study have received professional help from drug treatment counselors, probation groups, and the like and may therefore have adapted forms of "therapy speak."

In fact, almost half of the participants said at the time of the interview that they regularly saw some sort of counselor (usually a drug counselor, probation officer, or social worker) to work on their offending behavior or drug problems. The majority of this was described as "not real counseling":

> Er, yeah, I've got a drugs counselor. I don't get much counseling, though. All you do is go in and pick up your script [methadone prescription] and that's it. "How are you?" "I'm all right." That's it. They don't sit down and ask you nothing. (male, age 33)

> *Field note*: I ask K. [a rehabilitation client] why she "hates shrinks." She has no detailed explanation, except that those she knows are very "weird." She says she goes to a hospital once a month to get an "extra 20 quid [pounds] a week" on her dole check as a disability payment. She says when she is in the psychiatrist's office, she pretends to be "off her head" or paranoid, looking around the room or staring at the floor. She says she becomes so nervous about being "caught out" as a fake that she in fact does begin to shake, sweat, and behave in bizarre ways. "Loads of people do it," she assures me. At that moment, L. [another client] sits down to join us. K. asks her, "Do you see the shrink over at the hospital?" L. says that she does and illustrates her technique by beginning to shake as if uncontrollably with her head tilted toward her shoulder and her arm to her side. "'How are you today, L.?' 'Oh, I'm fine,'" she says, looking toward the ceiling. (7/22/97, field notes)

One potential source of bias in this sample may be the partial reliance on professional reintegration workers to recommend the "success stories" that they remembered among their former clients. As Lofland (1969) wrote,

> Deviants perceived by normals to have . . . high-value features [like intelligence, physical beauty, or unusual leadership ability] are more likely to be singled out, to be noticed, to be the objects of special recognition and treatment—to be, in short, more likely to have imputations of normality made upon them. They are, as a consequence more likely to be found among those ex-deviant normals who are paraded before the world as examples of successful "rehabilitation." (p. 222)

Certainly, the people "paraded" before me as success stories did seem to be, on average, slightly better looking and better spoken than those recommended to me for the persisting sample. Reintegration workers, like the rest of us, do not like to see "wasted potential," and one often hears phrases such as "The real shame of it is that he's a smart [or attractive or charming] kid." These helping professionals, therefore, may have largely introduced me to the people Schofield (1964) called YAVIS clients (young, attractive, verbal, intelligent, and successful). At least the AVI aspects may apply—I matched the samples on age, and of course, "success" was the discriminating trait I was seeking.

Nonetheless, self-presentation is not necessarily a permanent trait. Several desisting ex-offenders said, "You should have seen me 3 years ago," and 2 desisters actually showed me pictures of "past selves." In one photograph, a person who had struggled with alcoholism appeared to be 40 or more pounds heavier than he was at the time of the interview. In the other photograph, a former heroin user looked 20 or more pounds lighter, with gaunt eyes, a skeletal appearance, and nothing like the great skin and white teeth common among the so-called "heroin chic" fashion models. Indeed, part of the process of desisting might be finding enough value in one's self to maintain a presentable appearance. The ability to appear "respectable" and present oneself in a conventional manner, after all, is a consistent focus for rehabilitation and reintegration programs for ex-convicts.

The issue of IQ may be the more vexing problem. If indeed the desisting interviewees were significantly more intelligent than "average" offenders, and intelligence is indeed a stable trait of individuals (both big "ifs"), then this could provide an alternative explanation for the differences in the LDS narratives. Essentially, desisting persons may be more optimistic and see themselves as special or different, because, well, they are special and different, from other offenders anyhow. As I did not attempt to measure intelligence or IQ, this possibility cannot be dismissed. The samples are well-matched on other variables thought to be related to IQ, such as onset of delinquent behaviors. In addition, I asked all interviewees whether they "had trouble trying to read," "had difficulty paying attention in school," "enjoyed school," and whether they "got good grades while in school." There were no statistically significant differences between groups on any of these questions. The issue of IQ and criminality, of course, will not be settled with the LDS data set.

REFERENCES

Abraria, R. (1994, September 25). What ever happened to good old-fashioned shame? *Los Angeles Times*, p. E1.

Adams, K. (1997). Developmental aspects of adult crime. In T. P. Thornberry (Ed.), *Advances in criminological theory: Vol. 6. Developmental theories of crime and delinquency* (pp. 309–342). New Brunswick, NJ: Transaction.

Adler, P. (1993). *Wheeling and dealing: An ethnography of an upper-level drug dealing and smuggling community* (2nd ed.). New York: Columbia University Press.

Akers, R. L. (1985). *Deviant behavior: A social learning approach* (3rd ed.). Belmont, CA: Wadsworth.

Akerstrom, M. (1985). *Crooks and squares: Lifestyles of thieves and addicts in comparison to conventional people*. New Brunswick, NJ: Transaction.

Alcoholics Anonymous. (1939). *Alcoholics Anonymous: The story of how many thousands of men and women have recovered from alcoholism*. New York: Alcoholics Anonymous World Services.

Allen, F. A. (1981). *Decline of the rehabilitative ideal*. New Haven, CT: Yale University Press.

Alloy, L., & Abramson, L. (1979). Judgment of contingency in depressed and nondepressed students: Sadder but wiser? *Journal of Experimental Psychology: General, 108*, 441–485.

Alter, J. (1999, September 6). The buzz on drugs. *Newsweek*, pp. 25–28.

Amodeo, M., Kurtz, N., & Cutter, H. S. G. (1992). Abstinence, reasons for not drinking, and life satisfaction. *International Journal of the Addictions, 27*, 707–716.

Andrews, D. A., & Bonta, J. (1998). *The psychology of criminal conduct* (2nd ed.). Cincinnati, OH: Anderson.

Andrews, D. A., Bonta, J., & Hoge, R. D. (1990). Classification for effective rehabilitation: Rediscovering psychology. *Criminal Justice and Behavior, 176*, 19–52.

Augustine, St. (1968). *Confessions*. New York: Airmont.

Awiah, J., Butt, S., & Dorn, N. (1992). Race, gender and drug services. *ISDD Research Monograph, 6*.

Bandura, A. (1989). Human agency in social cognitive theory. *American Psychologist, 44*, 1175–1184.

Barnett, A., Blumstein, A., & Farrington, D. (1987). Probabilistic models of youthful criminal careers. *Criminology, 25*, 83–108.

Baskin, D. R., & Sommers, I. B. (1998). *Casualties of community disorder: Women's careers in violent crime*. Boulder, CO: Westview Press.

Bassin, A. (1984). Proverbs, slogans and folk sayings in the therapeutic community: A neglected therapeutic tool. *Journal of Psychoactive Drugs, 16*, 51–56.

Bateson, G. (1971). The cybernetics of "self": A theory of alcoholism. *Psychiatry, 34*, 1–18.

Baumeister, R. F. (1997). *Evil: Inside human violence and cruelty*. New York: Freeman.

Baumeister, R. F. (1991). *Escaping the self: Alcoholism, spirituality, masochism and other flights from the burden of selfhood*. New York: Basic Books.

Bazemore, G. (1998). Restorative justice and earned redemption: Communities, victims, and offender reintegration. *American Behavioral Scientist, 41*, 768–813.

Beck, A. (1979). *Cognitive therapy of depression*. New York: Guilford Press.

Beck, A. (2000). *Prisoners of hate: The cognitive basis of anger, hostility and violence*. New York: HarperCollins.

Beck, R. A., & Shipley, B. E. (1989). *Recidivism of federal prisoners released in 1983* (Bureau of Justice Statistics Special Report). Washington, DC: U.S. Department of Justice.

Becker, H. (1963). *Outsiders*. New York: Free Press.

Becker, H. (1964). Personal change in adult life. *Sociometry, 27*, 40–53.

Becker, H. (1966). Introduction. In C. Shaw, *The jack-roller* (pp. v–xvii). Chicago: University of Chicago Press.

Becker, H. (1998). *Tricks of the trade*. Chicago: University of Chicago Press.

Belenko, S. (1998). *Behind bars: Substance abuse and America's prison population*. New York: Columbia University, National Center on Addiction and Substance Abuse.

Bennett, J. (1981). *Oral history and delinquency*. Chicago: University of Chicago Press.

Bertaux, D. (Ed.). (1981). *Biography and society: The life-history approach in the social sciences*. Beverly Hills, CA: Sage.

Biernacki, P. (1986). *Pathways from heroin addiction: Recovery without treatment*. Philadelphia: Temple University Press.

Blackburn, R. (1998). *Psychology of criminal conduct*. New York: Wiley.

Blanton, H. (in press). Evaluating the self in the context of another: Assimilation and contrast effects in social comparison. In G. B. Moskowitz (Ed.), *The tenure of social cognition*. Mahwah, NJ: Erlbaum.

Blatier, C. (2000). Locus of control, causal attributions and self-esteem: A comparison between prisoners. *International Journal of Offender Therapy and Comparative Criminology, 44*, 97–110.

Blumstein, A., & Cohen, J. (1987). Characterizing criminal careers. *Science, 237*, 985–991.

Blumstein, A., Farrington, D. P., & Moitra, S. (1985). Delinquency careers: Innocents, desisters, and persisters. In M. Tonry & N. Morris (Eds.), *Crime and justice: An annual review of research* (Vol. 6, pp. 187–219). Chicago: University of Chicago Press.

Booth, M. B. (1903). *After prison—what?* New York: Fleming H. Revell.

Braithwaite, J. (1989). *Crime, shame and reintegration*. Cambridge, UK: Cambridge University Press.

Braithwaite, J., & Mugford, S. (1994). Conditions of successful reintegration ceremonies: Dealing with juvenile offenders. *British Journal of Criminology, 34*, 139–171.

Brickman, P., Coates, D., & Janoff-Bulman, R. (1978). Lottery winners and accident victims: Is happiness relative? *Journal of Personality and Social Psychology, 36*, 917–927.

Brickman, P., Rabinowitz, V. C., Karuza, J., Coates, D., Cohn, E., & Kidder, L. (1982). Models of helping and coping. *American Psychologist, 37*, 368–384.

Brown, J. D. (1991). The professional ex-: An alternative for exiting the deviant career. *Sociological Quarterly, 32*, 219–230.

Bruner, J. S. (1987). Life as narrative. *Social Research, 54*, 11–32.

Burgess, A. (1962). *A clockwork orange.* New York: Norton.

Burgess, A. (1988). Introduction: *A Clockwork Orange* resucked. In A. Burgess (Ed.), *A clockwork orange* (Rev. ed., pp. v–xi). New York: Ballantine Books.

Burnett, R. (1992). *The dynamics of recidivism: Summary report.* Oxford, UK: University of Oxford, Centre for Criminological Research.

Burnett, R. (1994). The odds of going straight: Offenders' own predictions. In *Sentencing, quality and risk: Proceedings of the 10th Annual Conference on Research and Information in the Probation Service* (pp. 47–74). Birmingham, UK: University of Loughborough, Midlands Probation Training Consortium.

Bush, J. (1995). Teaching self-risk management to violent offenders. In J. McGuire (Ed.), *What works: Reducing reoffending* (pp. 139–154). New York: Wiley.

Bushway, S., Piquero, A., Mazerolle, P., Broidy, L., & Cauffman, E. (2000). *A developmental framework for empirical research on desistance.* Unpublished manuscript.

Canter, D. V. (1994). *Criminal shadows.* London: HarperCollins.

Canter, D. V., Lundrigan, S., Maruna, S., Porter, L., & O'Keeffe, C. (1999). *Going straight: Transitions away from juvenile delinquency and implications for social reintegration policy* (Interim Report to the Joseph Rowntree Foundation). Liverpool, UK: University of Liverpool, Centre for Investigative Psychology.

Caspi, A. (1993). Why maladaptive behaviors persist: Sources of continuity and change across the life course. In D. C. Funder, R. R. Parke, C. Tomlinson-Keaser, & K. Widaman (Eds.), *Studying lives through time* (pp. 342–376). Washington, DC: American Psychological Association.

Caspi, A., & Moffitt, T. E. (1995). The continuity of maladaptive behavior: From description to understanding in the study of antisocial behavior. In D. Cicchetti & D. J. Cohen (Eds.), *Developmental psychopathology: Vol. 2. Risk, disorder and adaptation* (pp. 472–511). New York: Wiley.

Charland, R. (1985). *La resorption de la délinquence à l'adolescence* [The demise of delinquency in adolescence]. Unpublished doctoral dissertation, University of Montreal, Montreal, Quebec, Canada.

Chen, H. (1990). *Theory-driven evaluation*. Newbury Park, CA: Sage.

Chomsky, N. (1959). Review of verbal behavior by B. F. Skinner. *Language, 35,* 26–58.

Clarke, R. V., & Cornish, D. B. (1985). Modeling offenders' decisions: A framework for research and policy. In M. Tonry & N. Morris (Eds.), *Crime and justice: An annual review of research, Vol. 6* (pp. 147–185). Chicago: University of Chicago Press.

Clear, T. & Karp, D. (1999). *The community justice ideal*. Boulder, CO: West View Press.

Cline, H. F. (1980). Criminal behavior over the life span. In O. G. Brim & J. Kagan (Eds.), *Constancy and change in human development* (pp. 641–674). Cambridge, MA: Harvard University Press.

Cohen, S. (1985). *Visions of social control: Crime, punishment and classification*. Cambridge, UK: Polity Press.

Coles, R. (1989). *The call of stories*. Boston: Houghton Mifflin.

Conway, J. K. (1998). *When memory speaks*. New York: Knopf.

Conwell, C., & Sutherland, E. H. (1933). *The professional thief*. Chicago: University of Chicago.

Cooren, F. (2000). *The structuring property of communication*. Philadelphia: John Benjamins.

Cressey, D. R. (1955). Changing criminals: The application of the theory of differential association. *American Journal of Sociology, 61,* 116–120.

Cressey, D. R. (1963). Social psychological theory for using deviants to control deviation. In *Experiment in culture expansion: Proceedings of the conference on "The Use of Products of a Social Problem in Coping With the Problem* Norco, CA" (pp. 147–160). Washington, DC: National Institute of Mental Health.

Cressey, D. R. (1965). Social psychological foundations for using criminals in the rehabilitation of criminals. *Journal of Research in Crime and Delinquency, 2,* 49–59.

Crider, B. W., Byers, B., & Biggers, G. K. (1997, October). *Hate crimes against the Amish: A study of offender neutralization techniques*. Paper presented at the annual meeting of the Midwestern Criminal Justice Association, Cincinnati, OH.

Cullen, F., & Gilbert, K. E. (1982). *Reaffirming rehabilitation*. Cincinnati, OH: Anderson.

Cushman, P. (1990). Why the self is empty: Toward a historically situated psychology. *American Psychologist, 45,* 599–611.

Cusson, M., & Pinsonneault, P. (1986). The decision to give up crime. In D. B. Cornish & R. V. Clarke (Eds.), *The reasoning criminal* (pp. 72–82). New York: Springer-Verlag.

Dannefer, D. (1984). Adult development and social theory: A paradigmatic reappraisal. *American Sociological Review, 49,* 100–116.

de Charms, R. (1968). *Personal causation: The internal affective determinants of behavior*. New York: Academic Press.

Denzin, N. (1987). *The recovering alcoholic*. Newbury Park, CA: Sage.

Denzin, N. (1989). *Interpretive biography*. Newbury Park, CA: Sage.

DiClemente, C. C. (1994). If behaviors change, can personality be far behind? In T. F. Heatherton & J. L. Weinberger (Eds.), *Can personality change?* (pp. 175–198). Washington, DC: American Psychological Association.

Dodge, K. A. (1993). Social cognitive mechanisms in the development of conduct disorder and depression. *Annual Review of Psychology, 44*, 559–584.

Earls, F., Cairns, R. B., & Mercy, J. A. (1993). The control of violence and the prevention of nonviolence in adolescents. In S. G. Millstein, A. C. Petersen, & E. O. Nightingale (Eds.), *Promoting the health of adolescents: New directions for the 21st century* (pp. 285–304). New York: Oxford University Press.

Eaton, M. (1993). *Women after prison*. Buckingham, UK: Open University Press.

Elder, G. H., Jr. (1998). The life course and human development. In R. M. Lerner (Ed.), *Handbook of Child Psychology: Vol 1. Theoretical Models of Human Development*. New York: Wiley.

Eliason, S. L., & Dodder, R. A. (1999). Techniques of neutralization used by deer poachers in the western United States: A research note. *Deviant Behavior, 20*, 233–252.

Ellis, A., & McInerney, J. F. (1992). *Rational-emotive therapy with alcoholics and substance abusers*. New York: Pergamon.

Emmons, R. (1986). Personal strivings: An approach to personality and subjective well-being. *Journal of Personality and Social Psychology, 51*, 1058–1068.

Emmons, R. (1999). *The psychology of ultimate concerns*. New York: Guilford.

Epstein, S., & Erskine, N. (1983). The development of personal theories of reality from an interactional perspective. In D. Magnusson & V. L. Allen (Eds.), *Human development: An interactional perspective* (pp. 133–147). New York: Academic Press.

Erikson, E. (1968). *Identity: Youth and crisis*. New York: Norton.

Erikson, E. (1982). *The life cycle completed: A review*. New York: Norton.

Erikson, K. T. (1962). Notes on the sociology of deviance. *Social Problems, 9*, 307–314.

Evans, R. (1967). *Dialogue with Erik Erikson*. New York: Harper & Row.

Eysenck, H. (1989). Personality and criminality: A dispositional analysis. In W. S. Laufer & F. Adler (Eds.), *Advances in criminological theory* (Vol. 1, pp. 89–110). New Brunswick, NJ: Transaction.

Faller, L. B. (1987). *Turned to account: The forms and functions of criminal biography in late seventeenth- and early eighteenth-century England*. Cambridge, UK: Cambridge University Press.

Farrall, S., & Bowling, B. (1999). Structuration, human development and desistance from crime. *British Journal of Criminology, 39*, 253–268.

Farrington, D. P. (1986). Age and crime. In N. Morris & M. Tonry (Eds.), *Crime and justice* (Vol. 7, pp. 189–250). Chicago: Chicago University Press.

Farrington, D. P. (1991). Childhood aggression and adult violence: Early precursors and later life outcomes. In D. J. Pepler & K. H. Rubin (Eds.), *The development and treatment of childhood aggression* (pp. 5–29). Hillsdale, NJ: Erlbaum.

Farrington, D. P. (1992). Explaining the beginning, progress, and ending of antisocial behavior from birth to adulthood. In J. McCord (Ed.), *Advances in criminological theory: Vol. 3. Facts, frameworks, and forecasts* (pp. 253–286). New Brunswick, NJ: Transaction.

Farrington, D. P., Gallagher, B., Morley, L., St. Ledger, R. J., & West, D. J. (1986). Unemployment, school leaving and crime. *British Journal of Criminology, 26,* 335–356.

Farrington, D. P., & Hawkins, J. D. (1991). Predicting participation, early onset and later persistence in officially recorded offending. *Criminal Behavior and Mental Health, 1,* 1–33.

Farrington, D. P., & West, D. J. (1995). Effects of marriage, separation and children on offending by adult males. In Z. S. Blau & J. Hagan (Eds.), *Current perspectives on aging and the life cycle: Vol. 4. Delinquency and disrepute in the life course* (pp. 249–281). Greenwich, CT: JAI Press.

Feeley, M. M., & Simon, J. (1992). The new penology: Notes on the emerging strategy of corrections and its implications. *Criminology, 30,* 449–474.

Felson, R. B. (1985). Reflected appraisals and the development of the self. *Social Psychology Quarterly, 48,* 71–77.

Felson, R. B., & Ribner, S. A. (1981). An attributional approach to accounts and sanctions for criminal violence. *Social Psychology Quarterly, 44,* 137–142.

Felson, R. B., & Tedeschi, J. T. (Eds.). (1993). *Aggression and violence: Social interactionist perspectives.* Washington, DC: American Psychological Association.

Festinger, L., Pepitone, A., & Newcomb, T. (1952). Some consequences of deindividuation in a group. *Journal of Abnormal and Social Psychology, 47,* 382–389.

Finestone, H. (1976). *Victims of change: Juvenile delinquents in American society.* Westport, CT: Greenwood Press.

Fleiss, J. L. (1981). *Statistical methods for rates and proportions.* New York: Wiley.

Fogel, D. (1975). *". . . We are the living proof . . .": The justice model for corrections.* Cincinnati, OH: Anderson.

Foote, C. E., & Frank, A. W. (1999). Foucault and therapy: The disciplining of grief. In A. S. Chambon, A. Irving, & L. Epstein (Eds.), *Reading Foucault for social work* (pp. 157–187). New York: Columbia University Press.

Foote, J., Seligman, M., Magura, S., Handelsman, L., Rosenblum, A., Lovejoy, M., Arrington, K., & Stimmel, B. (1994). An enhanced positive reinforcement model for the severely impaired cocaine abuser. *Journal of Substance Abuse Treatment, 11,* 525–539.

Foucault, M. (1988a). The dangerous individual. In L. D. Kritzman (Ed.), *Michel*

Foucault: Politics, philosophy, culture—Interviews and other writings, 1977–1984 (pp. 125–151). New York: Routledge.

Foucault, M. (1988b). The ethic of care for the self as a practice of freedom. In J. Bernauer & D. Rasmussen (Eds.), *The final Foucault* (pp. 1–20). Cambridge, MA: MIT Press.

Foucault, M. (1988c). Technologies of the self. In L. H. Martin, H. Gutman, & P. H. Hutton (Eds.), *Technologies of the self* (pp. 16–49). Amherst: University of Massachusetts Press.

Fox, K. (1999a). Changing violent minds: Discursive correction and resistance in the cognitive treatment of offenders in treatment. *Social Problems, 46,* 88–103.

Fox, K. (1999b). Reproducing criminal types: Cognitive treatment for violent offenders in prison. *Sociological Quarterly, 40,* 435–453.

Frankl, V. E. (1984). *Man's search for meaning.* New York: Washington Square Press.

Frazier, C. E. (1976). *Theoretical approaches to deviance.* Columbus, OH: Charles Merrill.

Galaway, B., & Hudson, J. (Eds.). (1996). *Restorative justice: International perspectives.* Monsey, NY: Criminal Justice Press.

Garfinkel, H. (1956). Conditions of successful degradation ceremonies. *American Journal of Sociology, 61,* 420–424.

Garland, D. (1997a). "Governmentality" and the problem of crime: Foucault, criminology, sociology. *Theoretical Criminology, 1,* 173–214.

Garland, D. (1997b). Probation and the reconfiguration of crime control. In R. Burnett (Ed.), *The probation service: Responding to change* (pp. 2–10). Oxford, UK: University of Oxford, Centre for Criminological Research.

Gendreau, P. (1996). Offender rehabilitation: What we know and what needs to be done. *Criminal Justice and Behavior, 23,* 144–161.

Gendreau, P., & Ross, R. (1979). Effective correctional treatment: Bibliotherapy for cynics. *Crime and Delinquency, 25,* 463–489.

Gibbens, T. C. (1984). Borstal boys after 25 years. *British Journal of Criminology, 24,* 46–59.

Giddens, A. (1991). *Modernity and self-identity: Self and society in the late modern age.* Stanford, CA: Stanford University Press.

Glaser, D. (1964). *Effectiveness of a prison and parole system.* Indianapolis, IN: Bobbs-Merrill.

Glaser, D. (1978). *Crime in our changing society.* New York: Holt, Rinehart & Winston.

Glueck, S., & Glueck, E. (1940). *Juvenile delinquents grown up.* New York: Commonwealth Fund.

Glueck, S., & Glueck, E. (1945). *After-conduct of discharged offenders.* London: MacMillan.

Glueck, S., & Glueck, E. (1966). *Later criminal careers.* New York: Kraus. (Original work published 1937)

Goffman, E. (1959). *The presentation of self in everyday life*. Garden City, NJ: Doubleday-Anchor Books.

Goffman, E. (1961). *Asylums: Essays on the social situation of mental patients and other inmates*. Garden City, NY: Anchor Books.

Goffman, E. (1963). *Stigma: On the management of spoiled identity*. Englewood Cliffs, NJ: Prentice Hall.

Goring, C. (1919). *The English convict*. London: His Majesty's Stationary Office.

Gorringe, T. (1996). *God's just vengeance*. Cambridge, UK: Cambridge University Press.

Gottfredson, M., & Hirschi, T. (1986). The true value of lambda would appear to be zero: An essay on career criminals, criminal careers, selective incapacitation, cohort studies and related topics. *Criminology, 24*, 213–234.

Gottfredson, M., & Hirschi, T. (1990). *A general theory of crime*. Stanford, CA: Stanford University Press.

Gottfredson, M., & Hirschi, T. (1995). National crime control policies. *Society, 32*, 30–36.

Gove, W. (1985). The effect of age and gender on deviant behavior: A biopsychosocial perspective. In A. S. Rossi (Ed.), *Gender and the life course* (pp. 115–144). New York: Aldine.

Graham, J., & Bowling, B. (1995). *Young people and crime*. London: Home Office.

Grant, J. D., & Grant, M. Q. (1959). A group dynamics approach to the treatment of nonconformists in the Navy. *Annals of the American Academy of Political and Social Science, 322*, 126–135.

Green, L. L., Thompson, M., & Fullilove, R. E. (1998). Stories of spiritual awakening: The nature of spirituality in recovery. *Journal of Substance Abuse Treatment, 15*, 325–331.

Greenberg, D. F. (1981). Delinquency and the age structure of society. In S. L. Messinger & E. Bittner (Eds.), *Criminology review yearbook* (pp. 586–620). Beverly Hills, CA: Sage.

Greenberg, D. F. (1994). The historical variability of the age–crime relationship. *Journal of Quantitative Criminology, 10*, 361–373.

Greenwood, P. (1983). Controlling the crime rate through imprisonment. In J. Q. Wilson (Ed.), *Crime and public policy* (pp. 251–269). San Francisco: Institute for Contemporary Studies.

Greimas, A. J. (1990). *The social science: A semiotic view*. Minneapolis: University of Minnesota Press.

Groves, W. B., & Lynch, M. J. (1990). Reconciling structural and subjective approaches to the study of crime. *Journal of Research in Crime and Delinquency, 27*, 348–375.

Hagan, J. (1998). Subterranean sources of subcultural delinquency beyond the American dream. *Criminology, 36*, 309–341.

Haley, J. O. (1996). Crime prevention through restorative justice: Lessons from

Japan. In B. Galaway & J. Hudson (Eds.), *Restorative justice: International perspectives* (pp. 349–371). Monsey, NY: Criminal Justice Press.

Hamm, M. S. (1997). The offender self-help movement as correctional treatment. In P. Van Voorhis, M. Braswell, & D. Lester (Eds.), *Correctional counseling and rehabilitation* (4th ed., pp. 241–253). Cincinnati, OH: Anderson.

Hankiss, A. (1981). On the mythological rearranging of one's life history. In D. Bertaux (Ed.), *Biography and society: The life history approach in the social sciences* (pp. 203–209). Beverly Hills, CA: Sage.

Hanninen, V., & Koski-Jannes, A. (1999). Narratives of recovery from addictive behaviours. *Addiction, 94,* 1837–1848.

Harvey, J. H., Weber, A. L., & Orbuch, T. L. (1990). *Interpersonal accounts: A social psychological perspective.* Oxford, UK: Blackwell.

Hegell, A., Newburn, T., & Rowlingson, K. (1995). *Financial difficulties on release from prison.* London: Policy Studies Institute.

Henry, O. (1953). A retrieved reformation. In *The complete works of O. Henry.* Garden City, NJ: Doubleday.

Henry, S. (1994). Newsmaking criminology as replacement discourse. In G. Barak (Ed.), *Media, process and the social construction of crime: Studies in newsmaking criminology* (pp. 287–318). New York: Garland Press.

Henry, S., & Milovanovic, D. (1996). *Constitutive criminology.* Thousand Oaks, CA: Sage.

Hindelang, M. J. (1970). The commitment of delinquents to their misdeeds: Do delinquents drift? *Social Problems, 17,* 502–509.

Hirschi, T. (1969). *Causes of delinquency.* Berkeley: University of California Press.

Hirschi, T., & Gottfredson, M. (1983). Age and the explanation of crime. *American Journal of Sociology, 89,* 553–584.

Hirschi, T., & Gottfredson, M. (1994). *The generality of deviance.* New Brunswick, NJ: Transaction.

Hirschi, T., & Gottfredson, M. (1995). Control theory and the life-course perspective. *Studies on Crime and Crime Prevention, 4,* 131–142.

Hollin, C. R. (1989). *Psychology and crime.* London: Routledge.

Hoffman, P. B., & Meierhoefer, B. (1979). Post-release experiences of federal prisoners: A six-year follow-up. *Journal of Criminal Justice, 7,* 193–216.

Horney, J., Osgood, D. W., & Marshall, I. H. (1995). Criminal careers in the short-term: Intra-individual variability in crime and its relation to local life circumstances. *American Sociological Review, 60,* 655–673.

Hser, Y.-I., Anglin, M. D., Grella, C., Longshore, D., & Prendergast, M. L. (1997). Drug treatment careers: A conceptual framework and existing research findings. *Journal of Substance Abuse Treatment, 14,* 543–558.

Hughes, M. (1998). Turning points in the lives of young, inner-city men forgoing destructive criminal behaviors: A qualitative study. *Social Work Research, 22,* 143–151.

Ignatieff, M. (1983). State, civil society and total institutions: A critique of recent social histories of punishment. In S. Cohen & A. Scull (Eds.), *Social control and the state* (pp. 75–105). New York: St. Martin's Press.

Irwin, J. (1970). *The felon.* Englewood Cliffs, NJ: Prentice Hall.

Irwin, J. (1980). *Prisons in turmoil.* Boston: Little, Brown.

Irwin, J. (1985, November). *The return of the bogeyman.* Keynote lecture at the meeting of the American Society of Criminology, San Diego, CA.

Irwin, J., & Austin, J. (1994). *It's about time: America's imprisonment binge.* New York: Oxford University Press.

John, O. P., Donahue, E. M., & Kentle, R. L. (1991). *The big five inventory: Versions 4a and 54.* Berkeley: University of California, Institute of Personality and Social Research.

Johnson, R., & Toch, H. (Eds.). (2000). *Crime and punishment: Inside views.* Los Angeles: Roxbury.

Jolin, A. (1985). *Growing old and going straight: Examining the role of age in criminal career termination.* Unpublished doctoral dissertation, Portland State University.

Josselson, R., & Lieblich, A. (Eds.). (1993). *The narrative study of lives: Vol. 1.* Thousand Oaks, CA: Sage.

Kaden, J. (1999). Therapy for convicted sex offenders: Pursuing rehabilitation without incrimination. *Journal of Criminal Law and Criminology, 89,* 347–391.

Kasser, T., & Ryan, R. M. (1993). A dark side of the American dream: Correlates of financial success as a central life aspiration. *Journal of Personality and Social Psychology, 65,* 410–422.

Katz, J. (1988). *Seductions of crime: The moral and sensual attractions of doing evil.* New York: Basic Books.

Kellogg, S. (1993). Identity and recovery. *Psychotherapy, 30,* 235–244.

Kershaw, C. (1997, March). Reconvictions of those commencing community penalties in 1993, England and Wales. *Home Office Statistical Bulletin, 6/97,* 1–27.

Kershaw, C., & Renshaw, G. (1997, March). Reconvictions of prisoners discharged from prison in 1993, England and Wales. *Home Office Statistical Bulletin, 5/97,* 1–23.

Khantzian, E., Halliday, K., & McAuliffe, W. (1990). *Addiction and the vulnerable self.* New York: Guilford.

Kierkegaard, S. (1941). *The sickness unto death* (W. Lowrie, Trans.). Princeton, NJ: Princeton University Press. (Original work published 1843)

Kornhauser, R. (1978). *Social sources of delinquency.* Chicago: University of Chicago Press.

Knupfer, G. (1972). Ex-problem drinkers. In M. Roff, L. Robins, & H. Pollack (Eds.), *Life history research in psychopathology* (Vol. 2, pp. 256–280). Minneapolis: University of Minnesota Press.

Larson, R. W. (2000). Toward a psychology of positive youth development. *American Psychologist, 55,* 170–183.

Laub, J. H., Nagin, D. S., & Sampson, R. J. (1998). Trajectories of change in criminal offending: Good marriages and the desistance process. *American Sociological Review, 63,* 225–238.

Laub, J. H., & Sampson, R. J. (1993). Turning points in the life course: Why change matters to the study of crime. *Criminology, 31,* 301–325.

Laub, J. H., & Sampson, R. J. (2000). *Understanding desistance from crime.* Unpublished manuscript.

Leary, T. (1962). How to change behavior. In G. S. Nielson (Ed.), *Proceedings of the XIV International Congress of Applied Psychology: Vol. 4. Clinical psychology* (pp. 50–68). Copenhagen: Munksgaard.

LeBlanc, M., & Loeber, R. (1998). Developmental criminology updated. In M. Tonry & M. H. Moore (Eds.), *Youth violence* (pp. 115–197). Chicago: University of Chicago Press.

Leibrich, J. (1993). *Straight to the point: Angles on giving up crime.* Otago, New Zealand: University of Otago Press.

Leibrich, J. (1996). The role of shame in going straight: A study of former offenders. In B. Galaway & J. Hudson (Eds.), *Restorative justice: International perspectives* (pp. 283–302). Monsey, NY: Criminal Justice Press.

Lewis, D. A. (1990). From programs to lives: A comment. *American Journal of Community Psychology, 18,* 923–926.

Lewis, H. B. (1971). *Shame and guilt in neurosis.* New York: International Universities Press.

Lindesmith, A. R. (1968). *Opiate addiction.* Chicago: Aldine. (Original work published 1947)

Loeber, R., & LeBlanc, M. (1990). Toward a developmental criminology. In M. Tonry & N. Morris (Eds.), *Crime and justice* (Vol. 12, pp. 375–437). Chicago: University of Chicago Press.

Loeber, R., Stouthamer-Loeber, M., Van Kammen, W., & Farrington, D. (1991). Initiation, escalation and desistance in juvenile offending and their correlates. *Journal of Criminal Law and Criminology, 82,* 36–82.

Lofland, J. (1969). *Deviance and identity.* Englewood Cliffs, NJ: Prentice Hall.

Lombroso, C. (1911). *Crime: Its causes and remedies.* Boston: Little, Brown.

Lovejoy, M., Rosenblum, A., Magura, S., Foote, J., Handelsman, L., & Stimmel, B. (1995). Patient's perspective on the process of change in substance abuse treatment. *Journal of Substance Abuse Treatment, 12,* 269–282.

Luckenbill, D. F., & Best, J. (1981). Careers in deviance and respectability: The analogy's limitations. *Social Problems, 29,* 197–206.

Marlatt, G. A., & Gordon, J. R. (Eds.). (1985). *Relapse prevention: Maintenance strategies in the treatment of addictive behaviors.* New York: Guilford Press.

Martinson, R. (1974). What works? Questions and answers about prison reform. *The Public Interest, 35,* 22–56.

Maruna, S. (1997). Going straight: Desistance from crime and self-narratives of reform. *Narrative Study of Lives, 5,* 59–93.

Maruna, S. (1998). *Redeeming one's self: How reformed ex-offenders make sense of their lives*. Unpublished doctoral dissertation, Northwestern University.

Maruna, S., Naples, M., & LeBel, T. (1999, November). *Beyond "what works": Opening the "black box" in research on offender rehabilitation*. Paper presented at the American Society of Criminology conference, Toronto, Ontario, Canada.

Massaro, T. M. (1997). The meanings of shame: Implications for legal reform. *Psychology, Public Policy and Law, 3*, 645–704.

Matsueda, R. L., & Heimer, K. (1997). A symbolic interactionist theory of role-transitions, role-commitments, and delinquency. In T. P. Thornberry (Ed.), *Advances in criminological theory: Vol. 6. Developmental theories of crime and delinquency* (pp. 163–214). New Brunswick, NJ: Transaction.

Matza, D. (1964). *Delinquency and drift*. New York: Wiley.

Matza, D. (1969). *Becoming deviant*. Englewood Cliffs, NJ: Prentice Hall.

Matza, D., & Sykes, G. (1961). Juvenile delinquency and subterranean values. *American Sociological Review, 26*, 712–719.

McAdams, D. P. (1985). *Power, intimacy and the life story: Personological inquiries into identity*. New York: Guilford Press.

McAdams, D. P. (1992). *Coding autobiographical episodes for themes of agency and communion* (3rd ed., Rev.). Evanston, IL: Foley Center for the Study of Lives, Northwestern University.

McAdams, D. P. (1993). *The stories we live by: Personal myths and the making of the self*. New York: William Morrow.

McAdams, D. P. (1994a). Can personality change? Levels of stability and growth in personality across the life span. In T. F. Heatherton & J. L. Weinberger (Eds.), *Can personality change?* (pp. 299–313). Washington, DC: American Psychological Association.

McAdams, D. P. (1994b). A psychology of the stranger. *Psychological Inquiry, 5*, 145–148.

McAdams, D. P., & de St. Aubin, E. (1998). Introduction. In D. P. McAdams & E. de St. Aubin (Eds.), *Generativity and adult development: How and why we care for the next generation* (pp. xix–xxiv). Washington, DC: American Psychological Association.

McAdams, D. P., Diamond, A., de St. Aubin, E., & Mansfield, E. D. (1997). Stories of commitment: The psychosocial construction of generative lives. *Journal of Personality and Social Psychology, 72*, 678–694.

McAdams, D. P., Hart, H., & Maruna, S. (1998). The anatomy of generativity. In D. P. McAdams & E. de St. Aubin (Eds.), *Generativity and adult development* (pp. 7–43). Washington, DC: American Psychological Association.

McArthur, A. V. (1974). *Coming out cold: Community reentry from a state reformatory*. Lexington, MA: Lexington Books.

McCord, J. (1980). Patterns of deviance. In S. B. Sells, R. Crandall, M. Roff, J. S. Strauss, & W. Pollin (Eds.), *Human functioning in longitudinal perspective* (pp. 157–165). Baltimore: Williams & Wilkins.

McCorkle, J., Harrison, L. D., & Inciardi, J. A. (1998). How treatment is constructed among graduates and dropouts in a prison therapeutic community for women. *Journal of Offender Rehabilitation, 27,* 37–59.

McCrae, R. R., & Costa, P. T., Jr. (1987). Validation of the five-factor model of personality across instruments and observers. *Journal of Personality and Social Psychology, 52,* 81–90.

McGuire, J. (Ed.). (1995). *What works: Reducing reoffending.* New York: Wiley.

McIvor, G. (1992). *Sentenced to serve: The operation and impact of community service by offenders.* Aldershot, UK: Avebury.

Meisenhelder, T. (1977). An exploratory study of exiting from criminal careers. *Criminology, 15,* 319–334.

Meisenhelder, T. (1982). Becoming normal: Certification as a stage in exiting from crime. *Deviant Behavior: An Interdisciplinary Journal, 3,* 137–153.

Miller, J. (1998). Up it up: Gender and the accomplishment of street robbery. *Criminology, 36,* 37–66.

Mischkowitz, R. (1994). Desistance from a delinquent way of life? In E. G. M. Weitekamp & H. J. Kerner (Eds.), *Cross-national longitudinal research on human development and criminal behavior* (pp. 303–327). London: Kluwer Academic.

Moffitt, T. E. (1993). Adolescence-limited and life-course-persistent antisocial behavior: A developmental taxonomy. *Psychological Review, 100,* 674–701.

Monk, G., Winslade, J., Crocket, K., & Epston, D. (1996). *Narrative therapy in practice: The archaeology of hope.* San Francisco: Jossey-Bass.

Murray, H. A. (1943). *Thematic Apperception Test manual.* Cambridge, MA: Harvard University Press.

Nagin, D., Farrington, D. F., & Moffitt, T. (1995). Life-course trajectories of different types of offenders. *Criminology, 33,* 111–139.

Neitz, M. J. (1990). Studying religion in the eighties. In H. S. Becker & M. M. McCall (Eds.), *Symbolic interaction and cultural studies* (pp. 90–118). Chicago: University of Chicago Press.

Nelson, W. A. (1996). The new inquisition: State compulsion of therapeutic confessions. *Vermont Law Review, 20,* 951–980.

Neugarten, B. L., & Hagestad, G. O. (1976). Age and the life course. In R. H. Binstock & E. Shanas (Eds.), *Handbook of aging and the social sciences* (pp. 35–55). New York: Van Norstrand Reinhold.

Newman, G. (1975). A theory of deviance removal. *British Journal of Sociology, 26,* 203–217.

Niedenthal, P. M., Tangney, J. P., & Gavanski, I. (1994). "If only I weren't" versus "If only I hadn't": Distinguishing shame and guilt in counterfactual thinking. *Journal of Personality and Social Psychology, 67,* 585–595.

Nirel, R., Landau, S. F., Sebba, L., & Sagiv, B. (1997). The effectiveness of service work: An analysis of recidivism. *Journal of Quantitative Criminology, 13,* 73–92.

Northey, W. F. (1999). The politics of denial: A postmodern critique. *Offender Programs Report, 3,* 17–18, 30–32.

Nouwen, H. (1972). *The wounded healer.* New York: Doubleday.

Office of Population Censuses and Surveys. (1992). *1991 census.* London: Her Majesty's Stationery Office.

O'Reilly, E. B. (1997). *Sobering tales: Narratives of alcoholism and recovery.* Amherst: University of Massachusetts Press.

Osborn, S. G., & West, D. J. (1978). Do young delinquents really reform? *Journal of Adolescence, 3,* 99–114.

Palmer, T. (1965). Types of treaters and types of juvenile offenders. *Youth Authority Quarterly, 18,* 14–23.

Palmer, T. (1994). *A profile of correctional effectiveness and new directions for research.* Albany: State University of New York Press.

Parker, H. (1974). *View from the boys.* North Pomfret, VT: David & Charles.

Parker, H., & Kirby, P. (1996). *Methadone maintenance and crime reduction on Merseyside.* London: Police Research Group, Home Office.

Parker, H., & Newcombe, R. (1987). Heroin use and acquisitive crime in an English community. *British Journal of Sociology, 38,* 331–350.

Parry, A., & Doan, R. E. (1994). *Story revisions: Narrative therapy in the postmodern world.* New York: Guilford Press.

Patterson, G. R. (1993). Orderly change in a stable world: The antisocial trait as chimera. *Journal of Consulting and Clinical Psychology, 61,* 911–919.

Pawson, R., & Tilley, N. (1997). *Realistic evaluation.* London: Sage.

Pearson, G. (1987). *The new heroin users.* Oxford, UK: Blackwell.

Peele, S., & Brodsky, A. (1991). *The truth about addiction and recovery.* New York: Simon & Schuster.

Petrunik, M., & Shearing, C. D. (1988). The "I," the "me," and the "it": Moving beyond the Meadian conception of self. *Canadian Journal of Sociology, 13,* 435–448.

Pickles, A., & Rutter, M. (1991). Statistical and conceptual models of "turning points" in developmental processes. In D. Magnusson, L. Bergman, G. Rudinger, & B. Torestad (Eds.), *Problems and methods in longitudinal research: Stability and change* (pp. 110–136). New York: Cambridge University Press.

Popham, P. (1996, April 23). Gunfire across the Mersey: The shooting of seven people in five days has earned Liverpool the tag of Gun City, UK. *The Independent,* p. 1.

Prochaska, J. O., & DiClemente, C. C. (1992). Stages of change in the modification of problem behavior. In M. Hersen, R. Eisler, & P. M. Miller (Eds.), *Progress in behavior modification* (Vol. 28, pp. 184–214). Sycamore, IL: Sycamore.

Prochaska, J. O., DiClemente, C. C., & Norcross, J. C. (1992). In search of how people change: Applications to addictive behaviors. *American Psychologist, 47,* 1102–1114.

Quetelet, A. (1984). *Research on the propensity to crime of different ages* (S. F. Sylvestor, Trans.). Cincinnati, OH: Anderson. (Original work published 1833)

Rafter, N. H. (1997). *Creating born criminals*. Urbana: University of Illinois Press.

Ragin, C. C. (1994). *Constructing social research*. Thousand Oaks, CA: Pine Forge.

Rand, A. (1987). Transitional life events and desistance from delinquency and crime. In M. Wolfgang, T. P. Thornberry, & R. M. Figlio (Eds.), *From boy to man: From delinquency to crime* (pp. 134–162). Chicago: University of Chicago Press.

Reno, J. (2000). *Reentry court initiative*. Paper presented at John Jay College of Criminal Justice, New York, February 10.

Rex, S. (1999). Desistance from offending: Experiences of probation. *The Howard Journal of Criminal Justice, 38*, 366–383.

Rice, L., & Greenberg, L. (1984). *Patterns of change: Intensive analysis of psychotherapy process*. New York: Guilford.

Richardson, J. T. (1985). Paradigm conflict in conversion research. *Journal for the Scientific Study of Religion, 24*, 163–179.

Ronel, N. (1998). Narcotics anonymous: Understanding the "bridge of recovery." *Journal of Offender Rehabilitation, 27*, 179–197.

Rose, N. (1996). *Inventing our selves: Psychology, power and personhood*. Cambridge, UK: Cambridge University Press.

Ross, R. R., & Fabiano, E. A. (1983). *The cognitive model of crime and delinquency prevention and rehabilitation: Vol. 2. Intervention techniques*. Ottawa, Ontario, Canada: Ministry of Correctional Services.

Ross, R. R., & Ross, R. D. (1995). *Thinking straight: The reasoning and rehabilitation program for delinquency prevention and offender rehabilitation*. Ottawa, Ontario, Canada: Air Training.

Rotenberg, M. (1978). *Damnation and deviance: The Protestant ethic and the spirit of failure*. New York: Free Press.

Rotenberg, M. (1987). *Re-biographing and deviance: Psychotherapeutic narrativism and the midrash*. London: Praeger.

Rubin, L. B. (1976). *Worlds of pain: Life in the working-class family*. New York: Basic Books.

Rutherford, A. (1992). *Growing out of crime: The new era*. Winchester, UK: Waterside Press.

Rutter, M. (1989). Age as an ambiguous variable in developmental research; some epidemiological considerations from developmental psychopathology. *International Journal of Behavioral Development, 12*, 1–34.

Rutter, M. (1996). Transitions and turning points in developmental psychopathology: As applied to the age span between childhood and mid-adulthood. *Journal of Behavioral Development, 19*, 603–626.

Rutter, M., Quinton, D., & Hill, J. (1990). Adult outcome of institution-reared children: Males and females compared. In L. N. Robins & M. R. Rutter (Eds.),

Straight and devious pathways to adulthood (pp. 134–157). New York: Cambridge University Press.

Sagarin, E. (1975). The tyranny of isness. In E. Sagarin (Ed.), *Deviants and deviance: An introduction to the study of disvalued people and behavior* (pp. 144–154). New York: Praeger-Holt.

Sagarin, E. (1990). Deviance without deviants: The temporal quality of patterned behavior. In C. D. Bryant (Ed.), *Deviant behavior: Readings in the sociology of norm violations* (pp. 799–809). New York: Hemisphere.

Samenow, S. (1984). *Inside the criminal mind.* New York: Times Books.

Sampson, R. J., & Laub, J. (1992). Crime and deviance in the life course. *Annual Review of Sociology, 18,* 63–84.

Sampson, R. J., & Laub, J. (1993). *Crime in the making: Pathways and turning points through life.* Cambridge, MA: Harvard University Press.

Sampson, R. J., & Laub, J. (1995). Understanding variability in lives through time: Contributions of life-course criminology. *Studies on Crime and Crime Prevention, 4,* 143–158.

Sands, B. (1964). *My shadow ran fast.* Englewoood Cliffs, NJ: Prentice Hall.

Sapolsky, R. (1997). Testosterone rules. *Discover, 18*(3), 44–50.

Sarbin, T. (1986). The narrative as a root metaphor for psychology. In T. Sarbin (Ed.), *Narrative psychology: The storied nature of human conduct* (pp. 3–21). New York: Praeger.

Schaal, B., Tremblay, R. E., & Soussignan, R. (1996). Male testosterone linked to high social dominance but low physical aggression in early adolescence. *Journal of the American Academy of Child and Adolescent Psychiatry, 35,* 1322–1330.

Schofield, W. (1964). *Psychotherapy: The purchase of friendship.* Englewood Cliffs, NJ: Prentice Hall.

Schonbach, P. (1990). *Account episodes: The management or escalation of conflict.* Cambridge, UK: Cambridge University Press.

Schor, J. (1998). *The overspent American.* New York: Basic Books.

Scott, E. M. (1998). *Within the hearts and minds of prisoners: An in-depth view of prisoners in therapy.* Springfield, IL: Charles C Thomas.

Scott, M. B., & Lyman, S. M. (1968). Accounts. *American Sociological Review, 33,* 46–62.

Sealy, A., & Banks, C. (1971). Social maturity, training, experience and recidivism amongst British Borstal Boys. *British Journal of Criminology, 11,* 245–264.

Seligman, M. E. P. (1991). *Learned optimism.* New York: Knopf.

Seligman, M. E. P. (1993). *What you can change . . . and what you can't.* New York: Fawcett Columbine.

Shaw, C. (1929). *Delinquency areas.* Chicago: University of Chicago Press.

Shaw, C. (1930). *The jack-roller: A delinquent boy's own story.* Chicago: University of Chicago Press.

Shoham, S. G., & Seis, M. (1993). *A primer in the psychology of crime*. Guilderland, NY: Harrow & Heston.

Shover, N. (1983). The later stages of ordinary property offender careers. *Social Problems, 31,* 208–218.

Shover, N. (1985). *Aging criminals*. Beverly Hills, CA: Sage.

Shover, N. (1996). *Great pretenders: Pursuits and careers of persistent thieves*. Boulder, CO: Westview Press.

Shover, N., & Thompson, C. (1992). Age, differential expectations, and crime desistance. *Criminology, 30,* 89–104.

Simon, J. (1993). *Poor discipline*. Chicago: University of Chicago.

Singer, J. A. (1997). *Message in a bottle: Stories of men and addiction*. New York: Free Press.

Singer, J. A., & Salovey, P. (1993). *The remembered self: Emotion and memory in personality*. New York: Free Press.

Smith, C. P. (1992). Inferences from verbal material. In C. P. Smith (Ed.), *Motivation and personality: Handbook of theoretic content analysis*. Cambridge, MA: Cambridge University Press.

Solzhenitsyn, A. I. (1974). *The gulag archipelago, 1918–1956* (T. P. Whitney, Trans.). New York: Harper & Row.

Sommers, I., Baskin, D., & Fagan, J. (1994). Getting out of the life: Crime desistance by female street offenders. *Deviant Behavior, 15,* 125–149.

Steffensmeier, D. J., Allan, E. A., Harer, M. D., & Streifel, C. (1989). Age and the distribution of crime. *American Journal of Sociology, 94,* 803–831.

Stephens, R. C. (1991). *The street addict role*. Albany, NY: State University of New York Press.

Stewart, A. J., Franz, C., & Layton, L. (1988). The changing self: Using personal documents to study lives. *Journal of Personality, 56,* 41–74.

Sullivan, M. (1989). *Getting paid: Youth crime and work in the inner city*. Ithaca, NY: Cornell University Press.

Sullivan, M. (1996). Developmental transitions in poor youth: Delinquency and crime. In J. A. Graber, J. Brooks-Gunn, & A. C. Petersen (Eds.), *Transitions in adolescence* (pp. 141–164). Mahwah, NJ: Erlbaum.

Sutherland, E., & Cressey, D. (1978). *Criminology* (10th ed.). New York: Lippincott.

Sykes, G. M., & Matza, D. (1957). Techniques of neutralization: A theory of delinquency. *American Sociological Review, 22,* 664–673.

Talucci, V., & Solomon, A. (2000, January). From cell blocks to neighborhood blocks: Revisiting reentry. *American Probation and Parole Association Perspectives,* pp. 11–13.

Taylor, S. E. (1983). Adjustment to threatening events: A theory of cognitive adaptation. *American Psychologist, 38,* 1161–1173.

Taylor, S. E. (1989). *Positive illusions: Creative self-deception and the healthy mind*. New York: Basic Books.

Tedeschi, R. G., & Calhoun, L. G. (1995). *Trauma and transformation: Growing in the aftermath of suffering.* Thousand Oaks, CA: Sage.

Thomas, W. I., & Thomas, D. S. (1928). *The child in America: Behavior problems and programs.* New York: Knopf.

Thornberry, T. (Ed.). (1997). *Advances in criminological theory: Vol. 6. Developmental theories of crime and delinquency.* New Brunswick, NJ: Transaction.

Thune, C. E. (1977). Alcoholism and the archetypal past: A phenomenological perspective on Alcoholics Anonymous. *Journal of Studies on Alcohol, 38,* 75–88.

Tittle, C. R., & Paternoster, R. (2000). *Social deviance and crime: An organizational and theoretical approach.* Los Angeles: Roxbury.

Toch, H. (1963). The role of the professional in the promotion of change. In *Experiment in culture expansion: Proceedings of the conference on "The Use of Products of a Social Problem in Coping With the Problem* Norco, CA" (pp. 119–122). Washington, DC: National Institute of Mental Health.

Toch, H. (1969). *Violent men: An inquiry into the psychology of violence.* Chicago: Aldine.

Toch, H. (1987). Supplementing the positivist approach. In M. Gottfredson & T. Hirschi (Eds.), *Positive criminology* (pp. 138–153). Beverly Hills, CA: Sage.

Toch, H. (1993). Good violence and bad violence: Self-presentations of aggressors through accounts and war stories. In R. B. Felson & J. T. Tedeschi (Eds.), *Aggression and violence: Social interactionist perspectives* (pp. 193–206). Washington, DC: American Psychological Association.

Tocqueville, A. (1956). *Democracy in America.* New York: Knopf. (Original work published 1835)

Toukmanian, S. G., & Rennie, D. L. (Eds.). (1992). *Psychotherapy process research: Paradigmatic and narrative approaches.* Newbury Park, CA: Sage.

Trasler, G. B. (1980, September). *Aspects of causality, culture, and crime.* Paper presented at the Fourth International Seminar at the International Centre of Sociological, Penal and Penitentiary Research and Studies, Messina, Italy.

Travis, A. (1997, May 26). England and Wales top crime league. *The Guardian,* p. 1.

Travis, J. (2000). But they all come back: Rethinking prisoner reentry. *Sentencing and Corrections: Issues for the 21st Century* (No. 7). U.S. Department of Justice, Office of Justice Programs, National Institute of Justice.

Trice, H. M., & Roman, P. M. (1970). Delabeling, relabeling and Alcoholics Anonymous. *Social Problems, 17,* 538–546.

Turner, R. H. (1976). The real self: From institution to impulse. *American Journal of Sociology, 81,* 989–1016.

Turney, B. (1997). *I'm still standing.* Winchester, UK: Waterside Press.

U.S. Department of Justice. (1983). *Incapacitating criminals: Recent research findings* (Research in Brief). Washington, DC: National Institute of Justice.

U.S. Department of Justice, Federal Bureau of Investigation. (1996). *Crime in the United States, 1995.* Washington, DC: U.S. Government Printing Office.

U.S. General Accounting Office. (1991). *Drug treatment: State prisons face challenges in providing services* (Report to the Committee on Government Operations, House of Representatives). Washington, DC: Author.

Uggen, C. (1996, May). *Age, employment and the duration structure of recidivism: Estimating the "true effect" of work on crime.* Paper presented at the American Sociological Association conference, New York.

Uggen, C., & Janikula, J. (1999). Volunteerism and arrest in the transition to adulthood. *Social Forces, 78,* 331–362.

Uggen, C., & Piliavin, I. (1998). Asymmetrical causation and criminal desistance. *Journal of Criminal Law and Criminology, 88,* 1399–1422.

Vaillant, G. E. (1983). *The natural history of alcoholism.* Cambridge, MA: Harvard University Press.

Vaillant, G. E. (1995). *The natural history of alcoholism revisited.* Cambridge, MA: Harvard University Press.

Van Voorhis, P. (1985). Restitution outcome and probationers' assessments of restitution: The effects of moral development. *Criminal Justice and Behavior, 12,* 259–287.

Wagatsuma, H., & Rosett, A. (1986). The implications of apology: Law and culture in Japan and the United States. *Law and Society Review, 20,* 461–507.

Waldorf, D. (1983). Natural recovery from opiate addiction: Some social–psychological processes of untreated recovery. *Journal of Drug Issues, 13,* 237–280.

Waldorf, D., Reinarman, C., & Murphy, S. (1991). *Cocaine changes: The experience of using and quitting.* Philadelphia: Temple University Press.

Walters, G. D. (1998). *Changing lives of crime and drugs: Intervening with substance-abusing offenders.* New York: Wiley.

Warr, M. (1998). Life-course transitions and desistance from crime. *Criminology, 36,* 183–215.

Warren, M. (1971). Classification of offenders as an aid to efficient management and effective treatment. *Journal of Crime, Law, Criminology and Police Science, 62,* 239–258.

Watters, J. K., & Biernacki, P. (1989). Targeted sampling: Options for the study of hidden populations. *Social Problems, 36,* 416–430.

Weinberg, D. (1996). The enactment and appraisal of authenticity in a skid row therapeutic community. *Symbolic Interaction, 19,* 137–162.

Weiner, B. (1991). An attributional look at explanatory style. *Psychological Inquiry, 2*(1), 43–44.

Weiner, B., Frieze, I., Kukla, A., Reed, L., & Rest, S. (1987). Perceiving the causes of success and failure. In E. E. Jones, D. E. Kanouse, H. H. Kelley, R. E. Nisbett, S. Valins, & B. Weiner (Eds.), *Attribution: Perceiving the causes of behavior* (pp. 95–120). Hillsdale, NJ: Erlbaum.

Weitekamp, E. G. M., Kerner, H.-J., Schindler, V., & Schubert, A. (1995). On the "dangerousness" of chronic/habitual offenders: Re-analysis of the 1945

Philadelphia birth cohort data. *Studies on Crime and Crime Prevention, 4,* 159–175.

West, D. (1982). *Delinquency: Its roots, careers, and prospects.* London: Heinemann.

West, W. G. (1978). The short term careers of serious thieves. *Canadian Journal of Criminology, 20,* 169–190.

White, M., & Epston, D. (1990). *Narrative means to therapeutic ends.* New York: Norton.

Whittmore, H. (1992, March 15). Hitting bottom can be the beginning. *Parade Magazine,* 4–6.

Wilson, J. Q., & Herrnstein, R. J. (1985). *Crime and human nature.* New York: Touchstone Books.

Wolfgang, M. E., Figlio, R. M., & Sellin, T. (1972). *Delinquency in a birth cohort.* Chicago: University of Chicago Press.

Wolfgang, M. E., Figlio, R. M., & Thornberry, T. (1978). *Evaluating criminology.* New York: Elsevier.

Wootton, B. (1959). *Social science and social pathology.* London: Allen & Unwin.

Wright, K. N., & Wright, K. E. (1992). Does getting married reduce the likelihood of criminality? A review of the literature. *Federal Probation, 61*(3), 50–56.

Young, A. (1996). *Imagining crime: Textual outlaws and criminal conversations.* London: Sage.

Zamble, E., & Quinsey, V. L. (1997). *The criminal recidivism process.* Cambridge, UK: Cambridge University Press.

Zehr, H. (1990). *Changing lenses: A new focus for crime and justice.* Scottsdale, PA: Herald Press.

Ziedenberg, J., & Schiraldi, V. (1999). *The punishing decade: Prison and jail estimates at the millennium.* Washington, DC: Justice Policy Institute Report.

Zoccolillo, M., Pickles, A., Quinton, D., & Rutter, M. (1992). The outcome of childhood conduct disorder: Implications for defining adult personality disorder and conduct disorder. *Psychological Medicine, 22,* 971–986.

AUTHOR INDEX

SUBJECT INDEX

Neutralization, 40–41, 52, 112–113, 133–134, 142–144
"New Careers" movement, 129
Normal-smithing, 139–140, 142, 161
North, Oliver, 14

Ogletree, Charles, 164
Orwell, George, 165
Oxford University, 24

Parker, Howard, 65–66
Passive voice, 134
"Pawns," 76, 77
Personality, xvi, 57–59
Phenomenological research, 32–35, 55
Phoenix House, 103, 177
Positivism, 19
Poverty, 55, 59, 74, 101
Professional Ex-. *See* Wounded healer
Program evaluation, 111–112

Rational choice model, 23–24, 33
Rationalization. *See* Excuses and excuse making
Realistic expectations, 83–84
"Real me," establishment of, 88–92, 131
Re-biographing, 10, 89–90, 113, 140–141, 164–165
Recidivism, xvi, 55, 69–71
Redemption ritual, 155–165
  as construct, 158
  critical elements of, 158–162
  institutionalization of, 162–164
  and rebiographing, 164–165
  social impact of, 161
Redemption script, 85–108, 131, 147
  avoidance of responsibility in, 92–95
  beginning of, 87
  believability of, 85–86
  definition of, 87
  discovery of life purpose in, 99–105
  establishment of "real me" in, 88–92
  process of self-discovery in, 95–97
  role of environment in, 92–93
  stability of, 86–87
  suffering as positive experience in, 97–99

unique characteristics of, 87–88
Redemption sequences, 97, 174
Reentry courts, 163–164
Rehabilitation of Offenders Act, 164, 165
Reintegration ceremonies, 158
Reintegration programs, 11 n.1, 25, 50, 103, 114–115, 125, 129–130, 143, 155, 177
Relapse prevention, 114–115
Repentance, 121–124, 131–132, 145, 164–165
Responsibility
  acceptance of, 148
  avoidance of, 92–95
Restitution, 121–123

Sampling, 43–49, 174–179
Sands, Bill, 102, 142
Self-control, 58
Self-determination, belief in, 147
Self-discovery, process of, 95–97
Self-efficacy, lack of, 76–80
Self-narratives, 7–9, 38–43
  acceptance of responsibility in, 133–134
  believability of, 85–86
  changes in, 42
  comparisons to "real" criminals in, 136–138
  dynamic character of, 39
  neutralization in, 40–41
  and personal myth theory, 39–40
  purpose of, 40
  stability of, 86–87
Shame, 121, 131–132, 134, 138, 143
Shaming, 131, 143
Sharpton, Al, 164
Shaw, Clifford, 39
Shover, Neal, 34
Silbert, Mimi, 125
Singer, Jefferson, 78
Smokers, 17, 24
Social bond theory, 30–32
Social comparisons, 136–138
Socioeconomic status, 59, 63
Specific deterrence theory, 28
Street crime, 20, 62
Stuttering, 93

ABOUT THE AUTHOR

Shadd Maruna, PhD, is an assistant professor in the School of Criminal Justice at the State University of New York at Albany, where he teaches courses in community corrections, rehabilitative interventions, and drug addiction treatment. He has been a Fulbright Scholar, an H. F. Guggenheim Fellow, and a Fellow of the Joint Center for Poverty Research in Chicago. His doctoral thesis, "Redeeming One's Self: How Reformed Ex-Offenders Make Sense of Their Lives," was awarded the Phi Delta Kappa Outstanding Dissertation Award for Northwestern University in 1998. He spends his free time with his daughter Zara and volunteering as a tutor in a local correctional facility.